THE DAY OF THE AMERICANS

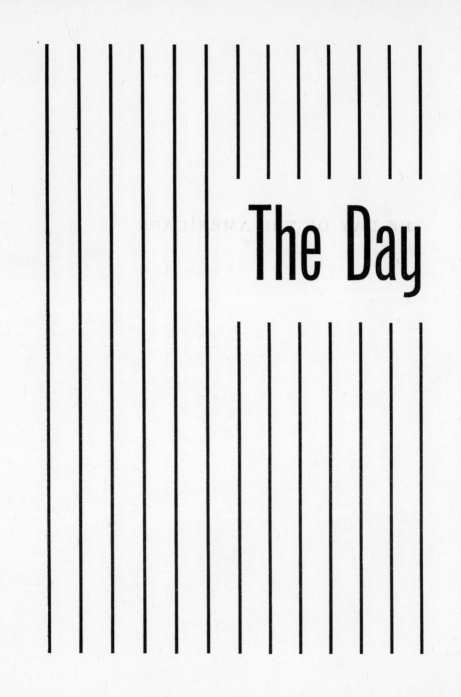

The Day

by Nerin E. Gun

of the Americans

FLEET PUBLISHING CORPORATION

230 PARK AVENUE, NEW YORK, N.Y.

To the dauntless soldiers
of the 45th Division and the 42nd Division
of the United States Army
who entered Dachau as liberators,
not as conquerors.

Contents

vii

THE DAY OF THE AMERICANS

1

The Gift

Since noon, a white flag has been flying from the watchtower beyond the moat. The three SS men are walking the last rounds of a guard duty that has gone on for twelve years. They still have their machine guns trained on us as if they were out for an everyday pigeon-shoot. But they have changed their get-up. No more of those black helmets that made them look like frogs; now, they have on worn gray-green tunics, without armbands, without piping, without decorations.

Down in our crowd, there are also some internees who have been waiting for eleven years, waiting for a liberation they no longer believe in. They are the least impatient ones. For them, time has lost all its relativity; they no longer count the days, nor the hours, nor the minutes, for in order not to go stir-crazy they have long since given up such arithmetic.

The white flag flying on this last Sunday in April seems to me also to be one of the cruel hoaxes of fate. Despite the repeated appearance in the livid skies of squadrons of silvery Flying Fortresses, despite the dull far-off thunder of cannon, despite the sudden stampede of most of the supervisory personnel, we refuse to allow ourselves even the slightest of hopeful speculations. Yesterday afternoon, after all, wasn't there one of these dangerous false alarms? The entire camp was electrified by a gigantic convulsion. Everyone turned out to shout for victory; we were hugging each other, laughing, crying, and a goodly number of German inmates, hiding under the eaves, unknown to anyone except a few insiders of the Resistance groups, had come down from their attic hideouts to take part in the rejoicings. Then came the order from the International Committee: "False alarm! Back to your barracks! Don't give the SS men the pretext they're looking for, to shoot into the pack . . ." After that we had surrendered to fate. The hours followed each other monotonously, and the only visible activity in the camp was the block orderlies continuing to pile up the corpses in the side alleys.

At the very moment when the camp had been the victim of this premature illusion of liberation, the people of New York City had been seized by a comparable mad enthusiasm. There had been snake-dancing in Times Square. An embarrassed President Truman himself had had to call in the press to issue a formal denial of the victory rumors.

I had got up rather late that Sunday, for I had stayed up practically all night. With the others, I had had to carry out the patrols around the barracks. The orders from our underground Resistance Committee were clear-cut: Make sure that none of the inmates venture out of doors, for any movement could only serve to provoke the SS men; keep a close guard so that those prisoners who for so long had made themselves the accomplices of our barbaric jailers could not escape from the camp at the last moment to elude our revenge; and watch for any attempt by the SS to carry out the liquidation by flame-throwers with which they had kept threatening us. We had a few stolen weapons and we were certainly ready now, for the first time in eleven years, to put up a fight against them.

Toward four in the afternoon, the sun, a pale Germanic sun, put in a timid appearance, as if it were just a prop in the overwhelming Wagnerian stage setting. From the doorway of my barracks, through the high-tension electric fencing, I could see only one piece of the diabolic jigsaw puzzle which was Dachau: one plot of gray earth, bordered by the russet walls of the crematorium, its factory chimneys clearly visible, and ending at a series of wooden sheds, which for us were the rim of the horizon.

This last Sunday in April had brought us, certainly for the first time in eleven years, a muffled calm to which I found it difficult to grow accustomed. It seemed like the deathly tranquility of a city right after a monstrous bombardment. It was a "no man's land" in time, during which you are not very sure whether you will go on living or are going to die, in which the silence is only an intermission between two tragedies. Of course, from hour to hour, there was a courier who came from Block No. 1, where the International Committee had its headquarters, bringing the latest scraps of news gleaned from the radio about advances by the Americans. But that afternoon there were no more debates about strategy, no more corner-café palavers, for by tacit agreement we had all decided to give up such narcotic pastimes. We had to spare our nerves. We all had a tremendous physical need for rest, and the wise ones took advantage of the lull to get some sleep.

I went to take a look around the rooms from which we veterans had moved out to make space for the new arrivals from Buchenwald, Auschwitz, Dora, and the other extermination centers. They were almost all Jews whom the Germans had been able just in time to spirit away from the camps under attack by the Allied armies, for even in his last agonizing spasms the monster was not ready to let go of his prey. They came to us tottering, bloody, their heads bandaged, some of them dragging themselves on their knees, others lucky enough to have been transported on stretchers improvised with staves torn from the sides of boxcars. Some of them had spent up to thirty days in those same boxcars, without food or water, and the rumor was that they had survived only by acts of cannibalism. They seemed like characters out of Dante's *Inferno,* so many Count Ugolini della Cherardescas, emerging from their Towers of Hunger. . . . We had put them all into one barrack and in a few minutes they had turned it into a stinking stable in which it was hazardous to walk because of the puddles of excrement and vomit. It had not been possible to take them to the showers, which were no longer operating, and they were crawling with vermin.

There were surely some dead among them, but it was hard to say who was simply sleeping or just too exhausted to give any sign of life. The others moaned unceasingly. Some of them recited Hebrew litanies, but their lamentations were drowned out by those who, on seeing me, called out to ask, to beg, to implore me to get them some bread, some clean straw, an aspirin, or merely some water. . . .

"Patience, just a little bit more patience. We're almost at the end. . . . The Americans can't be long now. . . . You have to hold out, victory is practically here . . ."

But they would not listen to me, and their groanings drowned out my voice. I tried to talk, in Hungarian, to a big redhead who on their arrival had shown his authority. He had put down the sowers of dissension who wanted to continue the feuds that had erupted during the journey.

"Come on, make them understand that we must have a little order, a little will power. . . . This can't last much longer . . ."

"Ah, Baron, how can you preach to drowning cows? For us, there has never been any liberty. You talk just like a rabbi. Only death can put an end to our troubles, and that's all we're waiting for. . . . Jehovah's will be done!"

And he went back to his mournful chanting.

What indeed did they know of the military situation, of the political elements at work; what of the devastation of German cities, the retreats, the exodus, the surrenders? Why should they have been fired with the burning faith of Resistance? No one had ever taught them respect for democracy. They had no more homes to defend; the Germans had destroyed them all. They had no more fiancées, mothers or children to go back to; the Nazis had probably cremated them. Living in abject poverty on their farms or in their ghettoes, having never received any other education than the rudimentary teachings of their synagogues, they had never understood the *why* of this cataclysm which had uprooted their lives. How then could they foresee the end of it?

They had been in Dachau only a few days. But many others also shared this same skepticism. They too had given up. . . . But those were the old-timers: the toughs, the Reds of the Dachau Commune, the jailbirds of the earliest days of Nazism. After eleven years, Dachau, for them, had become a way of life.

Every man, at the time of his arrest, is instinctively convinced that his captivity will last only a few hours. Judicial error, mistaken identity, miracle, escape—somehow he wants to believe that freedom is within his grasp. Then he tells himself it will be tomorrow, the next day, the end of the week, next month.

Hitler was not washed away by another tidal wave. The war came. It will last only two weeks, the experts said then. Aerial bombardments will "settle everything" just as the experts in our day now claim that an atomic exchange in a few hours will determine the fate of nations; but Hitler's war lasted six years, longer than any since the days of Frederick the Great, and he, at least, from time to time declared a breather.

The inmates had been told that they would be free the day the Germans entered Paris, then the day the Germans left Paris, after Stalingrad, after the rout of Rommel, the fall of Rome, the Invasion. The SS men had already started to open the doors of Dachau a chink when Count Von Stauffenberg's attempt on Hitler's life became known. Everything pointed to liberation in 1944, at Christmas, at Easter; next Christmas, next Easter. And now here we latecomers were talking about getting out in April, 1945. The tough oldsters looked at us derisively . . . 1945? Why not 1946? Or 1956? Or maybe never. Dachau had only one immutable law: "The only way out is up the chimney."

The day is ending and already the shadows of twilight are casting a red tint on the rooftops of the SS buildings. Some of the fellows are getting ready for the night. There won't be any soup ration tonight. But then, all of a sudden, like the call of the muezzin, there is a shout from the roof of the neighboring barracks, where one of the prisoners is acting as a lookout.

"Die sind da!" "Die Amerikaner!" The outcry is repeated, multiplied, blown up, and it echoes back to us like the chorus

of an opera, a chorus of 33,000 throats. And, as if the whole thing had been orchestrated in advance, we can now hear the cannon very near and the first full-blown burst of firing. These are no longer random shots from men on guard; a real battle has broken out. We are now all outside. How we got there I can't remember. But there we all are—outside near the ditch, peering at the end of the field, hidden in shadows, like children watching a show, waiting for the white knight to emerge from the wings now that he has slain the dragon.

The three SS men are still on their turret. But now they have pivoted their machine guns in the other direction, away from us, and they too are peering into the distance.

Here now, coming from behind a cement-mixer parked at the edge of the camp, an olive-drab shadow, with a spotted cape like a torero's and a helmet embellished with leaves and branches, moves cautiously forward, submachine gun in one hand, grenade in the other. He is still quite far away but I can already imagine that I see him chewing gum. He comes cautiously, yes, but upright, stalwart, unafraid. I almost expect to see him followed by a pure white charger.

For at that moment, for me as for all of us, for all those eyes that now saw him in one collective trance, he was like the cowboy of my youth, the one out of my favorite books and films, whom I was now seeing for the first time in flesh and blood.

You would have been able to count on your fingers the number of those in Dachau who at any time in their lives had known an American or visited the United States, which before the war had been a terribly distant and unimportant country. We knew America only through its films. And this first image of the liberation was truly one out of a tumultuous western, shot according to the time-honored rules. This soldier of the

3rd Battalion, 45th Combat Division, born in the American
Midwest of Polish parents and now come to Dachau, was for
us, in this moment of intoxication, the very incarnation of the
American hero; not one detail was out of character—his
bearing, his face, the way he held his submachine gun, his
slightly ridiculous helmet. . . .

The silence was broken again by a burst of hurrahs, *vivas,
siegs* and *dobres,* but all these Tower of Babel voices harmo-
nized to express the same cry of gratitude. We stood before the
fence, up on the roofs; some of us had climbed into trees and
raised our arms to the heavens, waving berets, handkerchiefs,
some even jackets, shirts, or any random rag; and this mass of
humanity, only a few minutes earlier so apathetic, so somno-
lent, indifferent, exhausted, was now alive with wild enthusiasm.

The GI with the somber uniform became aware of our
presence. He stopped, nonplused. He must have seen nothing
but a multitude of skeletons dressed in tatters, organized into a
frightful dance of death. He was dispatched as a scout and
now here he was in the entryway of a gehenna peopled by
phantoms straight out of the second act of *Fidelio*. He discovered there the emaciated, desiccated, haggard faces whose
boniness was even more accentuated by the contortions which
tried to express happiness; the atrophied bodies covered with
rags—for zebra-striped prison uniforms were still a sign of
great luxury at Dachau—climbing up one on the other like
tipsy cockroaches; the bleating, the nauseating stench of our
bodies and our clothing mingled with that of charred flesh
coming from the fallout of the crematorium smokestacks,
which clung to the nostrils. All of this must have struck him
like a hallucination.

And the man in the olive-drab uniform with the big helmet

covered with leaves and branches, who had crossed all of Europe to get to us, shrank back, turned, and went to hide behind the cement-mixer. We had frightened our liberator.

First GI at Dachau, we will never forget those first few seconds. Even those of us who have died since you freed them must have carried with them into the other world the memory of that unique, magnificent moment of your arrival. We had prayed, we had waited, we had lost all hope of ever seeing you, but you had finally come, Messiah from across the seas, angel and demon. You had come at the risk of your life, into an unknown country, for the sake of unknown people, bringing us the most precious thing in the world, the gift of freedom.

Today I know your name. But to me, to all of us, all of us who became brothers in that short instant of liberation, you will always remain the Unknown Soldier, the myth, and it matters not whether today, in your garage in Minnesota or Wyoming, you scarcely remember the episode of that afternoon in the course of an almost endless expedition. Even if you should read these lines, you won't be able to understand what your brief appearance meant to us, to what extent it changed our lives, our way of thinking, our very gospels. For you, we were probably nothing but statistics: so many prisoners, so many dead, so many Poles, so many Spaniards, so many Greeks. This might have been worth a decoration, a special furlough, even a citation in the day's communiqué, it might have been a good subject of conversation for the folks back home and, afterward, a good yarn to tell your kids.

For almost all of us in Dachau, as in the other hell camps of Europe, belonged to a cursed generation. We had been born during the other, the first, of the world wars—or shortly thereafter. We had grown up in the turmoil of the years that followed, lived through a series of devastating economic crises, inflation, unemployment, recession, adversity, only to be crushed in the meshing gears of ideological struggles: Fascism, Nazism, Spanish Civil War, fiery crosses, Iron Crosses, swastikas, arrow crosses, and just plain crosses. Then came this war, the fleeing, the destructions, the bombard- ments, the hunger, the prisons, the camps, and finally, perma- nent enrollment into this barbaric world of subhuman beings, reduced to the level of beasts. Our faces were hollow, our bodies transparent, our cast-off clothing louse-infested, but much more disgusting still were our souls that had lost all ideals, soiled by visions of horror, by so much remorse, so much cowardice, so many betrayals. If we were still alive, it was only because others, so many others, had died in our places, and we had willed those deaths, sometimes had even been responsible for them. What the enemy was now giving up to the Americans was in reality 33,000 enraged beasts cor- ralled into a barbed-wire enclosure.

But with a simple stroke of your magic wand, unknown GI of that twilight on the last Sunday in April, you changed all that. You made us suddenly understand that the world was still composed of human beings, that there were still men who were ready to give up their lives to save ours, without trying to strike a bargain, without asking anything in return.

For you came to liberate, and not to conquer.

You had come to prove to us that we had been right to hope, that there was still such a thing as justice, that the word "liberty" was not that obscenity which the SS men had had carved over the gateway to the camp; that the sacrifices of those who had perished had had some meaning. You opened a window to us on the world of our youth, a world we thought we had lost forever. . . .

If the Germans had suddenly taken down the fences and left

us free to go, if the SS men had suddenly deserted the camp, if the Gestapo had seen us quietly and safely home, one after the other, maybe our joy would have been as great, but nothing in us would have changed. It was you, unknown GI, coming from the shadowy edge of the field, with your submachine gun in your hand; you, carefree, brave and daring GI, who made men of us again.

In ancient times, Carrara marble pyramids might have immortalized your name; pouches filled with diamonds or gold might have seemed to you a more tangible proof of our gratitude. Nevertheless, unknown GI, first as you were out of a great army, your true reward must always remain our shout of gratitude that day twenty years ago. Thank you, in my name, in the name of all those you found still alive on that afternoon, thank you in the name of the hundreds and hundreds of thousands who died before you came but whose spirits were still prisoners in the limbo of the Dachau crematoria. . . .

The GI's hesitation didn't last long. He retraced his steps, accompanied now by some fifty foot soldiers. Then there was a burst of shots from up on the watchtower. We threw ourselves to the ground, terrified again at the thought of a possible massacre. Lying thus, face down in the dirt, we saw nothing of the advance of the Americans. One of the prisoners, in a sudden fit of madness, threw himself against the electrified fence, trying to scale it. He was immediately electrocuted and stayed there, the last scarecrow of our nightmare, his hands welded to the wires, his clothing singed black, his naked feet dangling. . . .

We started getting up, one by one, even before the firing had stopped. The Americans were now almost within reach, on the other side of the moat. They had forced the SS men to come down from their watchtower and line up one behind the other, hands on their heads. The charivari had now begun again, and already some of the GIs were throwing cigarettes to us, starting near-fatal scrambles.

During this time, another detachment had arrived at the main gate. An SS man opened it for them and saluted. Two prisoners, naked as jaybirds, stood there waiting, trembling with cold and fear. They were deeply involved in collaboration, but the deserting SS men had not allowed them to come along. And the members of the International Committee had taken away their clothes so that they might not be able to escape in the confusion of the first moments. An American major and other officers were getting out of their jeeps, and for the first time Americans and prisoners were hugging each other. A Polish priest, coadjutor of Cardinal August Hlond, who happened to be in the front row of the liberated, threw his arms around the neck of one of the officers and kissed him effusively. The officer submitted without resistance, but then laughingly freed himself from the embrace. He took off his blue-striped helmet. Golden locks fell down, and a pert, made-up face was revealed. The officer was a woman, a war correspondent, Marguerite Higgins of the New York *Herald Tribune.*

The priest was most uncomfortable, but the newspaper-woman seemed to be used to such mistakes. Anyway, she was not greatly interested in the enthusiasm of the prisoners about her. She wanted to know the fate of the important persons in the camp. Leon Blum, Stalin's son, Chancellor Schuschnigg—where were they? She wanted to cable their names to New York. Her paper would publish her dispatch on the front page, with a by-line reading, "Marguerite Higgins, First Woman to Enter Dachau." Readers would be amazed; circulation would boom; and the rival newspapers would be dismayed.

Miss Higgins and a fellow journalist, Robert Fust, on the highway leading to the camp, had picked up an SS man and ordered him to show them the quickest way to the Lager. The SS man had remained seated on the back seat of the jeep and, in the pandemonium that followed the arrival of the detachment, the prisoners, who had never seen an American uniform before and who at this point really had no reason to be choosy, thought the SS man was another one of their liberators. He too was showered with embraces, kisses, handshakes, and shouts of triumph. The SS man must have thought that either they had all lost their minds or else the hour of universal reconciliation had rung. It was only fifteen minutes later that O'Leary, head of the International Committee, ordered him arrested. The same evening, he faced a firing squad.

Contact having finally been cut off between the high-tension plant and the wire fences, the prisoners were at last able to get out and go to shake the hands of the American soldiers outside. The first wave of Americans had been followed by a second, which must have broken into the camp either through the crematorium or through the marshaling-yard, where the boxcars loaded with thousands of corpses had been parked. For, as soon as they saw the SS men standing there with their hands on their heads, these Americans, without any other semblance of trial, without even saying a warning word, turned their fire on them. Most of the inmates applauded this summary justice, and those who had been able to get over the ditch rushed out to strip the corpses of the Germans. Some even hacked their feet off, the more quickly to be able to get their boots.

One officer, with a silver cross on his helmet, jumped on a jeep and, in very bad German, announced: "We must pray, brothers. We must thank the Lord for this hour . . ." And then he went on in Latin. He could be heard very far away, for at that moment nobody dared to violate the silence any further, and his voice carried through the falling night and warmed our hearts. There were some who knelt to pray, others stood with their berets on their heads, still others hid their faces in their hands, weeping. Even the Russians were praying, and tried to imitate their neighbors in making the sign of the cross. Then the chaplain pronounced a benediction, four times, toward the four corners of the camp. Another officer got up at his side, and, still speaking German, but with difficulty, using words rather than sentences, said:

"Last night, Mussolini . . . brought down in Milan, lynched!" The words were repeated in French, Italian, Hungarian, Spanish, Greek, Serbian, in every language of the camp, by various prisoners.

"In Berlin the Russians are before the Chancellery. Munich is taken . . . Berchtesgaden destroyed. . . . The war is almost ended, you are all free, and you will soon be returning home. I salute you in the name of the United Nations. . . ." And at each phrase his words were interrupted by wild acclaim, ironically reminiscent of the way people used to applaud when Mussolini addressed them from his balcony in the Piazza Venezia.

Nobody slept that night. The camp was alive with bonfires and we all wanted to bivouac out of doors, near the flames. Dachau had been transformed into a nomad camp. The Americans had distributed canned food, and we heated it in the coals of the fires. We also got some bread, taken from the last reserves in the kitchens. But I for one was not hungry, and most of us did not think of eating. We were drunk with our freedom.

That night, the first for us, was also to be the last for the man who had weighed so heavily in our destinies. At the very moment when the Americans neared Dachau, Adolf Hitler, in a macabre ceremony, married his mistress, Eva Braun. But he spent his wedding night alone, while the thud of artillery fire shook his besieged bunker. Only his dog Blondi was with him. But Blondi was already dead. He had had him poisoned immediately after the mockery of the marriage ceremony.

Hitler was to commit suicide only the next day; yet, from the moment of our liberation, from five-thirty in the afternoon until midnight of that last Sunday in April, three hundred prisoners were to die.

The gates of the camp had been locked again, and the liberators of the first hour, on their way again, were already far off, toward Munich, toward the south, pursuing their war. Guards had been placed on the other side of the barbed wire. No one was allowed out any more. Already, at the end of this first day, the Americans wondered what they would do with this rabble of lepers.

We continued to sing, to laugh, to dream, before the flames of the bonfires. We knew nothing as yet of the three hundred dead, twice the daily average of the last weeks before the liberation. We could not foresee that this figure would go even higher in the months to come and that our captivity was still far from being over. We could not admit that there were some among us who would never leave Dachau alive, as its inexorable law demanded. Dachau was to become in a way the symbol of all Europe, which believed itself freed, but was really only changing masters. And in the same way, for many of us, the miraculous deliverance was to turn out to be only a changing of the guard.

2

The Rendezvous

The liberation of Dachau, seen from a strictly military angle, was an insignificant episode and did not quicken for one moment the disintegration of the German war colossus.

Therefore, this liberation was not foreseen in any general-staff plans, and it would be ridiculous to pretend that some American and some German soldiers had the hopes or the fears, if we go back in time a couple of years, say to January 30, 1943, that twenty-seven months later, destiny held in store for them a momentous meeting in the small Bavarian town of Dachau.

War is after all only a succession of individual rendezvous between combatants: they arrive, they meet; one kills, the other one dies.

I choose at random three of these fighters: two victors and one vanquished. I will try to sketch the paths they had to follow to keep their own personal rendezvous.

On January 30, 1943, the tide of German victories began to recede. On that day, the *Grossreich,* now including almost all of Europe, was celebrating the tenth anniversary of the day on which the German people, with Hindenburg at their head, had almost unanimously tendered power to Adolf Hitler. The good Germans did not know yet that on this same day at Stalingrad the greatest battle of the war was drawing to its bitter end. Gen. Paulus, whom Hitler had elevated to the rank of field marshal for the occasion, expecting him in reciprocity to fall on the line, was to let Hitler pitifully down. The Russians found him sobbing on his camp bed.*

At almost the same time, if memory does not betray me, I was in a phone booth in Budapest, dictating a dispatch to the *Gazette de Lausanne,* which I intended to be sarcastic but which I did not foresee would lead to many of my misfortunes: "I spent last evening at the German Legation where, while their men were dying at Stalingrad, Nazi diplomats danced a madly excited Conga."

Chief Glorious Eagle, living on an Indian reservation near Tulsa, Oklahoma, was a tall young fellow, with coppery skin, who worked at a garage on the main highway. Corporal Jeremiah McKenneth, of the U.S. regular army, was stationed at Fort Schafter, near Honolulu. *Unterleutenant* Heinrich Skodzensky, who had volunteered at seventeen, was then making his first trip to the front, in the vanguard of Ewald von Kleist's First *Panzerarmee,* which was still holding its ground in front of Mount Tabruz, the highest in the Caucasus, and trying in vain to avoid giving up the oil-rich territories around Maikop.

I will cut short the peregrinations of the German officer. His unit, forced to retreat, was obliged precipitately and sometimes in panic to cover all their conquered ground in reverse.

* The formal surrender actually took place in the basement of the *Univermag* department store, January 31, 1943, at eleven a.m.

After Rostov, the Donetz Basin, the Leningrad front, a sorry interlude in the Carpathians and the Rumanian catastrophe, Skodzensky was to spend two months in a hospital near Berchtesgaden. Thereafter, he was automatically assigned to the SS *Leibstandarte* Division and, no longer fit for active service, was sent in the late spring of 1945 as a "convalescent" to serve at the Dachau concentration camp, where his Iron Cross was due to mire itself in infamy.

The two Americans were to be incorporated into two divisions with poetry-laden names, names which were to sound to the people they liberated like archangelic titles, even though Madison Avenue has since degraded them with tasteless commercial uses: they were called "Rainbow" and "Thunderbird."

Thunderbird, named for the old Indian god of war and terror, had had as its emblem a swastika, weirdly coincidental for the outfit whose destiny it was to be to destroy Nuremberg, the cradle of Hitlerism. But when President Roosevelt reactivated it on August 31, 1940, he wisely directed the Thunderbird to change its insignia.

Chief Glorious Eagle answered the governmental greetings and reported to Fort Sill, where the division was in training. It was most appropriate for an Indian to belong to this outfit which, within the framework of the regular army, was taking over, from the National Guard, units that in the previous century had included many Indian tribes within their ranks. Their training was pitilessly tough, which explains why, later on, General Alexander Patch, commanding the Seventh Army of which the 45th Division was to become a part, described the Thunderbird as "the best damned outfit in the U.S. Army."

They were alerted on March 16, 1943. The division was to take part in Operation Husky, the invasion of Sicily. It was sent to Virginia, where it embarked on June 8, 1943. Chief

Glorious Eagle, now known as Cpl. Eagle, was seasick all the
way across. They landed at Mers-el-Kebir on June 22 and,
after additional amphibian maneuvers, there came, under the
command of Major General Troy H. Middleton, the assault
on the beaches of Cioglati. . . . Mussolini had sworn that the
"invaders would forever remain on that tide-swept sand-spit
which the fishermen call *"bagn'asciuga."* But, quite to the
contrary, the troops moved rapidly ahead and the populace
greeted them warmly. The Sicilian children danced with glee
when Glorious Eagle told them there were over a thousand
real Indians fighting with the division. "Where are your
feathers?" they wanted to know.

The 45th, after ending the conquest of Sicily at Messina,
took ships to Salerno, then foot by foot fought its way to
Venafro, advance post of the famous Abbey of Cassino. It
went back to Naples to be thrown into the breach on the
bloody sand at Anzio. That was how it happened that the
Second Battalion of the 157th Regiment—a unit worth remembering—commanded by Captain Felix Sparks, was completely annihilated except for its captain and radio operator.
But the 45th liberated Rome in an unforgettable day of glory,
before earning its well-deserved rest.

Then the Thunderbird was in for another sea voyage, and
once again Chief Glorious Eagle was seasick, before they
landed on the French Riviera, at St. Maxime. The division
was greeted with fruit and flowers and the kisses of beautiful bare-legged girls. It followed Napoleon's tracks, and its advance was as triumphal as the Emperor's return from Elba.
Along the way, there was the case of Clarence Coggins who
was temporarily taken prisoner by the Germans, until he
succeeded in bluffing them out of it and came back to the
outfit with 1,000 captive Nazis.

The real complications started at Sarreguemines, near the

German-French border, and there was a vicious battle at Bundenthal, which the division was to turn into a western Stalingrad. But there were to be still other Stalingrads along its way. At Reipertswiller, during the German offensive of January, 1945, coordinated with Marshal Gerd von Rundstedt's breakthrough at Bastogne, the Third Battalion of the 157th Regiment—still the same 157th commanded by the same Sparks who had now become a lieutenant colonel—was wiped out to the last man, except for its commander, who was decidedly running in luck.

Then the Nazi front collapsed. But those who still think that the occupation of the Reich was a walk and that the good Germans, once freed of the incubus of the swastika, quickly put down their arms, should ask some of the veterans of the Thunderbird about it. They'll tell you about the slaughter at Aschaffenburg, that charming little red-roofed town, which at a distance seemed to extend so warm a welcome.

The division had crossed the Rhine on March 24, and it was decided to push southward so as to upset the preparations for Operation Götterdämmerung, which was to be the final Nazi stand in the Tyrolean Alps. It arrived at the gates of Aschaffenburg on April 1. Hitler at the time was sealed off some twenty yards underground in Berlin. His closest associates had already deserted him. There was almost nothing left of the SS. The Gestapo had fled its headquarters, and still at Aschaffenburg the entire population, including women, children and old people, decided to defend their town, house by house. The commander in charge was not a Nazi but a Wehrmacht officer—yes, one of those regular army officers who today claim that they all served Hitler only under duress and did everything to sabotage his war, and who are filled with indignation if eyebrows are raised when one of them is appointed an ambassador or may marry a Dutch Princess Royal. The officer in Aschaffenburg was a Major von Lambert. His proclamation stated: "We must offer complete sacrifice to the Fuehrer. Not a single inhabitant can be excused from combat. Sitting down is hereby forbidden. Sleeping more than three hours a night is hereby forbidden. Our mission is to send the largest possible number of Americans to the devil."

Sixteen hundred and twenty died at Aschaffenburg. What was perhaps even worse, the bitter battle considerably delayed the advance of the 45th. Without this stumblingblock, it would probably have liberated Dachau ten or twelve days earlier, and torn from the jaws of death another 20,000 deportees. So, friend tourist traveling through Germany, do me a favor and, when you see the name of Aschaffenburg on a road sign, make a detour and skirt around it.

Under the command of Major General R. T. Frederick, however, the 45th went on with its liberating mission: on April 22, it was on the Danube. Two interesting prisoners had been taken, Mrs. Fritz Kuhn and her daughter Waldraut, the wife and child of the man who had organized the German-American Bund and tried to turn Manhattan's Yorkville into the American Nuremberg.

The 157th Regiment was now very near Dachau, this same 157th which had totally lost its Second and Third Battalions. It was the First Battalion's turn to lead the way. It spearheaded one of the three prongs aimed at Munich. The 157th, supported by the 191st Tank Battalion, gave battle to isolated SS units at Arnbach. Night layovers were made at Sigmetshausen and Rohrmoss.

It was only toward noon of April 29 that the First Battalion, commanded by Lieutenant Harold Mayer of Las

Vegas, New Mexico, reached the level of the Dachau concentration camp.

This was the 511th day of combat for the division, which had lost as many as 2,540 officers and 6   23 men, covered over 2,000 fighting miles and won eight C   ressional Medals of Honor.

Corporal Jeremiah McKenneth did not find many fellows from his part of the country when, on July 14, 1943, he arrived in the Cookson hills, where the 42nd or Rainbow Division was being reconstituted, for this outfit had no regional characteristics. It was an all-American amalgam, including every kind of ethnic group, every religion, and millionaires as well as farmhands. The 42nd may never have been as glamorous as the Thunderbird, but on the other hand it had a magnificent tradition dating from World War I. Organized on August 5, 1917, it had landed on October 18 at St. Nazaire, to take up positions at Luneville. The sector was a quiet one, and the first battle did not take place till July 18, 1918, in a village with the angelic name of Esperance. The division, which was later to pride itself on having had in its ranks William Donovan, organizer of the American OSS during World War II, was at Sedan when the armistice was signed.

Its commander in 1943, and right through till victory, was Major General Harry J. Collins, who could not have been more appropriately selected, for his daughter Patricia and her husband, captured at Bataan, were prisoners in a Japanese concentration camp, where they suffered quite as much as we did at Dachau.

The division had a "regimental sweetheart," a girl named

Peggy, whose picture could be seen inside every foot locker and on the barracks walls.

No doubt the soldiers hoped they would wait out the end of the war on their training grounds, and everything seemed to point that way. It was already October, 1944, and no preparations for a move had been made, when an urgent travel order arrived during the night. Everybody had to entrain for Camp Kilmer, near New York. There, two days' leave would be granted, just enough for a quick look at Broadway.

The strategic situation in Europe was getting complicated. Eisenhower was calling for reinforcements. It was decided that a special task force would be created, under the leadership of General Henning Linden, to be made up of the 242nd, 232nd and 222nd, to ship out immediately to Marseilles. It landed there on December 8, and the men, including Corporal McKenneth, who had been dreaming of La belle France, suddenly found themselves in a wet, cold, deserted atmosphere. This was another world: it was war.

The division, or rather the embryo division, was to meet the enemy in the very same Luneville sector in which in 1918 the 42nd had first gone over to the attack. But this time it was another story. The first shots were fired on Christmas Eve, and there was no let-up for the holidays. They fought their way to Strasbourg, but then de Gaulle was given permission to defend that city and the Americans were moved farther north. Their movement became difficult because of the clogged roads, as the civilian population, hearing that the Americans were withdrawing, started to flee in a new exodus.

On January 5, the Germans went over to the offensive, better armed and more experienced, and they were able to cross the Rhine and push toward Hagenau. The next days were hell: some of the companies of the 42nd saw up to half their men cut down. The German soldiers who were taken prisoner asked a strange question: "What is this Rainbow? Roosevelt's SS?" On January 14, after ten days of bloodbath, Hagenau was retaken and Alsace was saved.

Then it was the Americans' turn to go on the offensive. By March 15, the division, now up to complement, had advanced on the wooded Hardt Mountains, which continue from the Vosges, and on March 18 it attacked the Siegfried Line. At Dahn, a very significant incident took place. The Jewish chaplain of the division held Passover services. It was the first public Jewish religious ceremony in Germany since Hitler had taken over the Reich.

The god of war was now smiling on the 42nd, which went across the Rhine on Easter Eve. The local population welcomed them. They all boasted of their democratic feelings. Corporal McKenneth was speaking for all when he said: "There isn't a single Nazi. That Hitler must have been quite a guy. All by himself, he governed the country, built up an armaments industry, commanded an army, and without a soul to help him."

Wurzburg was a tough nut to crack. The Second Battalion of the 222nd Regiment had to pursue the SS men right down into the city's sewers. Then there was a hook-up through the north, Schweinfurt was taken, followed by Fürth. The SS men made another desperate stand at Donauwörth, and it was only on April 26 that the vanguard of the division was able to reach the beautiful blue Danube. The 222nd conquered Munster on April 26 and then went beyond the wild stream called the Lech. But on April 28, the advance had to slow down because of the rough condition of the motor highway, virtually all of its bridges having been blown up.

During the night of the 28-29th, there were two dramatic

developments: a broadcast of Radio Munich was monitored, announcing that *Staathalter* General von Epp had eliminated the Nazis and was suing for an armistice. Unfortunately, the putsch proved a failure. Then a deportee who escaped from the Dachau camp reached the American outpost: "Come, run, fly, as fast as you can. If not, we're all goners."

The decision was immediately made to constitute a new task force, under General Linden's command. Since the separating line between the 42nd Division and the 45th ran directly through Dachau, the Rainbow would attack from the west while the Thunderbird came on from the east. The Second Battalion of the 222nd Regiment, commanded by Colonel Henry L. Luongo, was given the risky task of leading the way ahead of the armor—the tanks, because of the state of the terrain, being too slow for the job. The First Battalion would support and the Third would mop up. There was such urgency about it that General Linden went ahead of everybody with a few jeeps and an armored car. Corporal McKenneth was in one of them, and the Dachau escapee was leading the patrol.

I will tell later what these brave soldiers of the Rainbow and Thunderbird Divisions were to find. Let us merely say that for these liberators Dachau was to be only a brief stop. Before night fell, they would be off again on their dash toward Munich.

And while we were singing for joy in Dachau, shortly after midnight, the soldiers of the ever-present First Battalion of the 157th Regiment were setting foot in front of the Burgerbrau- keller, in the very heart of the building that Hitler loved so much, their unique signature: "C.P. 157th Infantry, 45th Division, USA."

The Rainbow, which can lay claim to having arrived in the birthplace of Nazism at the same time, did not stop, but went on to pursue the enemy into the Tyrol. Thus, its men were able to capture, among others, Leni Riefensthal, Hitler's muse, who of course like everyone else claimed never to have been a Nazi, and Von Oberg, the demoniac butcher of Paris. Later, the division was to be part of the forces occupying Salzburg and Vienna.

The Thunderbird, slated to be shipped to Japan, had the good luck instead to be rotated home before the end of the year, and it was disbanded on December 7, 1945. But every member of the victorious outfit was to bring home with him that extra edition of the *45th Division News* (of which the first issue had been printed on the beaches of Sicily, making it the first American military unit newspaper to be published in invaded European territory), dated April 29, 1945, with the memorable banner headline: WE HAVE SEEN DACHAU. NOW WE KNOW WHAT WE ARE FIGHTING FOR.

3

The Waiting

On March 21, 1933, just a few weeks after power was offered to Adolf Hitler, a short item appeared in the *Muenchner Neuesten Nachrichten:*

"Yesterday, the first concentration camp was formally opened in the neighborhood of the city of Dachau. It can accommodate 5,000 persons. This measure has been taken, apart from any petty considerations, because we are convinced we are acting in the interests of national tranquility and according to the will of the population." *Signed:* Heinrich Himmler, Chief of Police.

The *Muenchner Neuesten Nachrichten* was the most widely read newspaper in Bavaria, and it was obvious that Himmler, far from trying to keep this secret, was eager for all Germany to know of his initiative.

The city of Dachau was not long in publicly expressing its gratitude to Himmler. Its finances were in a pitiful state, and it was delighted thus to welcome the conversion of an old munitions factory, unused since the last war. The mayor had been promised that the political convicts to be housed there would be employed at draining the sinister Dachauer Moor, the notorious peat bogs of the region. The Hitlerites were anxious to emulate Mussolini, who had so brilliantly reclaimed the Pontine Marshes between Rome and Naples. But of course, the Germans brought greater perfection to the Fascist methods. Instead of calling for volunteers, they used slaves.

The one-time munitions plant was rebuilt, enlarged, reequipped, and the KZ of Dachau became the model, the prototype of Nazi organization and subjection. It was to last a thousand years, like Hitler's Reich. Arrangements were made for important personages and foreign journalists to visit it. In 1938, the *Berliner Illustrierte,* which at the time was to Germans what *Life* magazine today is to Americans, was to publish a cover picture of the internees going to their work to the sound of bagpipes. Everything was alleged to be so impeccable in the camp that there had even been national elections, and the result of the plebescite had gone 99 per cent for Hitler. And later, during the 1939 mobilization, the camp was temporarily emptied of its regular inmates, and it served as billet for an entire SS division, the *Eicke.*

Alas, all this admirable Prussian order had degenerated into disorder by the spring of 1945. Thirty-five thousand inmates in a camp originally intended for 5,000 are a heavy load, and first typhus, then hunger had completely upset the mechanism. To make room for a group of hostages of honor, it had even been necessary to move the girls out of Block 31 and thus deprive Dachau of its most original attraction.

For Block 31 was the Puff, the prisoners' brothel. In fact, only the VIP German jailbirds and criminals made use of it, the political prisoners having determined to boycott it as a matter of principle. This did not really represent a great sacrifice, for the majority of the incarcerated were so famished, so weakened and so terrorized, that the idea of going to the whorehouse could only rarely be a temptation to them. But in theory the area was accessible to all except the Jews.

Each inmate received two marks per week for his work. During the earlier years he was able to use this money. It was not legal tender, but scrip that was honored in the camp, for which newspapers or toothpaste could be bought at the canteen. But soon these became unavailable, and the only place to spend the money was at the brothel, where the rate was two marks a trick. This worked out very well for the SS administration, for the whorehouse was self-supporting and the salaries paid to prisoners came right back to their source. The inmate had to put his name down in advance and then go for a medical examination. He presented his certificate to the Puff Fuehrer, who, after the usual sarcastic comments, had him draw a number out of a hat. The number designated the girl he was to have. Then he had only to wait his turn.

But even in a concentration camp, prostitution followed its own rules. Soon, the customer developed preferences, even a favorite. To achieve his ends, he had to subvert the SS man and then buy the favors and the silence of the girl so she would accept the infringement, agree to spend more time with him and be more complaisant. So he brought tobacco, food, stolen clothing, and it even happened that somehow he produced a Parisian gown, a well-known perfume, or a piece of jewelry. It seems that one of the Kapos succeeded in keeping one of the fifteen girls in the Puff all to himself for a whole year. She was off limits to all others.

However, the girls did not keep their earnings: just as in Montmartre, they had their "sweet daddies." For there were pimps operating in the camp: professionals who were inadvertently caught in a raid or picked up because they were also pushing drugs, or perhaps had "taken" some Nazi big shots for whom they had been procuring; and amateurs also. They could be seen at nightfall loitering near the windows of the whores' barracks, bargaining, checking on the "work" of their fillies, receiving their tribute. They were strong and good-looking, for with what they got from their women they could afford to eat well at the black market of the camp. They did a bit of white-slaving, and sometimes were able to transfer a girl from some other camp, sometimes succeeding in convincing a woman prisoner to volunteer for the Puff, perhaps by promising to save the life of her husband or child.

Normally the staff of the brothel was made up only of professional prostitutes, girls from houses in Warsaw, Lodz or Prague, who had simply been moved in to Dachau. Rarely were the women political prisoners forced into such pursuits. In the eyes of the Gestapo, that was no punishment, and moreover they would not have been satisfactory. As in any other craft, they wanted only experts at Dachau.

It was strictly forbidden for the SS guards to go to this establishment. They had their own, with equally professional "Aryan" German girls. It did sometimes happen that one of the higher SS officers lusted after a very beautiful woman captive or one of the secretaries, or the wife of a guard or even a woman SS jailer. Then, under one pretext or another—it was so easy in those days to denounce people or be denounced —they could have her locked up in the bunker and there seduce their victim quietly, by force or persuasion.

The reports at Nuremberg reveal, for instance, how the camp commandant, Obersturmbannfuehrer Weiter, secretly went to share the bed of a woman prisoner, H. L., in Cell No. 6 of the bunker. One night there was an air raid, and afterward all lights were turned on. The Obersturmbannfuehrer, who was naked, having hidden his uniform under the bed, had to stand flat against the wall to avoid being discovered by the guards. Meanwhile, the panicky SS men were looking everywhere in the camp for their commandant, and had already given him up for dead, a victim of the bombardment.

That there were pimps at Dachau should surprise no one. I would like to be able to say there had been nothing but heroes in the Lager, but that, unfortunately, would be untrue. We were a heterogeneous group. Among us, there were some of everything: Communists, members of the underground, criminals, anarchists, homosexuals—these wearing a little pink triangle, which was most appropriate, while the political prisoners wore a red one, the criminals a green one, and the admirable Jehovah's Witnesses a black one. The members of Jehovah's Witnesses, it must be said, showed such courage, daring, virtue, and stoicism in adversity that they deserve a special salute. They were rocks in a sea of mud.

Homosexuality inevitably finds fertile ground in any prison in the world. Hitler had wanted, however, perhaps because of his hatred for Roehm, his former boon companion, to lock up in Dachau every invert in the Reich. I sometimes doubt that these people gained anything from the lesson. To them, Dachau was a little like a "paradise found." They had succeeded in taking over certain jobs on the welcoming committees, those that were in charge of undressing the prisoners, shaving their pubic hair, creosoting them. For the pink triangles, these chores were happiness, and they could indulge in the boldest of caresses without risking reprisals. The prisoner who identified himself to them as one of their own would be treated with special favor, get a "connection"; as for the others, it was a matter of strength of character. From time to time, there were quarrels among the pink triangles, sometimes going even so far as actual crimes of passion. One might have been unfaithful, another might have become a threat to the peace of a "couple," yet another might have been seen going near the brothel. Their bodies were generally found the next morning in the showers, their faces raked with deep fingernail scratches.

Even among the "politicals," it was to be noted that sharp distinctions existed: for instance, among the Frenchmen, there was an abyss between the early Gaullists and those who had seen the light only after the landings in Normandy; between the Vichy vassals who had fallen into disfavor with the Germans for some reason and the volunteers of the Charlemagne Legion; the French SS men who had fought in Russia and who could no longer take it, as against the illegal wheeler-dealers from Paris, the stool-pigeons, the volunteer workers who had turned saboteurs or girl-chasers, the black-market boys, and those who had been arrested for pillaging after bombing raids. . . .

Beyond these, there were German deserters, court-martialed SS men, people who had simply been picked up on the street during indiscriminate roundups, or, as happened every day, drunkards or curfew-violators, who somehow found themselves in Dachau simply because their local jails were overcrowded to the bursting point. We were the Court of Miracles of Munich.

And then there were all those who actually felt completely innocent—in a word, those who had no idea what had landed them here. I had occasion to read a large number of their dossiers before they were destroyed, and I would guess that at least a thousand of these internees of the final period had been stupidly denounced by a wife, a girl friend, a secretary or a relative. Jealousy, spite, hurt feelings, meanness, whim—

whatever the motive, there is nothing more dangerous than a woman who knows a way to get rid of a man without running any risk herself. Some of the captives did not even know who had accused them. A neighbor woman, living across the corridor, might have seen the man going into the apartment of his girl friend, whom she secretly hated. Why was he there with the other woman when she herself was lonely that night?

All she had to do was pick up her pen and a sheet of paper, or just call the Gestapo. An old woman in the Briennerstrasse opened the telephone directory at random, let her finger fall somewhere on the page, and copied off the names. In this way, she turned in some 150 suspicious characters. All were arrested and then forgotten in confinement by the Gestapo, which by this time had more than it could handle.

These simple-minded creatures of course imagined they would immediately be freed, as soon as the mistake had been cleared up. The favorite game in camp was to impress the fact on them that they were here to stay and to paint a vivid picture of all the horrors of the place. The rookies hardly believed us, so we trotted figures out for them and showed them proof. It was cruel, it is true, but in a way practical, for they were then not too paralyzed when faced with the harsh reality.

Practically all nationalities were represented there and, according to the time and season, some were looked up to and some looked down on. In Dachau at first it was the Poles who were insulted, then came the turn of the Frenchmen, then the Russians, and finally the Italians and Hungarians occupied the bottom rung.

The only missing great nationality was the American. In one way that was unfortunate, as Edmond Michelet noted:

"Whereas all of Europe was represented at Dachau, not a

single American citizen, not one fighting man from the U.S.A. experienced the hell of the German concentration camps. I have often regretted that not one of our friends from across the sea had the possibility day after day to meditate upon an experience similar to our own. That he could not see the black science to which we were exposed. . . . I am afraid that Nazi barbarism will seem no nearer to them than that of the Assyrians. . . . On that score, there will be more than an ocean between us, there will be a whole world. . . ."

Alas, we could scarcely imagine then that in barely twenty years the President of our liberators would declaim in the middle of a public square largely filled with the accomplices of our former jailers, *"Ich bin ein Berliner!"* How much more secure the peace of the world would be if, instead, John Fitzgerald Kennedy had been able to say, *"Ich war in Dachau. . . ."*

The growing chaos of the final weeks also accounted for the elimination of the motion picture shows, usually restricted to the prominent prisoners, at which, along with documentaries about the glorious armies of the Reich, there were sometimes shown rather naïve Bavarian farces. The orchestra that, for reasons never explained, had made a habit of playing "My Old Kentucky Home," had disappeared. The SS had simply sent the musicians before a firing squad. And nobody wanted to hear any more of the lectures organized by the prisoners. There had been some on the Aztecs, on Roman law, on the life of Henry IV; and even I had discoursed, on Ataturk.

I had had to give up, some time back, my little clandestine newspaper which had a circulation of three copies. The title had been taken from that of the satirical French weekly, *Le canard enchaîné* (The Chained Duck), and each issue started with the report: "Today, the —— Hitler has still not died."

Countess Andrassy, now living humbly in a little house not far from the Canadian border, with no regrets apparently over her lost châteaux, parks, and armies of servants, still has a copy of it. There is an article in it signed by "Kurt," one of the camp dogs, suggesting that a factory be started for canning the bones of the prisoners, which the dog-author felt were being wasted in the crematorium. Then there is an interview with Countess Dampierre, wife of the French ambassador to Budapest, telling me of her plans for the post-liberation period. "I will give a sumptuous banquet," she says, "and invite the entire diplomatic corps. The menu will be worthy of the board of Louis XV. But, separately, in a special pot, I will personally cook up all my husband's dirty socks, which I will have allowed to go unwashed for a year, along with the dirt from his shoes, the sweepings from his barber's, a few old rats, and some good leather soles, and when this stew is ready, I'll pour it not into a bowl but into an old cap and serve it to the German ambassador. 'Your Excellency,' I will say, 'this is to repay you for the hospitality of your camp.' "

My little paper was scarcely exaggerating. That was just about what we were being given to eat and, there being no dishes, many of us had to eat out of our berets, if not out of our hands. You have to have seen it to believe the spectacle of a prince of Hohenzollern picking through the garbage cans of the SS mess hall! That is why nowadays I tend to laugh when my doctor talks to me about hygiene and sterilization.

However, there was a black market, with headquarters in the shower rooms, the same place the prisoners chose for having it out with knives when they were bent on killing each other. Brisk trade went on in canned goods received in packages, foodstuffs stolen from the SS men or the prisoners, hard-to-get daily necessities, and all sorts of trinkets. The medium of exchange was tobacco. There were real cigarettes, re-claimed butts, and ersatz smokes made from old newspaper and stable straw.

At Dachau, these smokes were perhaps responsible for more deaths than typhus and hunger. The smoker found camp conditions ten times harder than the nonsmoker. He was ready to betray, to kill, to sell himself for a cigarette.

I was sharing my bunk, a few weeks before the liberation, with a very nice Italian fellow, a Milanese, father of seven kids. Every day, he swapped his midday soup for one cigarette —that was the going rate—and there was no making him listen to reason. One morning I woke to the strange sensation of blood clotting on my chest. This was not my bedmate's usual hemorrhage. He had died during the night. In my arms. Of hunger.

We had a library, and in it were to be found the most disparate books, such as *The Three Musketeers* and *Babbitt*. But I was particularly proud of a little set-up which we had pompously named "Academy for Learning Not to Speak German."

It was a very petty kind of revenge against our jailers, but it had its justification. Dachau was certainly a Tower of Babel if ever there was one, and the multilingual prisoners had no choice, in order to communicate with each other, but to use German as a sort of Esperanto. But it was most distasteful to us to give universality to this language. So, within our acad-emy, the rule was that German might never be used, and beyond this its members made it a habit never to pass along orders in German, but to use a kind of international jargon: *Davai* was used for *Los; schleu* (the offensive French word for

German) to mean SS; *alerta* for *Appel; paella* for *Suppe;* and so on. Since we had our own French, Italian, Spanish or other pronunciations for the German words which nevertheless were unavoidable, the SS men on duty and the other Kapos could not understand what we were saying even when we spoke their language.

I had never had a chance to attend, but there was another school where our boys were taught to work hard without getting anything done. For instance, one crew was set to work building a bungalow for an SS man. The men built conscientiously, but when they turned the job over to the night shift, the latter undid everything that had been done during the day, and then set to work on another part of the project. The day crew then undid the night work, and so on, *ad infinitum.*

Despite our academy, the knowledge of German could be precious and account for highly prized jobs. In the SS clothing depot, where I kept books for a time, my main business was listening to the SS boss tell his political jokes. He would try them out on me before deciding whether to take a chance on them at the mess. Every day I had also to tell his fortune by reading his palm. My knowledge of palmistry has always been strictly nil. But I had some sort of idea of how to make a stab at it, which had sometimes been useful to me in Berlin as a pretext for getting into some pretty Gretchen's room. And being more or less aware of the boss's makeup, I was able to "read" a few truths to him and at the same time assure him he would live to a ripe and peaceful old age. In fact, other SS men came to me for readings, too.

Having been alerted by the boys in the administrative section that some of the SS men were to be sent to the front, I was able to foretell mysteriously that they "would spend Christmas in an icy place," while I promised others that nothing would happen to them. Pretty soon they all wanted to be assured that they would not be drafted for the front. I never gave this break to any of the SS men except those who could be useful to me. The others heard, to a man, that they would soon be heading east. And, since practically all of them went that way before the end, I turned out to be not such a bad prophet.

I was even asked to go to the homes of two or three officers' wives, and I got a good meal and a good chance to wash, out of it. I also took to reading coffee grounds, which for a time gave me a chance to sell these leftovers in the camp's black market. But unfortunately that did not last, for coffee at last became unobtainable, even to SS big shots.

I sometimes wonder whether it was my usefulness as an oracle which accounted for my surviving at Dachau, for, because of my fruitless attempt to escape, I was on the condemned list. Or perhaps it was because my serial letter T, for my nationality, came at the end of the alphabet, and the Germans perhaps never got around to me.

I was not the only would-be-fortuneteller around. There were a number of Gypsies who were adept at it, to say nothing of a hypnotist and a divining priest.

Our military information was a little more dependable, despite the disappearance of any newspapers coming from the outside. We had several radios, some of them equipped for short wave. One German Communist, Karli Horak, set up a permanent monitoring of the BBC. Another prisoner, a Frenchman, Felix Mauer, for two years remained in constant contact with the French intelligence service, though I never found out how.

News from the outside had a tremendous influence on the morale of the camp: when Paris was liberated there was dancing on "Liberty Street," but when the Rundstedt offensive scored its breakthrough toward Bastogne, everyone was downcast, there were suicides, and some of the sick refused treatment. At that time, a large number of German prisoners, dishonoring themselves and us at the same time, volunteered for the SS Dirlewanger Legion and went to fight on the Eastern front.

I still remember the excitement on the occasion of the attempt on Hitler's life on July 20, 1944. At that time, I was at Maria-Lanzendorf, a camp near Vienna, and the panicky commandant suggest that we take over the "management" of the camp while he, temporarily at least, took shelter. We were all convinced that Hitler was finally *kaputt*, so we were in no hurry to get out of camp and we decided to throw a huge banquet, with roast chicken and the varied wines of France that were to be found in the SS cellars. Unfortunately, the same night, everything was called off: Hitler was alive, the commandant came back to camp, and we went back to our cells.

At dawn on April 13, 1945—we were six hours ahead of American time—Dachau had the saddest moment of its whole history. The news came in by short wave. Roosevelt was dead. This was a terrible shock. To us, Roosevelt was more than a father; he was the man who had promised us freedom, not as a gift but as our right. There were twenty-five suicides in camp that day. I think that nowhere in the world was Franklin Delano Roosevelt mourned as he was at Dachau.

Mass was said in the chapel of Block 26, the priests' block. Entry to this chapel was only given to a privileged few, selected as carefully as applicants to the exclusive Jockey

Club, and even these were allowed in only during the final months.

This Block 26 had at first been open to all Catholic priests, as a kind of concession to the Vatican. Conditions there were better than elsewhere, and many packages were received from outside, thanks to the Archbishop of Munich. Then the German priests decided that all foreign priests should be excluded from it. It was equally off limits to all the rest of the camp's internees. A Bavarian priest stood guard outside the door, blackjack in hand, and woe to anyone who tried to get by him to take part in the religious service inside. Even old Schmitz, the ancient and highly likable Burgmeister of Vienna, had to kneel and cross himself from outside. These antics gave the SS men a good laugh.

Once more, I quote Edmond Michelet on the subject, since he, as a member of the hierarchy of the French Catholic Party, cannot be accused of religious irreverence: "Perhaps I am wrong to appear to hold a grudge against these poor German priests, subjected as they were to discipline. . . . We were thrown out of the chapel, sometimes with punches to boot. . . . The captive Church of Block 26 was a pitiful thing to see. . . . Of course, the Block was full of packages, the parishioners did not forget their *Pfarrer*. Where might it not have led if all the camp's starvelings had suddenly felt overcome by piety and thereby come into contact with the stores of foodstuffs kept in the priests' lockers? . . ."

It is difficult to give credit to any one person for the idea of setting up a prisoners' committee which, should the occasion arise, might take over the running of the camp. There was Patrick O'Leary, who claimed to be English, Canadian, Australian, and sometimes even Swedish, but whose real name was Albert Guerisse and his real nationality Belgian. Then, there was Haulot, who later became a minister in the Brussels government; the Pole Nazewsky; the amazing Albanian, Ali Kuci, who maintained to me that he was a direct descendant of Alexander the Great; and later, General Delestraint. The committee wanted to create a "Resistance brigade," avoid too much confusion in camp if it came to a pitched battle between the Americans and the SS men, set up an intelligence service, and especially, keep up the camp morale.

Kuci, who became propaganda minister in this rump cabinet, took me on as his assistant: it was to be my job to assemble the documents that would later prove to the world the unbelievable things we had lived through. We anticipated that the camp would be deliberately destroyed, and with it all proof. We knew that dossiers were already being burned, and that statistics were being faked before being sent to the OzTal.* Kuci introduced me to a pink-cheeked giant, mild as a child and faithful as a dog, who was called Ivan and came from Astrakhan. He talked some kind of dialect not unlike Turkish, so we could understand each other, albeit with difficulty. Ivan stuck to me like a shadow, and I owe him a great deal. He had a talent that was priceless in camp: he could steal with discretion and without detection. It was he who got me a Kodak camera. He had simply swiped it from the room of an SS man, who had probably confiscated it from an American paratrooper. We also got a can of newsreel motion-picture film from the depot of the SS propaganda company, and all we had to do was cut it up under a blanket in order to adapt it to the 35 mm. still camera.

That was how I was able, despite the risks, to get pictures of the camp, and once even to get inside the crematorium com-

* Where the Gestapo files were kept underground.

pound. . . . What struck me most there was the contrast between the piles of corpses on the lawn and the miniature house set up on a pole to welcome the birds. Feed was regularly put out for them. With the flowerbeds, this made an idyllic scene. There was also a Gypsy prisoner who sometimes played a harmonium. And I remember a sign that was posted: "Wash hands before touching corpses. Anyone who does not wash is a pig!"

Dachau was not destroyed, and the documentation I prepared was not required. I have never wanted to tell of these atrocities. Today, it all seems so unbelievable to me that, if I were to tell it, I would feel as if I were lying. Even when I look at the pictures I took, I feel, deep within myself, that they were faked.*

The International Committee needed weapons. We had made a few Molotov cocktails, found a bayonet, a few knives, and also—treasure of treasures—a Luger automatic. O'Leary had a Canadian pal, an aviator, Pat, a very handsome fellow. He had succeeded in attracting the interest of a big, strong, red-headed SS woman warder, who sometimes came to the infirmary supposedly to get medicines for the brothel girls.

The German woman in her death's-head uniform and the wretched prisoner took a fancy to each other. They would discreetly hold hands in an isolated corner of the Revier, and I think they even had a few rendezvous, very secretly, in a hothouse where exotic plants were cultivated. The Dachau

---

* Those who may want further proof of these atrocities, because they may doubt the word or the memory reflected in the many works written by former prisoners, should read the pamphlet *Dachau,* published by the Pentagon, OSS Section, 7th Army USA, Wm. W. Quinn, Col., at Dachau itself in July, 1945. It is as brief and succinct as a police report; in fact, it *is* a police report.

nursery was one of the most flourishing enterprises of the SS empire.

The German woman not only gave her affections, but also her promise to find us some arms. That was how we came to have the revolver, which was hidden under the bolster of a hospital bed. The Canadian prisoner had convinced his SS belle that the Fuehrer was done for and it would be all to her advantage to be on the good side of the International Committee. Whether out of love or self-interest, the Fräulein Unterscharrfuehrer became a precious ally to us. In exchange, we saw to it that she was not molested when liberation came, and I have been told that her one-time Canadian admirer still writes to her from time to time.

The fever was mounting, the camp was rife with unfounded rumors, and everyone was astir. Already a first convoy of Russians and Germans had been ordered out of camp, in the direction of Mittenwald. Going on foot, it was to be decimated on the way. The final Thursday, general evacuation of the camp was ordered. We dressed in all the clothes we could get on our backs and put our blankets around us. At my waist I had my messkit, my fork, my knife (they might be useful, my committee superior had pointed out to me; they were weapons, and we had decided to attack the SS men at the first opportunity). But O'Leary, tipped off by the Canadian flyer's German girl, decided it was better not to try anything yet. Instead, we sabotaged the roll call. After four hours of trying to get us started on our way, the SS men got discouraged with the whole idea, and sent us all back into our barracks, possibly because they were too anxious to go to join their fellows in the storehouses and offices who were stealing civilian clothing and even prisoners' passports and identity cards.

Ten times a day, we thought we saw the Americans coming. It was exactly the same hallucination as the Crusaders had had before Jerusalem, when they thought they saw St. George on horseback opening the gates of the Holy City to them.

The least sign was interpreted as the harbinger of imminent liberation. "Hope shone like a blade of straw," as Verlaine put it.

I can still hear, on that last evening at Dachau, the singing of the SS recruits who, after training exercises, marched back into their barracks as if nothing untoward were happening, their black figures silhouetted against the wild redness of the twilight.

No one that evening, not even O'Leary, was aware that at the very moment when Himmler was trying to negotiate an impossible armistice with Count Bernadotte, the camp commandant had before him an order signed by the selfsame Himmler:

"Flossenburg, April 14, 1945.
To: Commandant, *KZ Lager,* Dachau.
Surrender of the camp to the enemy is unthinkable. The whole camp is to be immediately evacuated. Not one prisoner is to fall alive into the hands of the Americans."

And this order was confirmed by another telegram, telling the commandant that, in case of necessity, he was authorized to utilize several military planes, which still remained intact at the air base of Schleissheim, near Munich, to massacre the entire population of the camp with napalm bombs and gas.

4

The Train

During the night of April 28, a ragged Jew, his face peppered with smallpox scars, knocked at the door of the camp. An old reserve soldier, attired in an SS uniform, opened the door to him, and was amazed to hear him say:

"I don't know anybody in Germany. On the outside, there's pandemonium. I'd rather go back in."

He had been in a convoy that had left Dachau three days earlier by rail. When the locomotive was hit by a bomb, the SS guards had taken to their heels. One of the prisoners, a priest, had taken refuge at a peasant's, and another stopped a passing truck to have the wounded loaded on it. The rest went ahead on foot foraging off the countryside as best they could. They grabbed whatever foodstuffs could be "liberated," put the fear of God into girls who saw them passing by, and had the unheard-of luxury of bathing in the large stream called the Amper. That was foolish: three of the escapees died of exposure and cold. The Jew who came knocking at the gate had wandered astray, terrified. Stones were thrown at him by civilians, and so he had decided to come back to the camp because, as far as he could remember, the prison was his only home.

The poor wretch was not entirely wrong in feeling bewildered when exposed to liberty. On this last day the murderous chaos which always precedes a victoriously advancing army had engulfed the region. That very morning the last detail had gone out of the camp to work in the town's shops. It was made up mostly of Germans and Austrians, tough nuts, some of whom were veterans of the International Brigade of the Spanish Civil War. The road from the Lager to the city of Dachau was lined with corpses—evacuees from other convoys who had died along the way of exhaustion or typhus or had simply been expedited by an SS bullet in the nape of the neck. It looked as though this was what was in store for this last work detail and its members decided to gamble everything in a desperate effort: they entered into negotiations with their SS guards, promising them immunity when the Americans arrived. The latter agreed, and turned their arms over to them. Otto Jendran, a veteran of the Spanish Civil War, took command of the troop and impressed some passing Volkssturm (uniformed German civilian home guards) into lending a hand. His men took control of the Rathaus, and he sent an envoy* out to carry the word to the Americans, who he hoped were very near. But the SS at Allach, when the rebellion was reported to them, arrived posthaste by truck, and a furious battle ensued. It was to last for five hours. More than half the prisoners of this work detail died during its course. The rest tried to get away into the countryside. But the skirmish served one very useful purpose. The camp commander, intimidated

---

* Actually one of the rebellious prisoners, Karl Reiner, succeeded in joining the Americans.

by this revolt, decided to give up any idea of mass evacuation of the prisoners.

The Americans, meanwhile, knew perfectly well what was going on. Their reconnaissance planes had been flying over the camp continuously and had seen all these comings and goings. Alerted to the fact that a detachment of SS men had left its quarters in Munich to proceed up the fateful Dachauerstrasse and perhaps make a deadly assault on the camp, they interdicted its progress with artillery fire. This was the source of the cannon thunder we were hearing at Dachau.

The whole world was talking then of Buchenwald, which had been liberated by the British. It would have been humiliating if the American army, for its first great camp liberation, found nothing but smoking ruins.

Fortunately, the situation in the German ranks was tumultuous. The former commandant of Dachau, Weiss, now inspector general of all camps, countermanded the orders received from Berlin. He informed the Americans by phone—yes, the general confusion was such that it was perfectly possible to establish telephone contact across the lines—that Dachau would be handed over to them intact. The Red Cross would act as the delivery agent. But the SS officers preferred not to wait for the surrender to take place. They deserted during the night. Command was turned over to a young survivor of the slaughters of the Russian front, a man who, as a result of administrative delays, had arrived at Dachau only two days earlier to spend his "convalescence" there. It was the Lieutenant Heinrich Skodzensky.

He was given a brand-new SS uniform, of which the warehouses were full, and he looked as though he had just stepped out of a bandbox. His decorations stood out richly against the gray-black color of the uniform. He was a hero from the front.

He therefore was in no danger, for it was well known that the Americans handled real fighting men with kid gloves. He knew little about Dachau. He never even had a chance to set foot into the confines of the KZ proper.

He was the one who gave the orders to raise the white flag over the Jourhaus. He was to spend the entire day there in the guard headquarters, awaiting the arrival of the conquerors.

The Jourhaus was the main gate of the camp. Its binational name was a throwback to the Napoleonic era, when the Prussians borrowed the French word *jour* from their opposite numbers. Through its portals, since 1933, each of the camp's damned had entered into this land of horrors. The entrance gate was made of wrought iron, the work of an Austrian deportee, and it bore the high-sounding legend: "Work will make you free."

In the city of Dachau, where there is a great, long-distance view from the malls of the château, the first American tanks had already been spotted, and bells had begun to ring. In the camp itself, an excited prisoner had pulled the switch of the alarm siren. Patrick O'Leary decided to call a full meeting of his International Committee in the library of the Schreibstube, which was the building closest to the Jourhaus. A large part of the garrison, like its officers, had bolted from the camp, but there were still several hundred SS men left; the machine guns in the watchtowers were still trained on the camp, and in the general confusion one could never tell what might happen. So, the committee had been in continuous session since 9:00 A.M., sending out repeated calls to remain calm, with sentries on the rooftops relaying its messages around the camp.

The Americans were not simply advancing; they were running, flying, breaking all the rules of military conduct, mounting their pieces on captured trucks, using tractors, bicycles, carts, trailers, anything on wheels that they could get their hands on. The Second Battalion, 222nd Regiment, 42nd Division, was coming brazenly, impudently down the highway, its general in the lead.

At the same time, the 45th Division, with its dauntless First Battalion, was coming across country from the east. They were the ones who were to meet the greatest resistance, for the SS men, who had decided to impede the enemy's progress as much as possible, had massed in that sector. They preferred to make their stand here, with the Lager filled with prisoners at their backs, rather than in the western part of the compound, where their houses were and their families lived.

Inside the camp, the International Committee was wondering whether or not it should order an assault on the watchtowers and try for a breakthrough to establish contact with the Americans.

Since dawn, two men, stark naked, had been standing near the Jourhaus gate. They were Mandzourian, the prisoner who had been the "administrative head" of the camp, and Wernicke, a Gypsy, who had run the internees' "self-police" force. Both of them for years had acted most barbarously toward their fellow prisoners. They had wanted to flee along with the SS men, but these, having other things on their minds, had left them behind without another thought. The International Committee, wanting to foil their escape, had confiscated their clothes, and they were thus readily identifiable. They stayed near the gate, shivering with cold and turning blue with fear. But if they had remained inside, they would have been pitilessly lynched. They, too, were hoping for some kind of miracle.

Then came the first American jeeps: a GI got out and opened the gate. Machine-gun fire burst from the center watchtower, the very one which, since morning, had been flying the white flag! The jeeps turned about and an armored tank came on. With a few bursts, it silenced the fire from the watchtower. The body of an SS man fell off the platform and came crashing loudly to the asphalt of the little square.

Patrick O'Leary had knelt behind the windowsill to protect himself from the bullets. He was never to forget the scene that ensued:

"I ascertain that the Americans are now masters of the situation. I go toward the officer who has come down from the tank, introduce myself and he embraces me. He is a major. His uniform is dusty, his shirt, open almost to the navel, is filthy, soaked with sweat, his helmet is on crooked, he is unshaven and his cigarette dangles from the left corner of his lip.

"At this point, the young Teutonic lieutenant, Heinrich Skodzensky, emerges from the guard post and comes to attention before the American officer. The German is blond, handsome, perfumed, his boots glistening, his uniform well-tailored. He reports, as if he were on the military parade grounds near the Under den Linden during an exercise, then very properly raising his arm he salutes with a very respectful 'Heil Hitler!' and clicks his heels.

"'I hereby turn over to you the concentration camp of Dachau, 30,000 residents, 2,340 sick, 27,000 on the outside, 560 garrison troops.'

"Am I dreaming? It seems that I can see before me the striking contrast of a beast and a god. Only that the Boche is the one who looks divine.

"The American major does not return the salute. He hesitates for a moment, as if he were trying to make sure that he is remembering the adequate words. Then, he spits into the face of the German,

" '*Du Schweinehund!*'

"And then, 'Sit down there!'—pointing to the rear seat of one of the jeeps which in the meantime have driven in."

A number of GIs had already surrounded the guard post and others were standing by the major. Among them was the corporal, recently promoted to sergeant, Jeremiah McKenneth.

Patrick O'Leary goes on:

"The major turns to me and hands me an automatic rifle.

" 'Come with me—'

"But I no longer had the strength to move.

" 'No, I stay here—'

"The major gave an order, the jeep with the young German officer in it went outside the camp again. A few minutes went by, my comrades had not yet dared to come out of their barracks, for at that distance they could not tell the outcome of the negotiations between the American officer and the SS men.

"Then I hear several shots.

" 'The bastard is dead!' the American major says to me.

"He gives some orders, transmitted to the radiomen in the jeeps, and more officers start arriving, newspapermen, little trucks. Now the prisoners have understood, they jump on the Americans, embrace them, kiss their feet, their hands; the celebration is on."

Lieutenant Colonel Will Cowling, who was among the first of the liberators, came very close to being mobbed by the mangy mass of humanity that swept him along like a tidal wave. The GIs had to fire into the air to make room around him. All the prisoners wanted was to get his autograph.

The detachment under the command of the American major had not come directly to the Jourhaus. It had made a detour by way of the marshaling yard, where the convoys of deportees normally arrived and departed. There they found some fifty-odd cattle cars parked on the tracks. The cars were not empty.

"At first sight," said Cowling, "they seemed to be filled with rags, discarded clothing. Then we caught sight of hands, stiff fingers, faces. . . ."

The train was full of corpses, piled one on the other, 2,310 of them, to be exact. The train had come from Birkenau, and the dead were Hungarian and Polish Jews, children among them. Their journey had lasted perhaps thirty or forty days. They had died of hunger, of thirst, of suffocation, of being crushed, or of being beaten by the guards. There were even evidences of cannibalism. They were all practically dead when they arrived at Dachau Station. The SS men did not take the trouble to unload them. They simply decided to stand guard and shoot down any with enough strength left to emerge from the cattle cars. The corpses were strewn everywhere—on the rails, the steps, the platforms.

The men of the 45th Division had just made contact with the 42nd, here in the station. They too found themselves unable to breathe at what they saw. One soldier yelled: "Look, Bud, it's moving!" He pointed to something in motion among the cadavers. A louse-infested prisoner was crawling like a worm, trying to attract attention. He was the only survivor.

"I never saw anything like it in my life," said Lieutenant

Harold Mayer. "Every one of my men became raving mad. We turned off toward the east, going around the compound, without even taking the trouble to reconnoiter first. We were out to avenge them."

"Now I know what we're fighting for," exclaimed Corporal Eagle—our friend Chief Glorious Eagle. "We can't live in the same world with them. They are nothing but animals. They must be destroyed."

In this very same station, at the very same time, German men and women, peasants or burghers from the town of Dachau, were in the process of looting the depot and the neighboring buildings. Their children were with them. The children played within touch of the corpses, while their parents piled their loot up on little carts or on their bicycles, totally indifferent to the dead on the train and to the nauseating stench of rotting flesh.

The ire of the men of the First Battalion, 157th Regiment, was to mount even higher as they got closer to the Lager of the deportees. The dead were everywhere—in the ditches, along the side streets, in the garden before a small building with chimneys—and there was a huge mountain of corpses inside the yard of this building, which they now understood to be the crematorium. And finally there was the ultimate horror —the infernal sight of those thousands and thousands of living skeletons, screaming like banshees, on the other side of the placid poplars.

When some of the SS men on the watchtowers started to shoot into the mobs of prisoners, the Americans threw all caution to the winds. They opened fire on the towers with healthy salvos. The SS men promptly came down the ladders, their hands reaching high. But now the American GI saw red. He shot the Germans down with a telling blast, and to make doubly sure sent a final shot into their fallen bodies. Then the hunt started for any other Germans in SS uniforms. Within a quarter of an hour there was not a single one of the Hitler henchmen alive with the camp.

In the SS refectory, one soldier had been killed while eating a plate of beans. He still held a spoonful in his hand. At the signal center, the SS man in charge of the switchboard was slumped over his panel, blood running down to the receiver, the busy signal from Munich still ringing in his unheeding ear. At the power plant, the SS foreman had been beaten to death with shovels by a Polish prisoner and his Czech assistant. After that, they had been able to cut the high-voltage current from the barbed-wire fences around the camp.

When there were no more SS men to go after, the GIs machine-gunned the dogs which were kept in the camp's huge kennel. One sheepdog, having only been wounded by the bullets, yelped desperately. He was finished off with a knife.*

Then came the time for fraternization with those who had just been saved, the mass of scarred, pate-shaven ones with their haggard, livid faces, their smiles grotesque because of their broken teeth, these human wrecks who embraced you, threw themselves on you, tried to tell you their stories in sign language, led you by the hand to show you the hovels they lived in, the dead outside the barracks, the dying in the hospital. The Americans gave them cigarettes, their rations, their chewing gum, their addresses, even the jackets or over-coats off their backs, or simply emptied their pockets to them.

---

* A week later a GI pilfering in one of the abandoned SS barracks, heard a growling coming from behind some cases in a dark corner. He approached cautiously and was startled to see a German Shepherd dog—his head was bloody from a bullet wound. The animal had apparently been hiding there without food and water for several days, licking his wound. The GI ran away and no one knows what happened to the wretched animal.

The symbol of liberation: an American distributes American cigarettes to the inmates.

An SS has his MG pointed toward the prisoners. (A photograph taken from the SS.)

Prisoners waiting. Photo by Gun.

Nerin E. Gun, before liberation, in the camp street. Photo taken with camera stolen from an SS guard.

Prisoners in the camp's streets.

The daily chore; putting the dead outside the block as though they were garbage. This photo was taken by Gun before the liberation, with a stolen camera.

The "shower." Photographed by Gun with stolen camera. This was, of course, the gas chamber.

Dead corpses in the crematorium. Photos taken by Gun with stolen camera before liberation.

The train loaded with dead corpses outside the camp.

The soldiers of the Second Battalion, 222nd Infantry, 42nd Division, "The Rainbow," fighting for Dachau.

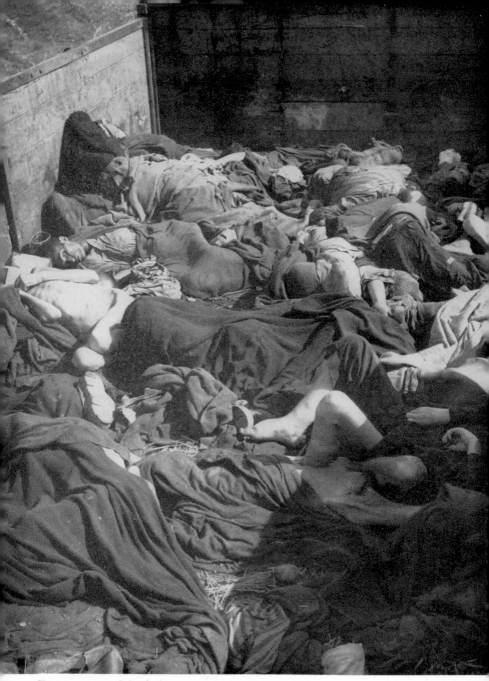

Every wagon of the train was full of dead prisoners.

SS killed by the Americans after the liberation.

During all this, at the Jourhaus, Patrick O'Leary was talking things over with the American colonel.

"We must press on to Munich," the colonel told him. "I will leave you a squad, to be under your command. But the camp gates must be kept closed. Nobody is to move away. You have carte blanche to enforce that."

"We need rations," O'Leary insisted.

"I have nothing with me," the colonel answered, "but I am advising headquarters. In the meantime, you are authorized to requisition whatever is necessary in the neighborhood."

The colonel went to his jeep to get two bottles of bourbon, which he gave to O'Leary. "To celebrate the liberation," he said.

Now Patrick O'Leary, who only that morning had been a prisoner like any other, was master of the camp. He sent out two deportees, escorted by American soldiers, to bring back some cows that were still on the special SS farm. During the night, they would be slaughtered and a first meat ration would be ready for the sick. He also authorized the confiscating of all supplies at the small canning factory at the edge of the compound. The contents were at once distributed to the freed prisoners, with what bread was left over in the SS refectory.

He was informed that Mandzourian, the Armenian Kapo, had been found hiding under a roof, and been rather severely beaten by his former fellow prisoners. With the help of the soldiers under his orders, O'Leary was able to save the Armenian, and he lectured his comrades: "We are civilized, don't forget. We do not kill out of hatred."

The Kapo was turned over to the American authorities. Two nights later he was shot down by a firing squad. The other murderer, the Gypsy, met the same fate.

O'Leary then went about disarming those prisoners who

had got hold of revolvers or automatic rifles. There was to be no summary settling of scores at Dachau.

This was an admirable and courageous decision. I can say it all the more sincerely, since later on I will take the liberty of severely criticizing certain decisions of the International Committee. Elsewhere, at Mauthausen for instance, there were veritable massacres among inmates, each wanting to get even for a beating, a piece of stolen bread, or an insult received. It was disgusting, for that was just what the Germans had wanted to make of us: stool pigeons and killers.

We had no right to take into our own hands the punishment of those who had made us suffer. First of all, because they were prisoners like ourselves, victims of the same circumstances; and secondly, because we were all guilty—all of us, at one time or another, out of selfishness or blindness or sheer madness, had wished for or brought about the death of a comrade. If we were alive this glorious evening, it was only because others had died in our place. In truth, the only ones responsible were those who had reduced us to this state.

In Reims, in the "little red schoolhouse," headquarters of SHAEF, a short paragraph was being dictated, for the communiqué of April 30, 1945, over the signature of General of the Armies Dwight D. Eisenhower:

"Our forces liberated and mopped up the infamous concentration camp at Dachau. Approximately 32,000 prisoners were liberated. Three hundred SS camp guards were quickly neutralized."

INTERLUDE

I

In Defense of an SS

. . . for a very brief period—and may the gods be thanked for this briefness, which explains how I escaped the common fate of all those who worked around the crematoria and who were periodically liquidated—I belonged to the team of prisoners in charge of sorting the pitiful herds of Hungarian Jewesses who were being directed to the gas chambers. My role was an insignificant one: I asked questions in Hungarian and entered the answers in German in a huge ledger. The administration of the camp was meticulous. It wanted a record of the name, address, weight, age, profession, school certificates, and so on, of all these women who in a few minutes were to be turned into corpses. I was not allowed inside the crematorium, but I knew from the others what went on in there.

The women, already completely undressed while answering our questions, were given an ersatz cake of soap, a darned towel, and were apparently told that they were going to the showers. Sometimes the internees tried to persuade those women who were carrying infants in their arms to let them take the children from them, for it was sometimes possible to stow babies away in the camp where devoted women would take care of them. Infants were not included in the figures of the statistics; they were, so to speak, traveling free, just as children do on trains, and the SS men cared little whether they died in the crematoria or lived in the camp. For infants alone, exact figures did not count.

But our arguments usually were of no avail. It was impossible to tell the victims what was going to happen inside, for they would not have believed it, or else, seized with panic, they would have started to scream. So the mothers refused to give up their children, and the babies were asphyxiated and burned with their mothers.

One of the SS men of the special detail—after all, even a wolf has a tender look and a caress for its young—became horrified by this spectacle and cried out in my presence, "*Mein Gott*, this is monstrous!" He had tears in his eyes, and his hair, like mine, was prematurely white. Then he regained control of himself and tried to find justification, perhaps in what had once been his conscience: "This is a terrible sacrifice imposed on us by the Fuehrer, a repulsive piece of work, but it is necessary to destroy these vermin, for they are the enemies of our people. The Fuehrer says that if we do not get rid of them they will take it out later on our own women, our own children."

I often think of the trial to which he might have been subjected, and I imagine myself being begged to serve as his defense attorney. I would have started my defense of this demon by having him describe the horror of what went on in the "shower room." The naked women, their sweating bodies pressed closely one against the others, the babies suffocating in their arms. Maybe one mother would have put her baby down on the floor to spare it the first shock of the expected spray of scalding water . . . then her face contorted with the horror of seeing her baby start coughing first, as the fumes of the gas issued from the floor, start to vomit blood, turn blue, violet, black, crushed under the weight of the bodies of the other victims slipping to the floor, like melted wax. . . . I would have asked the jury to think only of the suffering of that one mother. Was her anguish increased or diminished because other children and other mothers were dying at the same time, because there were two, four, six million human beings who were to be gassed as she and her child were? . . . No, my client's crime was not to be measured in units, however great the number of those martyred. It was to be judged in terms of this one baby lying in the horror of the gas chamber.

Then I would have asked the judge, the jury, and the spectators in the courtroom to remember the death of another baby of the same age, probably with cheeks as pink, with a body as tender, who had also been sleeping peacefully in his cradle before dying. His mother had looked at him with the same passion as had the Hungarian Jewess in the crematorium. She also had carried him for nine months. She had laughed and cried in the same way when he was born, and like the other mother she too had hoped for a future of roses and glory for her new infant. But now, suddenly, stealthily, the same horrible surprise as for the woman who expected a spray of hot water and instead inhaled a deadly gas; here now is a flaming bolt falling from the sky. This mother, too, like the other, probably saw her child consumed by flames. Is the despair, the pain of this mother any less important because her baby is the only one to die, in a house in London, instead of in a camp at Mauthausen, because there will not be a thousand, a million, six million of her race to die in the same way?

I would ask the jury to tell me whether pressing the button that opened the trapdoor through which the gas was released was a more criminal act than pressing the button that allowed a robot V1 or V2 rocket to spread death indiscriminately thousands of miles away. They are trying my client for having pressed the first button. Why then are they not trying the illustrious scientist who morally pressed the other?

So, for this trial, I would have called as a witness one scientist among the hundreds of scientists who worked on the Hitlerite war machines. It would have been easier to locate him than to find my SS man. For these scientists are working, most of them, because of the geographic accident of their capture rather than because of their real moral or political convictions, either in the United States or in Soviet Russia. I know one of them personally. This would have made my defense task easier, for I once put questions of this kind to Wernher von Braun.

"My SS man," I would have said to witness von Braun, "was an ignorant man, without political background, who had been continuously exposed to the brainwashing of Goebbels' propaganda. He thought he was doing his duty. But you, Dr. von Braun, belonged to a family of the upper bourgeoisie, had been given a complete education, were extremely intelligent and—you have proclaimed it a hundred times—savagely opposed to the Nazi ideology. But then how could it be that you could not distinguish right from wrong and made possible the murder of innocent children in London, Birmingham, Coventry, and elsewhere?

"My SS man had no choice. If he had refused to work at the gas chambers, they would have sent him away to a disciplinary camp or executed him. He could not sabotage the work, for he was carefully supervised, and he had to account for each of his victims. But you scientists, even if you were forced to work in the Hitler laboratories, no one could make you prove that you possessed genius. It may be possible to punish a general for losing a battle, a doctor for letting a patient die, but not a scientist for *not* having invented, for *not* having discovered. . . . For, to accuse someone of this kind of after-the-fact sabotage, it would be necessary to understand what the invention, what the discovery would be. And if that were known in advance—forgive the truism—then it would no longer be an invention or a discovery. Why, Mr. von Braun, could you not have been satisfied during all your years of work for Adolf Hitler, to search, and search, and search, and search, but never to discover anything?

"My SS man thought he was being a patriot. He was loyal to his Fuehrer. But you, von Braun, told me that you hated Hitler and his war. Then why did you build rockets for him which were bound to kill innocent children? You were horrified by the concentration camps where they gassed helpless babies, but at the same time you morally pressed the button that allowed flying rockets to go out and consume other babies.

"Did you do this out of patriotism, loyalty toward your native land? Then why did you desert that Germany, your fatherland, that country in which you grew up and which made of you a great scientist, at the very moment when it had the greatest need of you? You were not persecuted; the members of your family had not been arrested or killed; your wealth had not been confiscated; the Germany of post-1945 was free, democratic, and it loves and admires you, and welcomes you always as the prodigal son whenever you return.

It is immensely proud of you. And still you chose another country of your own free will. Therefore, could it not have been out of German chauvinism, out of Teutonic fanaticism that you helped in the launching of robot bombs aimed at London?

"The people of Huntsville, Alabama, consider you their most illustrious fellow townsman. An American judge has bestowed upon you the great privilege of American citizenship (let us point out, so as to avoid any partisan objections, that the German scientists working for the Soviets have been accorded the same distinctions and the same privileges). You have been richly rewarded, acclaimed; books and films have exalted your exploits; Presidents have been honored to shake your hand, and yet, if I were to demand that my SS man, now sitting in the dock, also be honored in the same way, triumphally acclaimed, given American or Soviet sanctuary, people would laugh me to scorn.

"Why? Because my SS man might do the same thing again? But, Herr von Braun, are you not once more working on the construction of giant rockets? Yes. Of course, this is for the progress of science, just as in a sense by perfecting Hitler's war machine you were also helping science. But these rockets might very well one day be aimed at your former German brothers, for the Germans who live behind the Iron Curtain are nevertheless your former countrymen. Don't you think that perhaps someday just such a rocket may murder a baby in East Berlin as in the past your V2 murdered babies in London?

"I know you are sincerely democratic, an honorable American and a good man, and that you don't want such things to happen. Some people—a tiny minority—have doubts about your sincerity. They point out that, after all, you *did* know how to lie to Hitler and to his Gestapo so cleverly that they never doubted you were one of them, otherwise you would never have been tolerated in one of their most vital factories, would never have been entrusted with such important secrets. I believe in your loyalty and I am sure that if by misfortune the United States lost a future war, you would not change your nationality a third time, nor proclaim that what you did at Huntsville, Alabama, was done under duress.

"So, honorable witness von Braun, I call on you to speak to the jury in favor of my client, the SS man, your former compatriot!"

"Your client," von Braun could have answered me, "simply had to go and serve the Russians as a mercenary in East Berlin, or the French in Indo-China, or the Africans in the Congo. Then he too would have been assured of impunity. So why take it out on me?"

Obviously, I would not get very far with this kind of defense . . .

Nostalgia

5

I have often noticed how a little dog, transplanted with his master to a totally strange place, follows this master step by step for fear of getting lost. So it was that Lorenzo, a simple garage worker from Taranto, whom the vicissitudes of war had turned into a chauffeur for an Italian reserve captain on duty in Rumania, never got a step away from his boss. For him, the outings in the invaded Russian provinces, as well as the hasty retreat through the Carpathian Mountains, were all in a day's work. He understood nothing about politics, was not very sure whom he was fighting against, and as far as he was concerned, Hitler, the King, Mussolini, Antonescu were just signori who, like all signori, were obviously in cahoots with each other.

The main thing, after the collapse of the Italian army, was not to get lost, so far away from Taranto, and he therefore never left his master. In exchange for this protection, he turned into a loyal and obedient serf. He was at his master's side when the reserve officer stupidly fell into the clutches of the Gestapo. Respectful of the immutable Prusso-Nazi police

74

regulations that decreed "like master, like chauffeur," they deported the officer and his Lorenzo to the concentration camp at Dachau. Same boxcar, same classification, same sentence, same specifications, same travel orders; only the names were different.

But once in Dachau, Lorenzo's destiny took another path. The Nazis were sick and tired of Italian reserve officers; they were a bothersome surplus. But a chauffeur was something else again, especially a chauffeur who knew about sports cars, for an *Obersturmfuehrer,* it just so happened, had "liberated" an Alfa-Romeo belonging to the "Badoglio" consul at Munich, and he needed a specialist to take care of it. So our Lorenzo, only a few days after his arrival at the camp, got himself a plum of a job, a real golden opportunity.

Other concentration camp prisoners put in years of humiliation and hard servitude, became involved with intrigue and even committed crimes, yet still needed lots of luck to get as far. For Lorenzo was no longer subject to work details; he was allowed out of the camp enclosure practically at will; the Kapos were powerless to give him even the slightest reprimand. He could thumb his nose at discipline and he spent most of his time in "his" garage, where life was easy and warm, listening to the radio and tinkering with motors.

It was his insignificant, wretched former master who unwittingly had been the reason for Lorenzo's lightning rise in the world.

At first, in the quarantine block, Lorenzo had remained his master's shadow. The officer was a century behind the times in his social ideas and still believed that some people were born to live and die as servants. He saw to it, therefore, that Lorenzo stuffed his mattress for him, brought him his messkit filled with soup; and he insisted on other services of this kind.

Dachau was certainly no bastion of democracy, but the fellow barracks tenants rebelled when they saw this abuse and forbade Lorenzo to do anything whatsoever for his master. One of the boys in the work office, being informed of the incident, saw to it that when the time came for them to go to one of the shops, Lorenzo was the one who was made the foreman. His master was put to sweeping, carrying heavy cases, and doing all the hard work under the orders of his former servant. The others thought the spectacle was side-splitting.

After a few days of this farce the officer rebelled and complained to a Dutch colonel who had some influence in the *Schreibstube* and who, for the international honor of the officer corps, insisted that Lorenzo be transferred.

So his card came into the hands of a clerk who was making out forced work assignments, and this is where Lorenzo's good fairy played a part: without her, the card would probably have been tossed on the pile of those assigned to outside work, from which it was so difficult ever to come back; but that very morning, the clerk had received a pressing call for a mechanic, preferably Italian, from an officer who couldn't start his Alfa-Romeo. Lorenzo's card read "Chauffeur, specialized mechanic." The SS big shot phoned again, insistently. He needed his *Haftling* right away! The weary and frightened clerk sent Lorenzo out on the job.

And for Lorenzo that was like winning first prize in the lottery. He was given an almost new blue-and-white-striped prison uniform with his number embroidered in silk on a red background (that had cost him ten cigarettes!), a good pair of boots (too big, of course, but still with usable soles), and woolen gloves (mismatched), but what did all that matter? He was allowed to let his hair grow, because the *Frau Obersturm-fuehrer* didn't like to see shaved pates. The other convicts stepped respectfully aside when he went past. There was a social order among the deportees which was as sacrosanct as the ukases of the SS itself. Even our skulking Oberkapo, the arrogant Armenian, answered his greeting. Lorenzo liked, of a twilight, to parade up and down the open street, clean and freshly shaven, dignified as one of those *corazzieri* who stood guard before the Quirinal, the King's Palace, in Rome.

Apart from this slight sin of vanity that might have been dreamed up by a Moliere, Lorenzo's sudden good luck had in no way corrupted his heart of gold. He remained obliging, generous, confiding, sympathetic, attentive, extremely discreet, patient, and understanding. Thanks to his influence on the *Obersturmfuehrer,* who could not get along without him, he got sinecures in the garage for some of our friends, among them his ex-boss, the officer, who showed no reluctance in accepting this time. Since Lorenzo ate at the garage, and sometimes even in the *Obersturmfuehrer*'s kitchen, he was able to afford the luxury of distributing his regular soup rations among friends in the *Stube*. In this way he helped save more than one life.

On occasion, rare occasions it is true, he drove the SS commander's car outside the camp and could therefore report to us about what was going on in town. His vocabulary was most limited but it did not detract from the effectiveness of his vivid descriptions, interspersed with "Mamma mias," "Madonnas," and "in gambas," of the red flames licking at the ruins of Munich, now in its death throes under a sheet of bombs.

Gasoline, which he swiped without danger, was a good medium of exchange; it was used for all kinds of heaters and was even transformed, though I never discovered how, into Schnapps and other liquors. The inmates who went out into the fields on work details could exchange it for food as the farmers were in dire need of fuel for their tractors, and I have always suspected that our Resistance group had stockpiled a supply for eventual use as "Molotov cocktails." Lorenzo also brought us tools, oil, an electric storage battery, rags—in fact, all kinds of things, not excluding the collection of cigar butts which the *Obersturmfuehrer* magnanimously let him have.

It was only normal that under such circumstances Lorenzo's friendship should be much sought after. The head of the *Stube,* worrying that Lorenzo might leave our block to go and live elsewhere, as he was entitled to, had set up a private bed for him in the vestibule. One of the newcomers had been delegated to wait on him. So now Lorenzo, in his turn, had his servant.

As there is no point in hurting former fellow prisoners, I will not use any names, but in Lorenzo's entourage there were many people who had been quite important in civilian life: a Magyar count, several marquis, a former ambassador to Spain, a bishop, two generals, an important Hungarian banker, the owner of the largest store in Budapest, a steel plant owner, the one-time manager of a hotel in Baltimore, and the former head of an automobile factory.

At first, Lorenzo had been duly impressed by these signori. He bowed to them and stepped aside as they went by. At that time, the signori had hardly been aware of his existence. Later, they deigned to refer to him as "chauffeur" or as "Lorenzo" and they addressed him in the familiar form customary in masters toward servants. But when Lorenzo went to work in the garage, a slow change set in. They started to say "Lorenzo" with a degree of friendship in their tone, and gradually the tone became more respectful. Soon he was

"Herr Lorenzo," sometimes "Herr Mekaniker," and even on occasion "Mr. Foreman."

They wanted to spend time with him; they asked after his health; and they began to show him the endless marks of attention which can take on such enormous proportions in the daily life of a death camp. There was always someone to fetch his cap for him if he had forgotten it at roll call; to see that he got the best place in front of the fireplace. He was now the first to be informed of any new bit of gossip; one of the boys who worked in the infirmary would bring him aspirin and wads of cotton; it was an honor to be the first to say good morning to him and find out how he was doing. When he spoke, he was listened to, and none would have dreamed of interrupting him without first saying "Excuse me."

Then there was the clique that set out to become his best friends. One lieutenant colonel had promised him that, thanks to his own influence with the Ministry of War, Lorenzo would be promoted to sergeant, decorated with the Silver Medal, and demobilized, all within three days after liberation. There was a diplomat who had figured out how he could get a pension. One of the bishops had promised him an audience with the Pope, and, in expectation of this great occasion, bestowed on him and his faraway family all sorts of blessings. The ambassador to Spain talked about adopting him later, and in the meantime started calling him, "My son, my dear son." He was assured of a job in a bank, as a factory foreman and as representative in America for an automobile company. The Hungarian banker, quite simply, transferred amounts mentally to "his" account. If Lorenzo brought him a slice of bread and margarine, a thousand pengös were deposited in his name; for a pair of shoes, it was ten thousand lire credited at the Banco di Roma. When the banker got a week in the infirmary, thanks to Lorenzo's pull, he rewarded Lorenzo with a block of stock in Fiat. I felt that, toward the end of our captivity, Lorenzo had certainly become a millionaire.

Yet Lorenzo did not neglect his former master, the reserve officer. Not only did he find him a goldbricking job in the garage, but he kept him fed, protected him when anyone bothered him, and I think he even took care of him like a son when the officer developed colic and later came down with pneumonia. To the officer, Lorenzo had now become a *fratello*. "If you are ever in need, Lorenzo, you can come and spend the rest of your days on my estate in Tuscany, tending the vineyards, hunting, taking it easy. . . ."

Then came the onrush of the Americans and days began to fly by filled with feverish activity, violence, turbulent events. But the more talk there was of liberation, the more a vacuum grew around Lorenzo. His conversation was no longer sought after. Of course, the slices of bread and sausage that he was able to "organize" were still welcome, but they were less avidly accepted, really just to make him happy. Eventually the time came when Lorenzo could no longer bring anything, because his SS commander had fled, the garage had been closed, and he was no longer allowed outside the confines of the camp.

During the final distributions of packages to the prisoners, Lorenzo never received any. Some of his "lifelong friends," including the bishop, parsimoniously deigned to share their chocolate, their sardines or their cigarettes with him, but most of the others now simply ignored Lorenzo's presence. He had suddenly ceased to be "Sir" and was plain "Comrade" or just "Lorenzo" when he was not referred to as "Italiano." The banker had ceased making imaginary deposits to his account. The father turned his eyes away from his adopted son. And, since Lorenzo had no more contacts with the outside world, all he could do now was listen silently and respectfully, knowing better than to dare take part in the badinage of his "good friends" who had all once more become shrewd strategists and political geniuses.

When liberation came, Lorenzo, like everyone else, was kissed by everybody, for at such a time joy makes no distinctions. But on the evening of that memorable day, I happened to notice Lorenzo squatting sadly in the corner of his barracks, staring straight ahead through the barbed wire, his ill-shaven face resting on one hand. For all the world, he was like a lost, forgotten puppy.

I was to see him often in the same posture. Most of his friends and entourage had moved away, into new quarters in the former SS barracks, to the GIs' area, or into the VIPs' block. Those who still remained in the barracks gave a very convincing impression of never in their lives having had any truck with Lorenzo.

Most of them eventually left Dachau without even coming to say good-bye to Lorenzo, but he did not become discouraged. Liberation had been responsible for great chaos, he rationalized, and it was only natural that his important friends, the *pezzi grossi*, the big shots, should be overwhelmed with a flock of new problems. He would be able to write to them later; he had made note of all their addresses.

The reserve officer was still on hand, and he remembered Lorenzo well enough to send him to liberate the commander's Alfa-Romeo. Thus, with Lorenzo at the wheel, they would be able to get out of the camp and head for the Italian frontier. But Lorenzo, like a good patriot, at the last minute had sabotaged the car so that the SS men could not use it for escape. It was a useless wreck.

Lorenzo left Dachau with his boss, the reserve officer, in an evacuation truck of the Vatican mission. The officer got in first, followed by Lorenzo, who was carrying two duffel bags in which the officer had accumulated boots, bits of fabric, statues, and any other odds and ends he could lay his hands on. The officer took his place on a seat which Lorenzo had carefully wiped off. Lorenzo squatted at his feet.

I was to meet Lorenzo again, fifteen years later, in Lima, Peru. He was working then as manager in a garage. He had emigrated with the financial help of the Italian government, which was available to all, and it was the consulate which had found him this job. His dream had been to set up in business for himself, but his friend the banker had been very slow in making good on the deposits. In fact, Lorenzo once received a money order for a few thousand lire but that was all he ever got. He had dutifully written to everybody, and a few of them had answered—mostly through their secretaries. He had, of course, received a few generalized and vapid letters of recommendation.

The bishop had sent along a papal benediction, made out to Lorenzo and his family, on an engraved parchment that accorded full remission of sins, along with a photograph of Pope Pius XII. This is still framed on his dining-room wall. I refrained from telling him such benedictions are for sale for a few lire in any of the shops of the Via della Conciliazione. He received a few Christmas cards the first years, in answer to his own, and then no more.

I had found his address on an official list at the headquarters of the Dachau Committee. He greeted me wildly, like a child who had found a toy he had thought lost forever, and insisted that I come to dinner at his house. *"Mia moglie, i bambini . . . ,"* he explained.

He had a large family, and there were a lot of friends, neighbors, and employees present. Lorenzo, in spite of his relatively modest situation, had remained a very likable, friendly, popular fellow, and the meal was a sumptuous one. He must have spent a month's wages on the wines alone. Lorenzo monopolized the conversation: he talked incessantly about *his* Dachau, *his* life there, *his* uniform, *his* responsibilities, *his* friends—the bishop, the ambassador, the banker, the general, the aristocrat, *his* adoption—and from time to time he would interrupt himself and turn to me for corroboration, which I dutifully supplied.

"I am so happy you came," he interjected, "because my friends, even my wife, would not believe that all this had happened to me. Tell them, my friend, that what I am saying is not a pack of lies.

"The *commendatore*," he reiterated, turning to his wife, "was there. Tell them, comrade, how I used to bring gasoline for the Resistance Committee. We were going to set fire to all the SS men with it. And when I announced the fall of Vienna—I had heard about it on the commander's radio. . . . And how my good friend, the head of Fiat in Bucharest, used to consult me, how he wanted to know what *I* thought of the Mercedes-Benz. . . ."

I got back to my hotel late that night. Lorenzo, still intoxicated with his triumphal evening, had insisted on accompanying me, so he could tell the hotel people that I was *his* guest and *he* would take care of my bill. He even phoned the *Correo,* so that they could interview me and take a picture of us together.

"You can't imagine the joy you have brought me," he said as we parted. "Everything here in Lima is so paltry, so unimportant. And how often I think of our daring, adventurous times together! We were caged lions then. . . . Ah, *amico,* in those days, I was really somebody, there at Dachau. . . ."

6

Milena

I met fat Piroshka again as she sat in the sun on a windowsill inside the barred window of a building which before the liberation had been the barracks of the SS noncoms, and now had been turned into a chaperoned residence for women prisoners. The American camp commander, even several thousands of miles away from his native Midwest, even in those days of the horsemen of the Apocalypse, had not been able to rid himself of the puritanical views which seemed to be part of the makeup of every New World officer. He had decided to have the "liberated" women guarded doubly, day and night, by patrols made up of both the volunteer disciplinary body of the internees themselves and American soldiers, all of them white. The women, some of whom had their infants with them, were thereby assured of invulnerability. Even those who claimed to be the husbands, fiancés, or long-established lovers of the women prisoners were not entitled to private visits, and after curfew the whole area was off limits. This building had been selected especially for the purpose, because all its windows were barred, and it was situated along a mall that was out of bounds in the evening.

On seeing me, Piroshka threw her arms toward the sky, and after giving thanks to the Holy Mother, asked if I had a cigarette. I did not, but I was able to give her a tube of toothpaste and a bottle of Jean-Maria Farina, which she accepted somewhat condescendingly. I had thought she was dead and most certainly she must have thought the same of me. Nevertheless, we passed the time of day—she behind her grille, her legs raised with her feet against the opposite side of the window frame, allowing her skirt to slip down toward her hips and show off a portion of her slack, grayish and bruised flesh, I self-conscious in my tropical shorts and with my flaming armband—just as if we had met casually in front of the terraces of the Ritz in Budapest, on a walk along the banks of the Danube.

Indeed, why should we have found it so amazing that one or another of the prisoners was still alive and free? The concentration camps were only a macabre lottery. Those who held the lucky numbers were bound to get out. The others, of course, all lost.

We had won. There had been the great mass enthusiasm of liberation. Unfortunately this enthusiasm was nothing but an aggregate of thousands and thousands of personal, animal, sensual satisfactions; the selfish satisfaction of still finding your own skin more or less in one piece. That others also had made it was virtually immaterial. The gambler who sees the roulette ball stop on the number he is playing pockets his chips without worrying too much whether other players shared his luck. If we had had to shout hurrah for every fellow prisoner spared by the avalanche, we would logically have had to weep over the disappearance of each of the dead. And that would have been a bad bargain because, for each survivor, there were a thousand gone forever.

Fat Piroshka claimed to be the daughter of a Hungarian aristocrat. Her father was supposed to have served as an ambassador in Teheran or in Bolivia.

I had first met her at the Maria-Lanzendorf Camp, near Vienna. Everybody called her Fat Piroshka because, working as she did in the kitchen, she had a nicely rounded belly and in fact looked pregnant. Even at Dachau, she had been able to maintain some of her plumpness.

She had left Maria-Lanzendorf in February, 1945, a considerable time after me, and was sent to the cursed Hartheim Castle where the Dachau administration kept the internees used as guinea pigs for the diabolical experiments of the doctors. Piroshka had been spared, or so she claimed, and had then been sent on to Dachau proper.

"Milena was there too," Piroshka finally said, in an embarrassed tone that seemed to forbid any further questions on the subject. Milena had been with us at the Maria-Lanzendorf Camp, but was taken away one day in October, 1944, in a police van normally used for carrying victims to the gas chambers. Milena had just turned seventeen. She was extremely pretty. All of us had been a little in love with her.

The Dachau Concentration Camp was an enormous spider's web whose steel threads extended to boundless extremities, throughout the Reich and even beyond. Maria-Lanzendorf had an appealing name, but, as was always the case with Nazi prisons, was horrible—foggy, marshy, and continuously exposed to punishing winds. It was a small correctional camp half an hour from Vienna by train; a sort of stopover between Dachau and Mauthausen. Dachau prisoners were sent to Mauthausen when they were to be exterminated in the latter camp's gas chambers and, in turn, Mauthausen sent prisoners to Dachau for liquidation there. On the way, they made a stop at Maria-Lanzendorf.

Maria-Lanzendorf was also a sorting area. The Gestapo, based in Vienna, held its victims here while making up its mind about their collective fate. Here interrogations took place, and it was to this camp that Dachau's political investigators brought prisoners from their camp for confrontations. It would obviously have been simpler to do all this at Dachau proper, but at that time Vienna was still a relatively agreeable city and I think the SS men used the pretext of doing this work at Lanzendorf so as to be able to spend their evenings off at the "Prater" or the "Grinzing." In addition, Lanzendorf was used to lock up deportees whose liberation had already been approved, but whom the authorities still wanted to have on hand for a few months: the Gestapo was always grudging about relinquishing its prey.

I was housed in a small building which, in the old days when the camp was only a large farm, had been used by agricultural workers. My lodging was a tiny room on the second floor with a door that barely closed. Beneath my room were three or four sordid cells housing American fliers who had been forced to parachute from their planes and who had been captured by local peasants armed with pitchforks. One of their number had been lynched by the farmers, and the rest were not in a very happy mood. The left wing of the house, completely isolated, had been made into a kind of dormitory stable for some hundred Italian *ergastoliani*, that is, lifers condemned for murder, who had no idea why the Germans had brought them here but were hoping they would be incorporated into an Italian SS division that was supposed to be in the planning stage.

For me, the stay at Maria-Lanzendorf was a relatively idyllic interlude between the horror of the death camps of Mauthausen, Auschwitz, and Dachau. This little camp, without a crematorium, reputed to be a gateway to freedom, seemed quite innocuous to me, aside from the obligatory attendance at the twilight punishments in the main square— fifteen to twenty-five lashes of the *Shlag* per prisoner disciplined, and the Friday hangings. The largest part of the population of the camp was made up of German or foreign workers sentenced to short terms for minor infractions of work rules.

My departure from Mauthausen had taken place under puzzling conditions. One rainy afternoon, we had been ordered out into the square for an inspection. I attempted to get out of the chore by claiming to have urgent work to do. But the Kapo, or barracks boss, a professional hired killer known by the innocent-sounding name of Willy, who had it in for all those he considered goldbricks and for me in particular, made such a commotion that I was forced to turn out with my group. The roll call was being held in honor of a "distinguished" visitor, the Gauleiter of Lower Austria. A Gauleiter was the title of the Nazi party's governor of a province, and this one was a friend of Hitler. His pleasure that day was a review of the group, made up mostly of Hungarian politicians, diplomats, and aristocrats. The Gauleiter stopped before the first man in each row to shout insults at him, laugh in his face and, when he felt like it, honor him with a couple of slaps. I thought I would escape this torrential rain of invective because, having arrived late, I was all the way in the back.

But the camp commander, an extraordinary specimen of Aryanism, resplendent in his gray silk uniform shimmering with carmine reflections, pointed me out to the Gauleiter.

"That one is a Turk," he said, "the only Turkish prisoner in the camp." He said it with the pride of a zoo director who might be displaying his white elephant from Siam. I was suddenly promoted to the rank of exotic curiosity.

"Aha!" the delighted Gauleiter exclaimed, "a spy, eh? What did you do to get in here?"

"Why, nothing at all," I replied in my most innocent tone, the more so since I meant it completely.

The Gauleiter looked at the camp commander. He in turn questioned an aide.

"We really don't know," the aide mumbled finally. "He's a newspaperman."

He seemed embarrassed and was probably kicking himself for having called the visitor's attention to a prisoner whose heinous crimes he could not detail to him. The Gestapo, whether through carelessness, laziness, or lack of organization, had thus far not forwarded my dossier to the camp authorities.

The Gauleiter eyed me perplexedly, then blurted:

"Of course, I remember now. We met at tea at Paula Wessely's, after the dress rehearsal of that Schiller play in Berlin."

The party suddenly came back to me. Paula Wessely was one of Germany's greatest dramatic actresses. At the Deutsche Theater I had covered the rehearsals of a Schiller play she was appearing in, *Hero and Leander,* because at that time I was attracted by the idea of being a stage director and had thought of trying to break in at this theater. The Gauleiter had indeed once come there. We had, in fact, had a long conversation. He knew Constantinople and had visited the tiny islet in the Sea of Marmara which now houses a lighthouse but which, according to legend, had been the meeting place of the lovers in the play.

"Why, if you're a Turk," he proclaimed, "that means you're a neutral, and you can't be kept here! Not in my *Gau!* This will have to be cleared up at once," he told the commander, who acknowledged this with a salute, as did his retinue of aides.

Two days later I had my travel orders. Half my comrades in misfortune were convinced I was headed back to freedom in Budapest, and started to load me down with messages and advice, but the other half merely prophesied that I'd meet a bitter end in the truck that was waiting for me at the gates of the camp. "They close the doors and then they turn on the gas," was their gloomy prediction.

But for me the transfer seemed something like a miracle and I think that the SS men who saw me arriving from Mauthausen by car and alive were dumfounded. As a result, they became very cautious of burning their fingers where I was concerned.

Even Dante created different categories in his Inferno, so I must therefore be excused for differentiating among these Schutzstaffel who, by vocation, had become the executioners of Europe. There certainly were some among them who were valiant men, who probably fought with honor, if the profession of warfare can be so considered; others who had been unwillingly assigned to the skull-and-crossbones units; and still others who had simply wanted to belong to a political group and who, at the start, had had no taste or desire for brutal violence.

Yet, there was no question that the major part of the SS corps was made up of abject criminals. But I must attest that the SS men who had come from Germany seemed to me just a little less cruel, less sadistic, and less perverted than those who had come from Austria. After all, the Austrian SS men had voluntarily chosen this criminal career after their own country became the victim of fratricidal aggression, when throughout the world it was already known that the branch of service they were joining was devoted simply to genocide. But there may well have been German SS volunteers who had come into the movement at a time when it was still only a vague kind of association of "patriots," exalted, embittered, thinking themselves to have been driven into an impasse and believing that they had heard the commanding call of an awesome German God. There may, indeed, have been some who had never foreseen abominations and had expected only easy victories.

Granted that Himmler and his crew were modern exterminating demons who, whether they worked through dossiers or through machines, wore white gloves and rarely got their own hands soiled. However, every time I witnessed acts of revolting brutality, they were committed by Austrian Nazis. Even worse were the prison guards who came from territories that had once been foreign provinces of the Hapsburgs and who had retained their assimilated Austrian traditions and dialects. These miscreants inflicted tortures not only under orders, but also because they derived a sort of sexual pleasure from them. Torturing prisoners—most of whom were miserable wrecks who no longer retained even the animal instinct to defend themselves until the end—was made a gala occasion, a macabre circus performance. The guards kept on the lookout for potential victims like cats eternally on the prowl for mice.

I particularly remember one little SS man, no more than five feet tall, who under other circumstances would have been considered ridiculous, with his fat belly oozing out over his belt and a nose like a potato. But, alas, none of us in the camps found anything funny about the physical aspects of SS men. The victim does not stop, as his head slides under the knife of the guillotine, to see whether the executioner is handsome or ugly.

We called this one "Napoleon" because of his size and his habit of slipping his hand between the buttons of his blouse, and also because of his custom each morning to announce a grandiose and imaginary victory of the Hitlerites in Russia.

Napoleon spent most of his time sitting on the edge of the watchtower, a wooden structure about eighteen feet high, from which the guards could view the entire central area of the camp. He held a fieldglass in his hands and, like an admiral on the poopdeck of his flagship, kept surveying the enormous expanse of the little square. No, he was not a Don Quixote in swastika uniform expecting a sneak attack by enemy paratroopers, but was merely supervising his prisoners at work.

As soon as someone within his field of vision appeared to be looking up, talking, or glancing toward the women's quarters —and very often, when real pretexts were too few and far between, our little Napoleon would invent infractions, without fear of contradiction, as can well be understood—the sadistic SS men would shinny down from his tower with an agility that under other circumstances might have been called admirable, jump on the motorcycle always at the ready at the foot of the tower, start it up, and come tearing through the courtyard at top speed without concern for anyone's safety. He would then hop from his cycle without turning it off and, like a motorized Tom Mix, throw himself on the poor prisoner and pitilessly down him with punches and kicks. The victim fainted or pretended to faint, for that was the only way to shorten the beating. Then Napoleon would pick up his motorcycle and rush back to his watchtower at the same breakneck speed. Fieldglass in hand, he would wait for the next bout.

Another of the SS men, a native of the Bachka (a Hungarian province bordering on Yugoslavia and inhabited by an Austrian minority), received visits two or three times a week from his fiancée. This was against regulations, but the commander was seldom there to know about it. This SS man was tall, well built, and had a certain amount of education, probably a couple of years of high school, which was rare among these usually illiterate mercenaries. One of his eyes was green and the other light brown, so we called him "Tiger."

His fiancée was beautiful. She could not have been more than sixteen, with curly ash-blond hair. She was perpetually smiling as if that was all she knew how to do. She was the village butcher's daughter. On each visit she brought a large package, the contents of which we could guess: sausages, ham, pork chops, and all those other kinds of meat whose taste we had forgotten ages ago. There were also bones for Tiger's dog, a mongrel sheepdog that was fond of nipping at the prisoners' calves.

When the blonde arrived, Tiger would bring her to our building. On the ground floor there was a sort of small cell which at times served as a shelter for the guard on duty. Tiger locked himself in there with the girl.

By coincidence, and there were only two or three exceptions to this during my stay at Maria-Lanzendorf, as soon as Tiger—who was an *Unterscharfuehrer,* a kind of sergeant— was locked in with his guest, it became "punishment time." Arbitrarily designated prisoners were tied down to a wooden sawhorse and one of the soldiers administered ten to twenty lashes with a whip. Usually the victim passed out after the first six lashes, after which he was revived with cold water and the punishment resumed.

Once, I was able to peep through a nail hole in the door and could see into the little room where Tiger and his pretty blonde were. They were standing near the window that looked out into the square so that they could get a good view of the whippings. She was completely undressed and stood there naked, her hands against the wall, her nose pressed to the windowpane, watching with fascination. From time to time, when she turned her head to kiss her lover, I thought I could detect the look of ecstasy on her beautiful face.

A long time afterward, I read somewhere in the memoirs of the gallant knight, Giacomo Casanova de Seingalt, how he seduced a lady of the court of Louis XV while she sat on her balcony experiencing a double thrill because she was simultaneously watching a hanging in the Place de Grève.

I never did find out how another *Unterscharfuehrer*, Tibor by name, got himself enrolled under the Jolly Roger. A prisoner does not ask that kind of question of an SS guard, even when the latter shows some humanity and condescends to talk to him. For Tibor was an unbelievable exception, I would even say unique. He mistreated no one. He insulted no one. He stubbornly avoided doing this, and I must say courageously (for their superiors severely disciplined the SS men who showed any signs of humaneness), and when under orders he was obliged to force the prisoners to march, to work, take them off to solitary confinement, or even read punishment sentences aloud in his nasal voice, he would do it with embarrassment and would try to smile humbly as if he wanted both to be pardoned for what he was doing and to soften the lot of his victims. When he was quite sure no other SS men were near, he would even venture to say a few words of encouragement, or announce some bit of good news, perhaps the arrival of a load of packages, and let the prisoners rest a while, offering one of those tiny favors which in a camp like this made the difference between the bearable and the intolerable.

For those who may be skeptical, Tibor did get into the SS voluntarily. He was born in the Siebenburgen, that province the Rumanians call Transylvania, and over which they fight, under all regimes, during all wars and all peaceful times, with the Hungarians, who call it the Banat. His family had emigrated there long ago, under orders, it was said, of Frederick the Great. His father had been a farmer, but Tibor had been satisfied to become the village postman. Then came the war and the greater Germany, and the boys were off to serve the ancestral Fatherland, now triumphant, as in other times they had gone off to the Crusades. Tibor had followed the others because it would have been too shameful to stay behind; and besides, the Rumanians were drafting all non-volunteers, and that prospect was even more distasteful. Himmler had decreed that all outland volunteers of German ancestry were automatically to be incorporated in to his Schutzstaffel as a tribute to their Aryanism. This was also a much handier way to keep an eye on them. They had practically all been assigned to the *Sicherheitsdienst* and turned into prison guards. Tibor, in spite of his dislike for violence, had meekly accepted his fate, for he was afraid to desert, and it seemed preferable to try to get by in Lanzendorf, only half an hour out of Vienna, than to serve as "wolf bait" on the steppes of the Lower Volga.

He was scarcely typical of the Teutonic knight: his hair was traitorously black and curly; he was slightly built and seemed fragile, with almost girlish skin. Even when he stood guard at the barricade in front of the north gate, he walked like a ballet dancer, but he was a good-looking boy and he modestly admitted to me that now, as he was in uniform, women found him irresistible. Of course, I could not help believing that he was also the prat boy of the head of the political section, which might explain why he had never been hauled up on charges and shipped off to Russia, but this was an area I carefully refrained from discussing.

We were able to talk almost every evening when Tibor was on guard. I was behind the little barred window in the ground-floor hallway, and he would lean against the outside wall. This was the time when the camp authorities expected wrongly that I was shortly to be liberated and they treated me with exceptional consideration. These bits of conversation were excellent entertainment. Tibor, in his legionnaire's lingo, described his conquests on the *Prater,* never leaving out any of the salacious details. He found the subject one of inexhaustible interest. He was probably trying to convince me, and also reassure himself, that he was the very embodiment of a fine masculine specimen. In exchange, I told him about Paris, about the girls on the Boulevard Saint-Michel and the Rue Soufflot, and about imaginary daisy chains in the Bois de Boulogne.

Tibor, handsome, charming, and good-natured despite his beast's uniform, was irresistible, but there was one hitch. That was Hildegarde, a statuesque blonde who lived in the 13th *Bezirk,* or ward, of Vienna, and who was Tibor's dentist. All the male dentists were either away at war or overloaded with patients. There were none in the camp.

"When Hildegarde rubs her big boobs against my shoulder, so that she can get a better look into my mouth," he would tell me, "it really does something to me."

But Hildegarde would not go any further than the rubbing, whether intentional or not. Every time Tibor tried to steer the

contact into more specific areas, Frau Zahnartzin very angeli-
cally discovered a new tooth to drill or one to extract.

"It seems like she does it on purpose," he speculated,
"because that's when she hurts me so that I have to control
myself not to yell."

Tibor confessed to me that he was not sleeping nights any
more because this sentimental standoff was so humiliating
him, upsetting him, discouraging him, and challenging his
masculinity.

"The worst part is that soon there won't be any more teeth
to drill, so I won't be able to go and see her any more," he
mourned.

And that was the first time I heard him talk about going off
to fight in Russia. He may not have been serious about it but
certainly there was not a prisoner in the camp who wanted to
see Tibor replaced by the regular bullies. Fortunately, I remembered reading in Stendhal's *The Red and the Black* that a
torrent of love letters will guarantee the eventual consent of
any woman. I think this maxim was borrowed from the
Russian General Kutuzov, who was famous for his conquests
—not the least of which was driving Napoleon out of Russia.

"A great idea," Tibor agreed. "But how can I do it? I'm
only an SS man, and what kind of letter could I write?"

I was dying of boredom and could think of nothing I
wanted more than a chance to write, to scribble anything, just
to hold a pen in my hand and blacken some paper. Tibor
accomplished miracles. He found an old typewriter for me and
got permission from the *Oberscharfuehrer,* who took advantage of the situation to have me type up his orders of the
day.

Whether Tibor had been wrong in his estimate of her, or
had rushed things too much, or later changed his tactics, my

letters, composed in classic German, produced the desired result. He returned glowing from a weekend pass, even bringing me a hunk of sausage and some potatoes, treasures in those days. And, as could be expected, he regaled me with a vivid description of his long night with the inaccessible Hildegarde. What is more, she would no longer accept payment for her dental services.

The story got to be known around the various barracks. It amused Camp Commander Schmidt, who, obviously impressed, came to see me. He gave me a cigarette and then, as if giving a distasteful order, added abruptly:

"We'll find something for you to do. You can't go on being fed without earning your keep. Report for the six o'clock roll call tomorrow morning. I have a job for you that's suited to your qualifications."

This was certainly good news. Having work meant getting out of my isolation, coming into contact with other prisoners, perhaps even with the outside, being able to listen to the radio, read a paper—and who knows what else. I was sure I was being sent to the *Schreiberstuben,* where some of the prisoners were employed at administrative jobs.

It was Tibor himself who the next morning escorted me to my new quarters. But they were not in any *Schreiberstube.*

"You are now," said Tibor, the only SS man who sometimes addressed a prisoner as "you" instead of the familiar *du,* "foreman of the shower room."

And he winked at me.

It was the women's shower. This was a large rectangular wooden shed, with a stone floor. A partition separated the shower room from a sort of dressing room which had a few benches in it. In one corner, some corrugated tin sheets formed a kind of cabin, which was my "office."

Germans, good, bad, indifferent, or ignorant, have a fixation about organization and scrupulously work out every detail. The women prisoners in the camp were undernourished, beaten, terrorized, many of them driven to the gas chambers. They were insulted, raped, bundled in stinking rags, piled three or four together on one mattress, driven through the streets of Vienna, heads shaven and hands tied; deprived of everything, even of the snapshot of a husband or child, even of a sanitary napkin, but by regulation, "in order to take care of their bodies and remain clean," they had to take a shower three times a week. This inane ruling took no account of the fact that there was practically never any soap, that afterwards they had to get back into the same unbelievably filthy, lousy clothes, and that on coming out of the overheated building they had to cross the freezing courtyard back to their barracks, with excellent chances of catching pneumonia that, under the circumstances, was invariably fatal.

Maybe this idiocy was intentional. It was decreed that the superintendent of the showers always had to be a male prisoner. This was another way of further degrading these poor women, who were obliged to go through the most intimate ablutions under the eyes of the supervisor and his male assistant.

Nevertheless, as far as the women were concerned, the shower sessions were practically the only distraction during their captivity. They got a chance to relax a bit in the warmth, out of the grasp of their SS matrons, and then, getting out of their clothes for a little while, naked and without the external marks of their penal condition, they were perhaps able to forget for the moment where they were. It was in some degree a recapturing of the normal lives they had once known, so far away in time and in space. Hot water, a towel, a warm floor—luxuries.

Shame hardly played a part any more. They had long since been hardened to the necessity of parading naked before the SS men and the Gestapo bullies. On the contrary, the showers gave them the only chances they had of any contact with men with whom they could talk, smile, or joke, without fear of being punished. Our stares, far from embarrassing them, were flattering. They felt they were being admired, desired. They imagined they had rediscovered their femininity which the camp regime tried forever to blot out. They could not know that with their shaven heads, their skeletal bodies, their breasts hanging down to their bellies like sheets flapping from a window, their blue and yellow skin, the clumps of hair soiling their crotches and their armpits, all they could inspire was pity and sometimes fear.

I never did know quite what the "adequate qualifications" were which had made me eligible to be supervisor, but I must admit the job was a sinecure. I had absolutely nothing to do, for Sasha, my assistant, did everything, even to turning on the faucets. Sasha was a Ukrainian from eastern Ruthenia who, according to the whim of the moment and the way the war appeared to be going, called himself a Russian, a Hungarian, or a Pole. He had come to Germany as a volunteer worker, but then had been turned in either for sabotage in the factory where he worked or for making love to some German woman whose husband was away at the front. Depending on the circumstances, his story was subject to change. He cleaned the room, heated the water, went to get fuel when it was needed, kept some kind of discipline among the bathers, and in his spare moments carried on a lucrative black-market business.

He left to me the job of being referee, for women in prison

are naturally prone to fighting. First of all, there was jealousy. The plump ones—and there were plump ones, either new arrivals who had not yet lost weight, or those who were lucky enough to work in the kitchens—complained of being persecuted by the "Moslems," as they called the women who had become nothing but skin and bones. They were always settling scores because of a gesture or a smile that some male prisoner had allegedly made toward one or another of them. As if, at over two hundred yards and across rows and rows of barbed wire, it was possible to be sure.

There was the constant fighting over the soap—since only one bar of soap was the week's ration for two hundred women. On the outside, the Viennese claimed that the soap of the wartime Reich was made from the fat of Jews killed off in the death camps, but I have always been unable, despite the evidence, to bring myself to believe in such a horror. The women were not concerned with the origin of the soap which, for them, even though sparingly used, was a matter of life and death. They fought each other, nails to cheeks and fists at breasts, to get at the bar of soap.

Then there were the girls who tried to take advantage of the confusion to trade off their rags against some other woman's, not that there was any advantage to this, for one set was as disgusting as another. My poor diplomatic talents were sorely tried and I must admit that Sasha, who roared and threatened to turn a cold hose on them, got better results in shutting them up if not in calming them down.

Sasha and my predecessor had got things well organized. The girls rarely came to the showers empty-handed. For instance, there was Natasha, a Lithuanian who had pull in the kitchen. She "organized" bits of meat (finally confessing that they were scraps of beef intended for the commandant's wolf-dog). Others brought what they could—potatoes, vegetables, sugar, salt, as occasion allowed. They hid these treasures in their blouses or stockings, and used them as payment for lengthier use of the bar of soap. Two little French girls who cleaned house for the SS families used to swipe newspapers and books. Liselotte, an Austrian girl turned in by her cousin for sleeping with a Belgian house painter, stole pass blanks from the political office where she scrubbed the floors. These might be useful in case of escape.

Fat Piroshka, the very same Piroshka whom I was to meet again at Dachau after the liberation, also worked in the kitchen. Gianfranca, a Venetian girl, did mending in the uniform shop and was able to steal scraps of material. Others would wash our clothes for us.

Sasha had in his employ a gang of Russian girls who got their hands on an unbelievable assortment of goods—aspirin tablets, electric light bulbs, shaving soap, baby clothes, and so on. And he carried on a brisk trade in all this, tobacco being the recognized medium of exchange. I believe he even had customers among the SS men.

I did not dare try to stop him, for he was an inventive cook who knew how to turn stolen potatoes and slices of ersatz sausage into truly mouth-watering dishes. When an SS man came in on an inspection tour, Sasha got around him by simply treating him to one of his culinary masterpieces. Or, failing that, to some prize from his smuggled stores.

Sometimes he would give food or medicine, or even a rag, to one of the girls who seemed to need it most; but we had to be careful, because if we showed too much favoritism to any of the women, the others would have ganged up on her.

I had quickly become used to the routine of the women undressing, dressing, and displaying their nakedness, which

almost invariably only accentuated their ugliness. I was reminded of Henryk Sienkiewicz, in his *Quo Vadis,* having
Petronius say:

"Ten thousand naked women along the banks of the Tiber
arouse me much less than one alone. . . ."

Milena changed all that. She came to us direct from the Foe
Utca Prison in Budapest, having been picked up with her lover
in a raid. He had documents on his person that implicated him
with a group of Croatian partisans. She was a high-school girl,
barely seventeen, and beautiful as a Madonna. During the
police interrogation, her lover had tried to escape by jumping
through a window, but one of the interrogators had brought
him down with a pistol shot. The poor terrified girl was able
only to kiss the bloody lips of her dying lover once more.

Milena's emerald-green eyes, deep as the sea off the coast of
Abbazia, sometimes seemed to reflect this last grim vision. At
times like that they turned into eyes of ice which saw nothing
else. She still had intact her long red hair which she wore in
braids, for the Gestapo were not yet finished with her interrogation and they had sent her to Maria-Lanzendorf only to
intimidate her. She was allowed to keep her good looks in this
morass of ugliness so that the threat of destroying her angelic
face might have more effect.

However, she rarely alluded to these interrogations or the
misfortune of her arrest. She never joined in the chatter of her
fellow prisoners. She thanked Sasha with a trace of a smile
when he slipped her a bit of bread or some clean linen. Sasha
called her *draga* ("dear one"), and made no mystery of the
fact that he was mad about her. I felt the same way.

Since Milena had started coming to the showers the atmosphere of our sorry, somber and primitive barn had been
completely transformed. Milena in our eyes was like one of

those heroines of a Charlie Chaplin picture, diaphanous angels made up of equal parts of poverty and poetry, whom one would not dare touch lest they vanish instantly. Neither Sasha nor I tried to pay court to her; such things were for people who are free. Our attentions, our little favors, our silences, even our attempts at modesty, were all a bouquet of declarations of love.

It started when Milena begged us not to make her undress with the others, but to let her take her shower without being watched. With anyone else, Sasha would have thrown a fit at such an idea. He would have shouted at the top of his voice, stamped his feet, sneered, and threatened to call the commander, for any such breach of discipline drove him crazy. As for me, I never would have dared indulge such a change in the rules, if only out of fear of rebellion by the other prisoners who were always ready to jump at any sign of favoritism. But Sasha did not object; and later, to assuage the others, he made a free distribution of paper towels and even brought a jar of margarine out of his hidden supply. My permission was given tacitly, as if this favor were the most natural thing in the world. I told the other women that I did it under orders.

Nevertheless, I expected some violent reactions. The girls might, I knew, take their first chance to get even with the too-beautiful Milena, and I was resigned to the idea that I might have to go back to solitary confinement in my room if the thing exploded.

But the other women, at least while they were at the shower building, showed the strangest kind of tolerance toward Milena. They never complained seriously when Sasha gave her a new cake of soap, which she readily offered to share, or when he brought her a chemise, a pair of socks, or a woolen shawl, got from heaven knows where. Natasha, whose bad disposition was as great as her pull in the kitchen, pretended not to notice when we gave Milena a share of the victuals she stole for us. Soon, she began to bring an extra bit of sausage or a pancake specially for the girl. The others too began to show attentions to her, to give her little presents, do her favors, and speak kindly to her. Fat Piroshka became Milena's best friend.

The women prisoners rarely used each other's real names. Nicknames were easier to remember, and often less dangerous. So for them all Milena became Engelchen or "Little Angel."

Finally, we were even able to get her an easy job in the infirmary. Natasha was responsible for this; you get all kinds of power when you work in the kitchen. And now, except for the interrogations, which Milena never mentioned but which hurt us as much as they did her, Milena's life at Maria-Lanzendorf began to be bearable.

She sometimes came to see us in the evening. As a nurse she had the right to go about the camp, and she would talk to me about her home village on the shores of Lake Balaton, where whitewashed houses surrounded the painted steeple of the church, the shore was unendingly caressed by the waters of the lake, and dances were held in the main square when the wine was new and the spring was intoxicated with sunshine. . . .

One morning she came to the showers alone. The SS man who brought her had been given explicit orders: she was to be disinfected, shaved, creosoted, and made ready for transfer. He would come for her at the beginning of the afternoon. Our Milena was going to leave us. She did not seem to be concerned about her new destination. She was so young, and the idea of a change did not seem overly to alarm her.

"They're probably taking me back to Budapest," she told us, "but just the same I'll be sorry to be leaving you."

We were heartbroken. Especially after Liselotte, the Austrian girl who worked in the political office, came to tell us that Milena was leaving in the special prison van headed for an extermination camp. "I saw the orders myself: Dachau!"

This was the second time I heard about the truck with the hermetically sealed sides, whose driver, during the course of the trip, pushed a lever and gassed the passengers. On arrival, the truck-turned-hearse delivered its corpses. This motorized method alleviated a lot of checking and administrative red tape. Dead on arrival!

The terrible news spread rapidly through the women's barracks. Those who were able came over to the showers to say good-bye to Engelchen, regardless of the rules and defying all risks.

One brought her an apple; another a handkerchief, her most prized possession; and Natasha, the despot of the galley, brought her—marvel of marvels!—a hardboiled egg. Of course, it had begun to smell a bit already, but that didn't make it any less valuable. Everyone greeted her with shouts of "Good luck," "Remember us," "Call my mother," and so on, for they all pretended to believe she was headed for release. Liselotte's information remained a secret that burned our hearts.

Sasha had prepared a package for her, slices of bread with margarine and a nice soft cheese. I had put in my whole supply of six cigarettes and a pencil and some paper. Piroshka was the only one who could not keep from crying.

And then, for the first time, chastely, unaffectedly, swiftly, as if she had never done it any other way, Milena undressed before all of us. She went in to the shower with all the others, then came back naked into the dressing room and remained standing near the bench where her clean clothes were.

The order specified that her hair had to be cut short so as

to reduce danger of infection. She was standing there completely nude before me, still smiling, still without the slightest embarrassment, as if to say: "Thanks for everything. You see, after all, I have become one of you. I have become equal to the others. I am no longer ashamed."

I cut off Milena's hair, carefully, tenderly, the way you cut the ribbon that holds a bridal gown in its box. The red strands, long and heavy, sank down one after the other to the moist stones of the floor. Sasha, overcome by the whole thing, had forgotten to turn the hot-water faucets off and the water and steam were filling the dressing room.

Still smiling, as if she were getting ready to go for a walk in the park, she got dressed, fastidiously, without haste, without the slightest hint of modesty.

That was how she left us.

I in turn was sent on to Dachau a few weeks later, but by train. Piroshka told me that she had been taken there the same way as Milena, in the same hearse-truck. There was no gassing. It was far worse. She had been delivered to that castle whose name I no longer want to pronounce, for it must be a thousand times damned, which was under the jurisdiction of the Dachau camp and was used for the most abominable medical experiments. Piroshka found Milena there, alas, a thousand times alas, still alive.

Piroshka, who had always been lucky in her misfortunes, was consigned to use in metabolism experiments, because she was fat and the doctors wanted to discover a practical reducing formula. But this was 1945, and the project no longer had any kind of priority, considering the level of nourishment in Germany and in the rest of Europe. It might even have been termed a superfluous notion. In the early days of March, Piroshka was transferred to Dachau proper, where her dossier simply joined the thousands of others in the file. She remained there until the liberation.

Milena, she said, had slept in the same dormitory with her, in the north tower of the castle. But she was no longer Milena, our beautiful Milena, our Engelchen. She scarcely spoke, treated Piroshka as if she were a stranger, and spent her time stone-still near the window which had been strung with barbed wire.

Milena was being used in experiments dealing with erotic reactions. She would be placed naked between two men, both also prisoners and both also completely naked. Electrodes were then attached to different parts of their bodies. To the organs, the heart, the brain, the tips of the toes—in short everywhere. The reactions were endlessly recorded, evaluated, interpreted. Piroshka told me that Milena's hair had all grown back again—gray.

Toward the end, before Piroshka left, there had been talk of liberation. The news of the Russian advance to the outskirts of Berlin and of the Allied seizure of the Ruhr had reached even into the confines of the cursed castle. One evening, the women in the dormitory were talking about what they would do once they were free. They talked of their relatives, of home, of their first meal, their first walk through their native city.

That was the night Milena hanged herself, under the shower in the bathroom. She had run the slightest trickle of cold water, so as not to attract attention. She was found too late, asphyxiated and half-frozen. Piroshka told me that she did not have the courage to look at her dead body.

For a long time after I left Dachau, an undefinable distress, a shiver of remorse, regret, tenderness, overcame me every time I heard water running from the faucet in a bathroom.

7

Two French Generals

The SS men of the camps, no doubt because of their animosity toward the Wehrmacht, had nothing but scorn for those prisoners who were top-ranking officers. Thus they violated the immemorial international solidarity which prescribed that enemy generals show each other every imaginable courtesy and sometimes even embrace each other, entertain lavishly, exchange reminiscences, and with the most excessive politeness instruct each other in strategy while the troops under their command continue pitilessly to massacre each other. The SS men seemed to feel that generals were far more contemptible than other captives and that there was no reason why these men, because they owned caps adorned with stripes, stars, oak leaves, anchors, eaglets, and other assorted fruit salad should, barring accident, continue to die in bed. They therefore were even tougher on generals than on most prisoners.

General Delestraint had come to Dachau from the camp of Nazweiler early in the summer of 1944, along with the bishop of Clermont-Ferrand, Monsignor Piguet. They arrived in a state of pitiful exhaustion, having served as whipping boys for their guards during the whole trip.

General Delestraint was without doubt the most important of all the French deportees at Dachau, and was readily acknowledged by them as such. According to Edmond Michelet, who had already met him at the prison of Fresnes, he had been selected by General de Gaulle from among all the active army generals remaining in the unoccupied zone of France to organize the secret army which was to offer effective opposition to the Germans in French territory before and during the invasion. Delestraint, then known as Vidal, had been arrested by the Gestapo only a few months after he assumed this command and had been incarcerated at Fresnes, just outside Paris. Later, at Dachau, he would claim that he had been sold out by Communist elements who would not willingly tolerate the presence of a career officer among the clandestine high command of the underground movement.

Still, the Germans had not fully realized the importance of the man who had fallen into their net and they were satisfied merely to deport him.

He maintained his fine military bearing despite fatigue and deprivations. His deep azure eyes were commanding and yet filled with kindness. His "class" energy had not been lost. Even in his convict's garb he was the military aristocrat who commands, demands, expects, and expresses his thanks only with the condescension of a mighty lord. He had no use for those Frenchmen interned in the camp for any reason other than active resistance. He could not accept the fact that not all his compatriots had followed him in his "rebellion."

An effort had been made to put him up in the *Revier,* but the Communist Kapos had refused to accept this "militarist" intruder in the infirmary, and shortly afterward he had been transferred to Block 24, which housed mostly Frenchmen. Perhaps in order to bask in the glow of his insignia, they immediately accepted him as their leader.

I rarely spoke to him, for he was not readily accessible to any except military men of high rank or to those prisoners who spontaneously placed themselves under his command and could be regarded as his soldiers.

He was a shrewd man who, as the occasion demanded, knew how to be affable and persuasive. He bucked up both the morale and the prestige of the French group, and was responsible for forming a prisoners' International Committee at Dachau.

I would see him standing in the twilight at the corner of the large square discoursing with authority to a small group of courtiers who crowded close to hear him and also to protect him from the small fry. Seeing him thus, one could imagine him still wearing his monocle and believing himself back at St. Cyr imparting his wisdom to the cadets.

It was this superb military bearing which accounted for his bad end. According to Michelet, the authorities had lined up in front of Barracks 24 all those who were still unassigned to specific work detail. Delestraint was among them and, as if it were the most natural thing in the world, he was in the front row. Despite his small stature, he had a way of sticking out his chest which could not go unnoticed.

That day we had the distinction of a visit from a colonel who was an inspector of the SS. Curious about Delestraint, the *Obersturmfuehrer* proceeded to interrogate this French bantam with the blue eyes and the forceful manner.

"Your profession?"

"General of the French Army," Delestraint boldly replied,

"now serving under General de Gaulle who once served under me."

Whether because the answer impressed the SS officer, or the Gestapo had already learned of the role Delestraint had assumed at Dachau, or by simple administrative coincidence, the order from Berlin having been some time in arriving, the general was presently transferred to the VIP bunker.

This "honor" bunker was situated behind the kitchens at the southern extremity of the compound. There was nothing honorific about this bunker, which was a place of torture and abomination. But the prisoners had given it its name because certain important inmates had been accorded the painful honor of being put there in solitary, either as a security measure or for "special" treatment.

It was an immense box of reinforced concrete. It must originally have been intended as a military fortification, without doors or windows—and I was to see similar ones, much later, at Cape Canaveral, where they were meant to protect technicians during the blast-off of space rockets. Heavily armed and helmeted SS men kept constant guard around the building, and other prisoners were forbidden near it. Today, twenty years after liberation, that bunker is still being used, to house SS men held for trial, and later American soldiers from the Munich garrison awaiting court-martial or serving their time. It appears that, from time to time, important prisoners whose identities must be kept secret are locked up there. On several occasions, the last being in the spring of 1965, I tried to visit the place. But now the American army, as in the old days the SS men, always forbade my getting near it.

It was there that Delestraint was assigned to one of the cages, and at first he was delighted by this mark of distinction. The treatment he received was indeed an improvement. He was even allowed to dress in the uniform he had worn the day of his arrest. And on the pretext of going on sick call he could renew contact with his fellows.

He was not the only VIP in the bunker. With him were the bishop of Clermont-Ferrand, the famous Protestant pastor Niemöller, the mayor of Vienna, and many others.

But perhaps the most interesting of these prisoners was one Eller, alias Georg Elser, a bizarre character whose presence in the blockhouse further emphasized the *Tales of Hoffmann* ambiance that characterized the place.

Of the seven known plots against Hitler's life, the one organized by the Communist carpenter Georg Elser appears to have been the best conceived. On the evening of November 8, 1939, twenty minutes after Hitler had delivered his annual screed commemorating the anniversary of the disastrous Putsch of 1923,* a bomb had exploded killing seven members of Hitler's Old Guard and wounding sixty-three others. The bomb had been planted in a pillar directly behind the speaker's platform.

All Germany knew that Hitler and his top brass, the elite of National-Socialism, were to take part in the memorial ceremony, the most important date in Nazi folklore. The Buergerbraukeller is the most popular meeting place in Munich. People come there to tie one on and have a good time without class distinctions. Hitler liked to meet his old cronies there, and usually he stayed far into the night, cutting up old touches with his accomplices of the ill-fated Putsch, swapping experiences, discussing the current political situation. The time and

---

* Hitler at that time, flanked by General Ludendorff and Goering, had tried to take over the headquarters of the Bavarian government, but in front of the Feldherrenhall the army had opened fire, Ludendorff had continued to advance, Goering had been brought down by the shots, while a terrified Hitler turned and fled.

place could not have been better chosen. The bomb would have been enough to decapitate the Fuehrer and his whole general staff, thereby avoiding the possibility of a war that promised to be devastating.

But Hitler's speech that night was shorter than usual, and he suddenly left the place, followed by his retinue.

Only one newspaper, the *Voelkischer Beobachter,* Hitler's own publication, the next day announced the failure of the attempt on his life, at the same time accusing the British Intelligence Service of having instigated it. And on November 21, Himmler told an increasingly gullible Germany that the man directly responsible for the explosion, one Georg Elser, had been arrested. The culprit not only confessed his act, but was proud of it. Moreover, he implicated his British co-conspirators.

The whole story seemed fantastic, and many of my German friends took it with a grain of salt. Himmler apparently did not feel he was on very solid ground, for Elser was never brought to trial. There had been no execution either—an extraordinary circumstance in view of the wholesale massacre which was to follow the assassination attempt of July 20, 1944—and the whole thing seemed fishy.

Quite the contrary, Elser was treated most deferentially, first at the camp of Sachsenhausen, then at Dachau. He was given a large comfortable cell, and allowed a workshop for tinkering; he had a zither which he played, and he received somewhat better rations. Himmler had ordered him kept in solitary confinement, but during bomb alerts he was allowed to come down into the bunker's shelter and talk with the other inmates. It was there that Pastor Niemöller had been able to talk to him. Elser, who in the camp was known by the name of Eller, maintained that he had been nothing but the willing tool of the Gestapo, which had ordered him to take part in the staging of a mock plot.

On April 5, 1945, the *Reichssicherheitleiter* sent a top-secret message from Berlin to the Dachau camp commander: "The superior authorities have discussed the case of prisoner Eller. During one of the next enemy air attacks on Munich, Eller is to be 'fatally wounded.' In view of this, you are ordered to carry out the elimination of Eller in complete secrecy, only the fewest possible people to know of the action. You will announce his death to me officially in a telegram to be worded as follows: 'On such and such a day, at such and such an hour, prisoner Eller was mortally hit during a terrorist air attack.' Destroy this letter after execution of my orders."

General Delestraint had noticed the sudden disappearance of Eller but assumed that he had been evacuated to the southern Tyrol, as had been the case with so many other "big shots." He himself had left the bunker proper, to go into a neighboring isolated barracks that, because it was so much more comfortable, was referred to as the "sorority."

The general was devout and insisted on serving at the mass which was daily celebrated by Bishop Piguet. On April 19, the Americans were no longer very far away, and Delestraint was receiving communion when an SS sergeant came in with the order: "The French general is asked to leave immediately; he is to gather up his effects without delay—" A few seconds later, Delestraint disappeared.

Shortly after mass, the SS noncom returned to the barracks and, almost jocularly, explained that soon everybody was going to be transferred to Innsbruck. There had been a car waiting with one empty seat in it, so the general had been taken along. . . . "You'll be seeing him there again in a day or two."

A few hours later, before the wall of the crematorium, General Delestraint, naked, but with head held high, after having dug his own grave, was wiped out with two pistol shots.

The name of the other French general, the one who became my friend, is irrelevant. I don't think he played an important part in the Resistance, but had merely been taken as a hostage because he was in command of some obscure garrison in Savoy where the maquis held sway. He should have been on the retirement list long since, for he was well over seventy. He was a tiny fellow, barely over five feet tall, with silver hair and a round face that made him look like King Louis-Philippe, and he habitually spoke just above a whisper. He had arrived in Dachau toward mid-April after tortuous detours. The Gestapo, which had never even interrogated him, panic-stricken by the American advances, was now dipping into its dungeons and randomly picking people to fill up the last convoys of deportees. I had been put in charge of welcoming the French contingent, of which the "little general" was a member, and it was thus I saw him arrive, awkward, dragging painfully behind the others, then when he fell too far behind, starting to run to catch up with them.

"Why, they're sending children to us now," was my first reaction, and I was on my way to inform the barracks chief that a mistake had been made, for the poor man had been decked out in the most unimaginable outfit: a pair of short trousers that barely reached his knees, old sneakers with holes in them, a striped sailor's T-shirt, and a reddish brown overcoat that covered only half his body. His bare arms stuck out of the sleeves and he could scarcely move. On his head, he wore a sort of bersaglieri hat that still had some rooster feathers in it. In one hand he held a filthy enameled messkit and in the other a big aluminum spoon. He looked like a carnival lampoon of a warrior and, God forgive us, occasions for amusement being so few and far between, the spectacle struck us as so grotesque that the next quarter-hour was nothing but hoots and laughter.

In the supply room, he had fallen victim to a drunken SS man or one of his sidekicks. When he naïvely identified himself as a French brigadier general, the low-ranking Hitlerite, stimulated by having at his mercy this little old man who claimed to be a general, bore down heavily on him.

We had a political leader in the barracks, a French Resistance colonel who was a friend of the Kapo and who, now that liberation was at hand, was virtually commanding in his stead. He didn't laugh when he saw the little man but, snapping to attention, saluted him with a "Welcome to the block, General." The little general shook his hand and was then formally introduced to us.

"The absurdity of your clothing, General," the leader said to him, "is just another ruse of the Nazis to try to humiliate us, to make us feel inhuman, to reduce us to the lowest possible level. Everything they do is calculated. I won't be able to make any change in your equipment because, if the SS man should come on an inspection, he might, on the pretext that we had violated his capricious directives, get even tougher with you. So we'll just have to put up with it, one way or another."

But the general wasn't in the least concerned. In fact, each morning as we got dressed he would find a new way of making a good thing out of his misfortune: "When I get out of here I'll be a headliner in a circus," or "When the Americans get here the Nazis will wish they could trade their uniforms of infamy for my little overcoat. . . ."

Because of my many transfers to various camps and prisons other than Dachau, I had lost the doubtful privileges of seniority, and on my last arrival, like everyone else, I should have been dumped into a quarantine block. This was one of the worst of fates. As long as you were there you were considered untouchable; there were no privileges; you often had to sleep on the floor (if you were permitted to sleep); the food, if any, was even more unpalatable than elsewhere; and at all times there was the risk of being selected for the most dangerous kind of work detail. But an old friend from the showers had arranged to have me switched into the French colonel's block.

I must say, to the credit of nearly all the French deportees of my concentration-camp world, that they never hesitated to adopt as one of their own a fellow victim who spoke French, perhaps because they didn't find too many of such. The majority of the inmates, apart from the Jews, were of Slavic or German background, and the Frenchmen, who were not great linguists, felt isolated from them. So I turned into a sort of liaison man for them.

As a journalist possessing fairly fresh news from the outside world, and being in a position to offer a reasonable evaluation of the situation, I was immediately of interest to the colonel, who took me under his wing. Through friends working with the Gestapo section of the camp he had familiarized himself with my dossier. In it could be found the details of my first arrest, in Berlin in 1940. . . .

I had just come back from a trip as a correspondent to Paris, only recently occupied by the Germans. In a series of articles in the Swiss newspaper *La Tribune de Geneve* I dwelt on the deplorable living conditions of the French refugees as they fled before the enemy, and with silly schoolboy emotion I wept over the presence of German boots in "my Latin Quarter." Goebbels and his people would probably have paid no attention to these pieces by a journalistic neophyte, had it not been for the International Red Cross, which used them as the basis for asking the Hitler government to let them organize refugee relief. I don't know what the Wilhelmstrasse replied, but one afternoon, while I sat slicing a watermelon, some revolver-toting mugs broke into my room and, slipping hand-cuffs on my wrists, dragged me off through the streets of Berlin to the notorious Alexanderplatz jail. I remained in detention for three months without knowing what I was ac-cused of.

At that time prisoners who came through filled me in on the horrendous things they had seen at the camps of Dachau and Oranienburg, and I had had a chance to speak with the first wagonloads of Jews swept up from the various quarters of the capital, who now told me they knew they were headed for nightmarish death. All of this in 1940, in the heart of Berlin, capital of a Germany that has since sworn a thousand times that it knew nothing and saw nothing of the Hitler crimes of genocide.

Freed as suddenly and unexpectedly as I had been arrested, I found myself unemployed, for *La Tribune de Geneve*, claim-ing that I had "deserted my post," dismissed me, refused to pay me my salary for the months I was in jail, and replaced me with a "true" Swiss, who was in no danger of deserting *his* post for he made no secret of his enthusiasm for the Greater Reich.

Colonel Didier, a name I suppose was assumed for war purposes, was in full control of our block. He was a delightful man who never took advantage of his position, was capable of intelligent conversation, and was always on hand when morale needed bolstering. He made me his assistant for the processing of newcomers and introduced me to the underground activities of the resistance movement which had been organized in the camp. I owe my life to him, for I had been put automatically on a list of those assigned to an outlying work yard from which few ever returned. A request to Colonel Didier, and he quietly got the list from the Kapo and whispered a few words in his ear. My name was removed. He confirmed this to me a few hours later between two bits of gossip, as if it were the most routine thing in the world.

There was another French officer in the block but he was a character who apparently had somehow escaped from one of Courteline's military farces. He insisted on being referred to only as "Major," demanded recognition of all of his prerogatives and titles, and was always pressing for full field inspections as if he were the commander of the Dachau "Training Task Force." Each day, he had some new plan for an armed assault on the Kommandantur, for the organization of an army of Dachau "desperadoes" which would march off to conquer Munich, Berlin, Vienna and, weather permitting, Moscow and Vladivostok. He was extremely touchy, ever insistent on being treated with due respect.

Colonel Didier handled him admirably by making him feel that no decision was ever made without first consulting him. Didier would have been delighted to be rid of the man, but he was too respectful of the traditions of the career officer ever to consider putting him in his place. He didn't bother me, and I patiently listened to the recitals of his military exploits, which made it abundantly clear that in the end he and de Gaulle would be the only two triumphant conquerors of this war.

But Didier, like his colleague, had great friends in the

rooms of the "leaders," and often they would leave us for long periods of time, while my little general was a constant companion, good-natured, loyal, sharing all of our daily troubles. He and I, along with a handful of other Frenchmen, including a physician from Toulouse, a mechanic from the 17th arrondissement, two men from Lorraine, and a young Corsican with a baby smile, had become inseparable.

The little general would talk to me about his mountain châlet in Savoy and invite me to visit him there for Christmas, for the skiing season, for the midsummer holidays, and for the various first-communion celebrations of his innumerable great-nephews. He would tell me about the olden days when he, too, wrote poetry; about his first meeting with the girl who was to become Madame la générale, and especially about his grandchildren. I think there was only one miracle he hoped for, and that was to retrieve the pictures of the children that had been confiscated when he was arrested.

We speculated about being freed. The mechanic from Paris had already spotted a pickup truck in one of the SS motor pools, and the plan was that the general and all our group would requisition it when the time came and take off for Savoy, where we would rest and put on some weight before heading back to our respective homes. The little general had promised that he himself would cook us the first *fondue*, then he would recite from memory all the famous vintages in his cellar.

Then there was the matter of Red Cross food parcels. A large number of them were issued to the prisoners during the last days of our captivity. The Germans no longer knew what to do with them. Because of the Allied advance, the only road open to the supply trains of the International Red Cross from Switzerland was the road to Dachau. So all the food packages intended for all other prison camps had been funneled to Dachau. The camp commander, probably thinking he was making points for himself in the final days, decided to distribute them among the internees. It was manna from heaven, for food had become extremely scarce in the camp and the statistics of those dying of starvation had soared.

But the Geneva International Red Cross had a very "Swiss franc" concept of human solidarity. It had laid down the rule that the packages could be given only to nationals of those countries which contributed hard-currency dollars to the organization. Therefore the food could legally be given only to Frenchmen, Belgians, Dutchmen, to some Poles, to Scandinavians, and other citizens of Allied countries. Russians, Germans, Italians, and Jews were entitled to nothing. Turkey, a belligerent only the day after victory was assured, was not recognized by the Red Cross. So I was never eligible for any packages.

These windfalls turned out to be the cause of serious trouble, arguments, sometimes bloody fights. Each parcel call meant that the following night there might be up to a hundred dead. The Russians, true to their Bolshevik catechism, used force to seize the packages belonging to others. They took out after the weakest ones. At night they burrowed under mattresses to get at what was hidden, sometimes killing their victims as they slept, and if caught at it, the Russians in turn were done away with. The Poles, even though they got their own packages, wanted more, and organized regular armed expeditions to get them. The German Kapos demanded their rake-off. Inmates struggled because some were unwilling to give up the packages they had already sold, at the time when they had nothing, to comrades for an extra bread ration or a favor. Fights arose over what terms had been agreed on for a swap, because someone had got a half-destroyed package, because another one was not considered eligible. The French, for example, were furious because the Saarlanders had suddenly discovered that they had never, never been Germans but were really French. The Greeks would not recognize Macedonians as their countrymen, and the Belgians insisted that former collaborators, even though now deportees, should not be included. The Poles were unwilling to share anything with Polish Jews.

It was, as usual, a case of jungle law. For a package, or even half a package, in those fateful days, might be the difference between a painful death and hope of liberation. It was like a branch held out to a drowning man.

The little general, as soon as he received his first package, came to me and declared peremptorily: "No arguments now; we're sharing everything. When it's your turn to get something, you'll do the same for us."

In that way he and his friends put their precious possessions into a common pool. And the little general turned out to be a meticulous accountant. He divided a chocolate bar evenly down to the hundredth of an inch, and when we heated a can of food he counted out each pea, each spoonful of sauce. I also got my ration of Gauloise cigarettes. Since I didn't smoke, I wanted to give them back to the boys. But the general insisted that I take something else instead, so that the smoker had to give me two *petit-beurre* from his share in exchange for the cigarette from his own package!

We had decided each morning to have two sardines in oil for breakfast. This became a ritual. The general, with a pocket knife, cut each sardine into equal parts, making proper allowance for heads and tails. Then in turn we passed before him with our meager pieces of bread and he poured out of the can an equal share of oil for each one. When the sardines were all gone, we were entitled to one wipe each at the inside of the can with a forefinger.

The little general was the first person I embraced when liberation finally came. We were dancing around in a circle and, since the general was too slow to keep up with us, we picked him up in our arms like a doll, while he laughed, wept and babbled about his grandchildren.

Because of my activities in the International Committee, I was soon allowed outside the quarantine block and, at the first chance to ransack the SS stores, I made it my business to bring the general a handsome uniform bedizened with silver icing, a cape, boots, a military belt and gloves. But he only put on the pants and went on playing *belote* in his shirtsleeves. Each evening when I got back to the block, followed by my shadow, Ivan the Mongolian, who pushed the cart loaded with merchandise, I turned the whole load over to the general. He proceeded to divide it all with such scrupulous fairness that nothing was left for him.

When I found living quarters in the half-demolished apartment of an SS officer I suggested to the general that he come there to live with me.

"Thank you," he said, "but I don't feel like moving. I'm all right here in the block. The arrival of the first French mission is expected soon and I'll probably be able to leave with them. I may be smiling, but down deep I'm tormented by the craving to see my wife and my little ones again. Move in alone, my friend. I'll come to visit you each day."

I didn't realize it, but little by little freedom was making strangers of all of us who only yesterday were ready to die together; it was returning us to what we had been "before" . . .

It was the highfalutin major who moved in with me. He was crazy about boots, and since I had a knack for getting them he followed me in my expeditions. "Today, we'll have to pick up some for horseback riding," he would say. Was he thinking of outfitting his next regiment, or did he intend to open a shoe-store when he got back to Paris? It remained a mystery to me.

The little general came to visit us, but then I got sick and was taken to the American field hospital, so all my contacts with the outside world were necessarily interrupted. When, several weeks later, I was out of danger, the little general was no longer there. Now it was his turn; he was very ill. His trouble was not typhus, but general fatigue. Age, privations, emotions—all had contributed to weakening his heart.

Thanks to the complicity of an American soldier, I got in to see him. He scarcely recognized me. I spoke to him in a carefree manner, joking about his indolence, telling him he had to get into the fresh air, that Savoy was waiting for us. But I doubt whether he listened. The chart at the foot of his bed was explicit enough: he did not have long to go. He gave into my safekeeping a scrap of paper on which he had scribbled a few sentences, and a rosary, the bit of red material on which his prison number had been marked, and a bottle of toilet water we had "liberated" together.

"You'll be getting out ahead of me," he told me. "Write to my wife from Paris. Send her all these things. Tell her about the happy hours of our deliverance, of the joys we had then. . . ."

One evening, the Belgian friend who worked in the office of the American commander notified me that the little general's wife had arrived at Dachau in a special convoy arranged by the Vatican. She had come to get her husband. If I wanted to, I could go and see her. I could have a visitor's pass. I answered that I was busy with my own departure and would write to the lady when in Paris.

For the little general had died the day before.

I had not gone back to see him a last time, and I never went to see his wife. I sent her the things he left and wrote her from Paris, much later, as he had requested.

That was the only time at Dachau that I was really ashamed —ashamed of myself, ashamed of being alive, ashamed for other human beings, ashamed of fate. . . .

INTERLUDE II

Statistics

. . . we often were visited, of an evening at the camp at Mauthausen, near Linz, by a Frenchman from Toulouse, a bartender by trade, who liked to reminisce about the good old days when he worked at the Negresco in Nice or the Baur-au-Lac at Zürich. At the camp he was a scribe and he was rarely without a huge ledger he carried under his arm. It was the death register of the camp. He had to enter after each prisoner's number whether the inmate was living, sick, dead of illness or dead "by accident." The ledger was unusually thick, yet he made his entries in a tiny hand, almost illegible to the naked eye. There was a good reason for this: the *modus operandi* of the camp was to do away with the ledger once it was filled, and at the same time to do away with the scribe in charge of it. When a new book was opened, a new record keeper took the place of the one who had gone up in smoke through the crematorium chimney. Neither document nor witness being left they could start again with No. 1.

It is totally childish to imagine that the Gestapo for twelve years preserved all the records of imprisonments. Those that fell into the hands of the victors at the time of liberation give only sketchy notion of the real statistics. The serial number worn by a prisoner had often been used before him by a dozen other victims, who might have been transferred to other camps, freed, drafted, or dead. The Germans were meticulous, but circumstances often made a correct census impossible. When a raid was carried out in a poor neighborhood and everyone at hand was loaded into trucks for Dachau, the militiamen rarely bothered to make up identification lists. The horrible deaths in the cattle cars were certainly ignored in the statistics, and the evaluations based on witnesses' testimony were equally undependable. Those who managed to survive in a camp from beginning to end were rare indeed. Even rarer were those whose testimonies could be relied upon, for often this excessively long survival was due to compromise and complicity with the jailers. Even if they were sincere, these few witnesses never had any real idea of the overall picture. There were so many secrets in Dachau! Then there were those who died in the auxiliary camps, on the work details, or in the underground factories. . . .

So it is with some skepticism that I report here certain statistics compiled after the liberation. First, there are those of Domgala, who figured that 206,204 persons went through Dachau. I would put the figure closer to 450,000.

Dachau being a sorting point and not, like Auschwitz, a camp where prisoners were sent to die, the number of Jewish prisoners was relatively low. I estimate it at 5,000, but do not include those who arrived in the last days before the liberation or those whom the Americans found dead outside the camp gates. It is impossible to ascertain the number of deaths in the camp from 1933 to 1940. It was certainly more than

The Americans enter the Jourhaus, April 29, 1945, 5:37 P.M.

The Americans arrive in Dachau. (1st Battalion, 157th Regiment, 45th Division.)

An SS guard, knocked to the ground, is insulted by the prisoners.

The American soldiers killed all the SS men in the camp and, after this, all their dogs. One dog, pictured here, had his throat cut.

"James Ortoleva, my liberator, in front of the Dachau swimming pool, used solely, of course, by the SS men."

Photo of James Ortoleva, taken by Gun, in front of the crematorium.

The crematorium with the birdhouse, the flowers, and the dead bodies. This photo was taken by Gun with a stolen camera.

Urns used for ashes of people burned in the crematorium. They were then sold to relatives for 50 marks ($100).

Love in Dachau.

Liberated women in Dachau.

The pretty nurse to whom James Ortoleva introduced me.

The American cafeteria in Dachau.

An American soldier practicing golf in Dachau.

American girls.

Inside the gas chamber. The Zyklon-B bomb made by the German industrial giant, I. G. Farben, was dropped on the floor. Prisoners were told they were going to take a shower.

The gas chamber. At the moment of liberation, the hour of the last operation was still written on the door. Since then, Germans have tried to deny that there was a gas chamber in the camp. This photograph is proof: it was taken the day of the liberation.

15,000. From 1940 to the liberation, a former camp inmate, Domgala, a responsible witness, accounts for 27,830 deaths, but that figure must be a minimum. In fact, more than 100,000 died at Dachau, or approximately one out of four inmates. Of these, 3,166 were gassed.

A few days before the emancipation, the captive population of Dachau included:

Albanians	44
Americans	11
Arabs	3
Armenians	4
Belgians	989
Bulgarians	54
Chinese	2
Danes	1
Germans	6,118
British	13
Estonians	3
Finns	1
French	5,706
Greeks	338
Dutch	836
Italians	3,388
Japanese	1
Canadians	1
Croatians	818
Latvians	230
Lithuanians	3,250
Luxembourgers	211
Norwegians	77
Iranians	1
Poles	14,994
Portuguese	8
Rumanians	69

Russians	13,536
Swedes	7
Swiss	12
Serbians	516
Slovaks	244
Slovenes	1,746
Spaniards	286
Czechs	1,974
Turks	86
Hungarians	12,067
Homeless	17

Too much faith cannot be put in the nationalities in this classification. It was not the German authorities who determined the nationalities, but the prisoners themselves. Each prisoner could give whatever nationality he felt most favorable to the inmate in charge of gathering this information. Some of them, so as not to upset the Nazis, called themselves Czechoslovakian or Yugoslavian. Others, particularly Russians who did not want to lay themselves open to the reprisals of the Soviet government, claimed to be Turks, Chinese, Japanese, or Arabs, so as to avoid forced repatriation. Still others, especially Jews, alleged themselves to be Swiss or Canadians, just as certain Germans, arrested for desertion and fearful of the firing-squad, maintained they had been born in Chicago or were refugees without nationality. I myself, in order to protect my friend Ivan, had attested to the fact that he was 100 per cent Turkish, and I have good personal reasons to know that in all of the huge Greater German Reich there was only one prisoner of Turkish nationality. The nationalities of the other 85 on the list were therefore imaginary.

At the time of liberation, April 29, 1945, the Americans made up this official listing:

Germans	1,173	including 6 women
Belgians	843	
Danes	1	
British	8	
Estonians	11	
French	3,918	
Greek	195	
Italians	2,184	
Croatians	103	
Serbians	79	
Slovenes	2,907	
Latvians	27	
Lithuanians	39	
Alsatians	36	
Luxembourgers	133	
Dutchmen	558	
Norwegians	79	
Poles	9,082	including 96 women
Rumanians	50	
Russians	4,258	including 9 women
Slovaks	44	
Albanians	30	
Americans	1	
Maltese	1	
Arabs	2	
Armenians	2	
Finns	1	
Iraqis	1	
Iranians	1	
Turks	3	
Spaniards	194	
Czechs	1,632	
Hungarians	670	including 34 women
Bulgarians	8	
Portuguese	4	
Swiss	2	
Austrians	253	
Sudetens	5	
Jews	2,539	including 225 women

It can be seen that the American statistics, with a total of 31,432, differ from the census taken by the prisoners on April 26. The first list shows 67,665 inmates. Let us not forget that a large number of the liberated died during the American occupation, on the road back, or in the hospitals to which they had been evacuated.

Dachau remains, even after twenty years, a symbol of death and of terror. However, these statistics, terrifying as they are, are pale indeed compared to those of all the civilians who died through World War II, which I have taken from a German work (Putzger's *Historische Weltatlas*). Besides the 19,070,-000 soldiers who died in Europe and North Africa, there is a horrifying proportion of civilians killed in the camps, the prisons, the gas chambers and during bombing raids:

Civilians, non-Jews:

British	60,000
Belgians	40,000
Dutchmen	90,000
Germans	3,640,000
Austrians	40,000
Hungarians	80,000
Greeks	80,000
Poles	2,500,000
Russians	6,000,000
Esthonians	140,000
Latvians	120,000
Italians	70,000
Czechs	70,000
Yugoslavs	1,300,000
Rumanians	40,000
Lithuanians	170,000

To this total of 14,440,000 must be added the 5,978,000 Jews— who were systematically eliminated.

Civilian Jews:

In	
France	90,000
Holland	90,000
Denmark	1,500
Germany	170,000
Czechoslovakia	260,000
Italy	15,000
Greece	60,000
Bulgaria	7,000
Soviet Union	1,720,000
Belgium	40,000
Luxembourg	3,000
Norway	1,500
Austria	40,000
Hungary	200,000
Yugoslavia	55,000
Rumania	425,000
Poland	2,800,000

These statistics, coming from official sources, are in my estimation incomplete. There is no way of accounting for those Jews who may have concealed their identity, for the purpose of escaping persecution, those who had changed their names; those who had emigrated to other countries where they were seized by the Nazis; or children born during the occupation, in prison and in the camps. The proportion of 72% of the Jews of Europe thus massacred appears to me to be on the light side. In my view, Greater Germany was responsible for the deaths of at least 8,000,000 human beings of the Jewish faith.

I am immensely proud of the fact that the Germans saw fit to send me to a concentration camp (the only regularly accredited foreign correspondent in Berlin during the war to meet such a fate) for having been the first journalist living in

wartime Germany who told the world of the existence of a
Warsaw Ghetto and of the first roundups of Jews destined for
the extermination camps. I think I was also able to help, far
too few, unfortunately, some of the Jewish victims. Nothing
seemed so horrible as the spectacle of those children with the
Star of David inked on their chests who were thrown like so
many packages into the crematorium furnaces; nothing more
unjust or bestial than to make human beings suffer merely
because they were accused of having hooked noses or their
names happened to be Moses, Ashkenazi, or Cohn.

I hope I may be pardoned if I seem to be an iconoclast, but
here I would like to try to destroy that legend which the
surviving Jews and their co-religionists have created, which is
solidly implanted in the United States, and which would have
us believe that the Jews alone were the victims of the concentration camps and the only civilians persecuted by Hitler.

Every time I talk about the camps, there is some American
who innocently asks in surprise, "But if you were not Jewish,
what were you doing there?" The American press almost
always equates the notion of "persecuted by the Nazis" with
that of being Jewish. All the associations of deportees, of
relatives of victims, even those who demonstrated before the
White House to celebrate the liberation, are exclusively Jewish. Reference is never made to common struggles, to common suffering. They have never invited their non-Jewish comrades in captivity to join in their meetings or their activities.

All this has tended to create the belief in America and
elsewhere that the Jews alone were unjustly persecuted by
Hitler's Germany.

Nothing could be less true, or more unfair. The statistics
show it: there were almost as many Catholics massacred by
Hitler as there were Jews, and the active Resistance against

him and his Germany was not the work of one group or one religion or one people, but of a whole world, united in a common goal.

I am writing this not to create dissension, but in the interest of my Jewish comrades and brothers. For they allow the Germans to believe—these Germans of a new generation who like the others might someday plan a new massacre—that Hitler and the Reich had only one enemy, the Jewish race or religion, and that therefore their only crime was to want to wipe out that race. By thus limiting it, they attenuate the guilt of Hitler. Those who are still anti-Semites will consequently be sympathetic to Hitler and will hold only one thing against him. I heard it said in Munich by a secretary at the offices of an illustrated magazine, "Hitler's only mistake was that he did not get around to gassing all the Jews. . . ." The others will dismiss it with "Hitler was crazy; he had a mania about wanting to wipe out the Jews, but apart from that he was normal, and the Germans around him were normal." Perhaps without even intending to, they blame the Jews for being the main cause of the worldwide hostility toward Germany.

But if we remind the Germans, and the whole world, that between 1933 and 1945 they were gassing not only Jews but people of all nationalities, all religions, all classes, all political opinions, and that all, not only a minority of Jews, hated, resisted and fought in combat against the Third Reich, then the notion of this "universality" may perhaps effectively intimidate Germany and preserve our children from a new catastrophe.

To compensate these 20,000,000 dead and the 3,000,000 victims of persecution who succeeded in escaping with their lives, the German government allocated a sum of 90 billion dollars. The figure, at first blush, seems impressive. But it is tiny compared to the present prosperity of Bonn, Germany. A pittance, really.

What is not disclosed by German Minister of Finances Rolf Dahlgre is that a large share of this sum went to cover losses by German citizens, a great majority of whom can in no way be classified as victims of Nazism. Another part remains within the coffers of the government, and still another share, equally large, had been paid out to the government of the State of Israel, and so must be considered political financing, not compensation.

The average sum received by each former prisoner, once administrative costs were deducted, was about $500. If allowance is made for interest accumulated over twenty years, it can be said that Germany, which pretends to be so generous, has merely repaid the equivalent of the cost of the clothes, the contents of the valise, the wedding ring or the pocket money confiscated from the prisoner. Nothing was paid for the automobiles, the stocks of merchandise, the factories, the bank accounts; for the forced labor done; or for the gold teeth extracted from the mouths and hoarded in Swiss banks. Germany is the most prosperous nation in Europe, perhaps because it had at its disposal the gold, the currency, and the paintings stolen from camp inmates; perhaps because we were forced to work for Krupp, I. G. Farben, Mannesman, Messerschmitt; to dig tunnels in their mountains; build factories in their salt mines; and reclaim their marshes. The original investment of West Germany was the sum total of our sweat, our belongings, our dead, and on this investment it has grown fat. Such restitution is made grudgingly, for it takes years of effort to obtain compensation, and every care has been taken to ensure that the great majority of victims remain unaware of the availability of even such compensation. A few marks at a depressed rate: good Lord, how easy it is to appease one's conscience!

The poor Hungarian Jews who were forced into the gas chambers cared little that someday the country of their murderers was going to try to compensate their heirs. Had they thought of such a possibility, they might have earmarked the compensation for cousin Sarah or grandfather Geza. If they had been told that the wedding rings torn from their fingers would one day serve to finance a future nation whose existence they knew nothing of, for the simple reason that it did not yet exist even in name, they would certainly have thought that this was some new form of mental torture.

The State of Israel is admirable. It is a progressive, democratic, enlightened nation in the Middle East, and the Arab despots and petty dictators who try to prevent its growth reveal stupidity and blindness. Israel has every right to her place in the sun.

But the dead of Auschwitz and Dachau did not die for Israel, and no one, not even such a prosperous and victorious state, has a right to speak in their name. No one can ask the dead to give their consent.

If Germany wants to finance Israel, that is its business. If Israel chooses to accept, that is her right, just as it is her right to buy armaments with Bonn's money. Since, alas, we must accept that a submachine gun is criminal only in the hands of an SS man, but is a gift of God in anyone else's hands.

The gassed victims of Dachau never delegated to the State of Israel the function of receiving restitution in their names nor in the names of the survivors who are not its citizens. Any other view amounts to exploiting, betraying, and desecration of their ashes.

I become just as indignant when the State of Israel kidnaps

Eichmann or any other Nazi monster and judges him in the name of the gas-chamber victims, for at the time of their deaths these victims were Germans, Italians, Poles—not Israelis at all.

If we were to tolerate such deviations from international law, then tomorrow Gabon might demand of the United States compensation for the Red Indians massacred by the cowboys, and the Congo might kidnap and execute Governor Wallace in retaliation for the Negroes lynched in Alabama. Italy might make demands on the Queen of England because her indirect ancestors, in the days of Henry VIII, massacred Catholics, and so on ad libitum. . . .

But what I think is worse is that, by taking such an attitude, the State of Israel plays into the hands of the anti-Semites. Anti-Semitism was not invented by Hitler. It existed long before him, and he only put into practice the subconscious wish of a great many Germans. The persecutions, arrests, and even massacres of Jews had a perfectly legal basis and form. There were the Nuremberg laws, the laws for security of the Reich, those against espionage. Hitler did not say "Kill the Jews because they are bad Germans," but "Kill them because the Jews are not Germans, Italians, Frenchmen or Poles, but enemy subjects, working for the enemy, in league with the enemy." The German who denounced a Jew in theory did so not because of his race, his religion, the shape of his nose, or the color of his skin, but because he was a "foreigner," a traitor, a person dangerous to and fighting against Germany. Just as, in the case of a war against the Soviet Union, "good" patriots would denounce Communists in their midst.

If today we are told that Schultz was not a German, Cohen not an Austrian, Rothschild not a Frenchman, Pilsky not a

Pole, but that all of them were citizens of the future independent State of Israel, then, at least on the surface, Hitler is being proved right.

I prefer to read the statistics in my own way, and to see Cohen, Schultz, Rothschild, or Pilsky only as innocent human creatures who were pitilessly murdered because they did not suit the people responsible for these statistics.

One of the Secrets
of Dachau

The Café Backus, with its clean glassed-in veranda, its flowered terrace, its tables with immaculate tablecloths, its red bricks, is located near Venlo, a few hundred yards from the German-Dutch border. It is a prosperous establishment. Germans come there from the other side of the frontier to get a good cup of mocha or pick up a supply of tobacco, and it seems probable that despite the closeness of the Dutch Customs office, the café has always been a meeting-place for petty smugglers.

But on November 9, 1939, an unusual thing took place there. The circumstances were typical of the then "phony war," but its consequences were to be disagreeable to all concerned. Almost all of them, cops as well as robbers, would find themselves together again in Dachau less than six years later.

On that November 9, the café had been selected as the

scene of an unexpected assemblage. British Intelligence agents
were to meet there with a group of German conspirators,
including a Wehrmacht general, who had tried to overthrow
the regime. It had first been planned that Hitler himself, made
prisoner by the general, would be turned over, bound hand
and foot, to the men who came there from The Hague.

This fantastic plot had been afoot since the first days of
September, right after war broke out. Captain (preferring to
be called Mister) S. Payne Best, whose functions within the
British Intelligence service remain shadowy even today, but
about whom we can guess that he was head of its European
network, had been contacted by a German anti-Nazi emigré,
Dr. Franz. Some German officers, Franz had told him, were
planning a revolt and wanted the support of Great Britain.
Mr. Best asked the home office to give him competent military
advice. They sent him Major R. H. Stevens. Since it was an
important affair, at least in the imagination of the British, the
head of the Dutch Secret Service, Major General van Oor-
scholt, had also been brought in on it. The latter respected the
obligations of neutrality in his own way, and did not hesitate
to plunge into this international intrigue, which had earmarks
of a Hollywood thriller. He delegated Lieutenant Dirk Clopp,
to whom the British were to give the code name of "Captain
Coppers, of His Gracious British Majesty's Guard Regiment,"
to represent him, and contact was established with the plotters.

Meetings were held near the frontier, for the Germans
could not afford to be seen in neutral territory, much less stay
away from their garrisons for any extended time. There was a
Major Grosch, a Colonel Martini, and a Major Schaemmel.
Their plan, or more precisely that of the generals whom they
represented, was to form a South American-style junta, cap-

ture Hitler, smuggle him across the border, and sneak him on to a submarine anchored outside of Rotterdam.

"But," Major Schaemmel specified, "above all we are Germans, and the interests of our country are dear to us. Before we do anything at all, we demand the assurance that France and Great Britain will grant us a just and honorable peace."

Mr. Best could not give any such assurances on his own. He contacted London, and to keep up a liaison with the conspirators without committing anything to writing, gave the German officers a short-wave transmitter which could operate on the clandestine wave-length of the London Secret Service. Negotiations were carried on by radio and once an agreement in principle had been reached, the final meeting was arranged at the Café Backus.

That very morning, the German radio had announced the failure of a plot against Hitler, but Best did not let this worry him. He thought it might be a ruse designed to explain the disappearance of Hitler, already in the hands of the plotters.

But when they arrived the British spies scarcely had time to open the doors of their car. The café was surrounded by a commando of German soldiers, from the very regiment whose commander was supposed to be revolting against the Nazis, and Best, Stevens and the company saw the barrels of submachine guns pointed at them. They did not even have time to get over their surprise before the handcuffs were on their wrists.

"We're trapped like a bunch of rabbits," Stevens is supposed to have said. These were the last words to be exchanged between them for the next five and a half years.

The Dutch lieutenant had tried to escape and had emptied his revolver at the aggressors, breaking one of the windows of the grayish Mercedes-Benz, but he was quickly brought down.

He died a few hours later. While the shooting was going on, the Britishers had been moved across into German territory where, in the Nazi customhouse, they were formally arrested. The fantastic kidnapping had taken only a few minutes.

Dr. Franz was a double agent, acting, he was to claim later, under coercion. "Major Schaemmel" was in reality *Obersturmfuehrer* Schellenberg,* a Gestapo big shot, as were the other pseudo-plotters. The plot, the palace revolution, the whole business was nothing but a farcical sham which the Gestapo had elaborated.

One of Himmler's henchmen even called the British Intelligence Service on the short-wave radio Best had thoughtlessly given them, and after a few engaging remarks he told them point-blank that their men were in a Nazi prison, and ended the broadcast with a stentorian "Heil Hitler!" followed by the cocky notes of the march, *"Denn wir fahren gegen Engelland"* ("We are marching off to England").

This adventure might have proved laughable to all of Europe, were it not for the fact that the Germans had tied the capture of the Britishers in with the aborted plot against Hitler in the cellar of the Burgerbrau. Stevens and Best, accused of being the instigators of the murder attempt, were given up for dead by public opinion. In reality, they were sent to the Sachsenhausen concentration camp, where they were secretly locked up in the "honor bunker." In 1941, Stevens was transferred to Dachau. Best was not to join him there till the first days of April, 1945. The story of their liberation is told in another chapter.

Captain Best, who was fifty at the time of his arrest, had all

---

* Schellenberg, at the end of the war, was to negotiate, in Himmler's name, a partial surrender of the Reich to the Swedish Count Bernadotte. The others involved in this adventure, having fallen from grace, all ended up at Dachau.

the leisure he wanted in prison and was even allowed a typewriter. He was able to write a book in which he related all the tiresome details of his time in captivity. But he carefully avoided explaining what he was really doing in Holland at the time, or how much, if at all, he was implicated in the unfortunate affair at the Burgerbrau. One could hardly expect a secret service professional to reveal details of this sort. It would not be cricket.

His discretion is understandable. The part he played had been ridiculous, and the farce staged by the Gestapo, which never had the reputation of being a brilliant organization, had been so side-splitting that going into it any further could have had no effect but to send members of the Intelligence service scurrying down into the Piccadilly underground station to hide their shame.

This unbelievable inefficiency of the information services of Germany's enemies largely explains the smashing successes of Hitler's blitzes. In 1939, these word-famous intelligence outfits remained blindly convinced that Hitler was surrounded by enemies continually looking for a chance to wring his neck, that every good German who was having to go without butter was ready to rebel, that the army of the Reich had only papier-mâché tanks, and that its planes would never be able to take off because Goering was too fat. Whereas, on the other hand, the Allies were invincible.

"We will win because we are the stronger," one could read on the walls of Paris just a few days before the breakthrough at Sedan. The "experts" almost daily announced new plots by Nazi generals. But that was what was fashionable at the time.

Even that extraordinary historian, my old Berlin colleague William L. Shirer, fell into the trap. In his magnificent work, *The Rise and Fall of the Third Reich,* the best book ever written about the Hitler decade, he bogs down in this labyrinth of military conspiracies which, with two exceptions, were never anything more than barracks scuttlebutt. Too bad. The Germans would have an excellent alibi if they were able to prove that their military men were thinking of going against the one-time corporal at a time when he was still a victorious leader, distributing marshals' batons right and left.

Why were Best and Stevens not immediately executed as spies? Why were they given preferential treatment? It must be understood that the presence of Best and his friend and the other distinguished captives such as Schuschnigg, Léon Blum, Schacht, and the rest, within the confines of the camp, was a purely geographical one and not necessarily connected with other inmates. The camps were immense places. They included bungalows for field-grade officers, farms, factories, cafés, restaurants, barracks for the SS, guardhouses for the SS, lodgings for temporary guests, jails, bunkers, and finally the Lager itself, the compound into which the real *KZ Haftling* were herded. That part was hell. The Haftling were the ones who were starved, molested, beaten, hanged, or gassed on the slightest pretext. Their heads were shaven, their clothes were rags, they had a number on their chests or tattooed on their wrists, they were put to the hardest labor in the mines, and were exposed to being horsewhipped or flogged by ordinary criminals. Their contact with the outside world was cut off. For them it was truly *Nacht und Nebel* (night and fog).

On the other hand, the prisoners of honor were detained either in prison cells or in the bunker. Some of them lived under conditions of remarkable ease. Best himself, in his book, admits that if he had remained free he would have known greater deprivation in wartime England, not to mention the risk of being buried under a German bomb. Chancellor Schuschnigg had a private villa at Buchenwald where he lived with his wife, whom he had married after becoming a prisoner. A little daughter, Maria-Dolores, nicknamed Sissy, was born to them there. To establish a comparison, many a KZ inmate would gladly have cut off his own arm with a pocketknife just for a glance at a picture of his wife or daughter and a word to reassure him of their safety.

I am not saying this to diminish the merits of these illustrious captives, for five or seven years in solitary confinement is a devilish punishment, even if the prisoner is allowed, as was the case with Best, to keep his monocle, his personal possessions, a typewriter, a radio capable of receiving London broadcasts, and to get double the normal SS ration of food. They, like the rest of us, lived in constant terror of tomorrow. Each dawn might be the one of their execution. Yet the public, interested in the fate of these personages, might well fall into the misapprehension that all the rest of us at Dachau, Buchenwald, and Sachsenhausen were treated just as well.

Many of these "VIP prisoners" have emerged with a hazy recollection of what their captivity was really like. Chancellor Schuschnigg told me only recently that the 138 Dachau hostages, whose story I tell elsewhere, have remained closely tied through the years and maintain friendly relationships. He does not realize that in saying this he is lumping together courageous men like Pastor Niemöller, General Garibaldi, and himself; honest men like Léon Blum or the mayor of Vienna, Schmitz, on the one hand, and on the other some former accomplices of Hitler, some of whom were later tried for war crimes. The fact that these Hitlerites were persecuted at the end by their former chief, that they were imprisoned along with real Resistants, may entitle them to our pity but certainly not to our sympathy.

S. Payne Best relates that one day Himmler came to see him, and said, "We are doing our best to make life agreeable for you. I trust you will bear witness that all those atrocity stories printed in the *White Paper* were nothing but Jewish inventions."

Best claims that he protested vigorously at the time, but when you read his memoirs you feel he had more affection for his SS guards, whom he considered to be nice everyday people who had somehow been forced to don a uniform, and worried more about what would happen to them than he did about the poor prisoners dying all around him. One even gets the impression that our temporarily unemployed chief of the British Intelligence served as an adviser at times to camp commander Keindl and in a way helped him win the governing of Sachsenhausen. Perhaps there is a professional solidarity which is hard to overcome, even when you are at war.

Nor am I trying to cast the first stone, for I, too, when I was on occasion recipient of some specially favored treatment, found it hard to conceive that these guards who were obliging to me were the same who, a few minutes later, would sadistically torture other less-favored prisoners. That in itself was one of the paradoxes of the camps: it could happen that in one and the same place, with the same warders, under the same regime, one group of prisoners might be treated almost royally, with a diet more splendid than that of the most elegant *pension* of the Riviera, while at the same time, across the way, the bloodiest of slaughters might be carried out.

Dachau was all of that, and it was also the repository of numerous state secrets, some of which will forever remain buried in the bloody dust of the execution yards.

Georg Elser, the enigmatic perpetrator of the November 8, 1939, attempt on Hitler's life and, according to Goebbels and

Himmler, the associate of Best and Stevens, occupied a neighboring cell, No. 13, in the Sachsenhausen bunker. While Stevens was moved to Dachau in January, 1941, Elser was sent there only in February, 1945, a short time before Best.

Georg Elser had grown up in the lower depths of Munich. Much of his youth was spent in the reformatory. He was an orphan whose mother had died in childbirth and whose father was killed on the Ardennes front in World War I. He was raised by an uncle who himself died when Georg was only fifteen. Nevertheless, he became a good auto mechanic, only to be forced into unemployment by bad times. He joined a gang of Communists, was picked up in a raid, and in 1937 was sent to the Dachau concentration camp, at the time the most fearsome in Europe. He was able to withstand the mistreatment, and because of his mechanical skill, even obtained a reduced sentence.

Elser, it seems, was then approached by the authorities who proffered a bizarre bargain to him. Would he be willing to manufacture a small bomb, alleged to be the one used in a so-called plot against Hitler, in exchange for his freedom and a life of tranquillity in Switzerland? His choice was limited. If he refused, he would undoubtedly be sent up the chimney of the crematorium the same night.

Fishy story? It happened often that the Gestapo used camp prisoners for this kind of undertaking. They could be sure that the prisoner would keep quiet, for he would be too terrified of being re-arrested. The camp was an efficient machine when it came to testing a man's real character. It was easy enough for the Gestapo to find out which prisoners were cowards, ready to accede to any kind of betrayal to save their skins.

On the other hand, why tell an Elser any details about so secret and important a plan? It would be just as easy to tell him where to place his bomb, without revealing the political circumstances.

Nevertheless, he was freed and taken by car to the Burgerbraukeller. There he was shown the column in which the bomb was to be placed. All he had to do was to saw a panel of sculptured wood and move a few bricks in order to have a niche in which to put his charge. In a neighborhood store he bought a Swiss alarm clock, an electric battery (he already had plastic explosives), a detonator, and the wherewithal for installing a device which would allow him to determine the exact moment of the explosion by pressing a button under a table over near the counter.

Elser claimed later that the Gestapo had given him an envelope stuffed with Swiss francs and had suggested that he cross the Swiss border between Bregenz and St. Gallen. I know the spot well, for during my escape from Dachau, I tried, unsuccessfully, alas! to get through the barbed-wire barrier there. Elser had set me a sad example, since he was stopped and arrested there by Nazi customs agents. In the meantime, his name had become a household word. Two days earlier, his bomb had narrowly missed Hitler but had cut down several members of his entourage.

Brought back to Berlin, Elser was informed that, for reasons of political propaganda, he was being asked to stay in custody until the day when he might be produced as a prosecution witness in a spectacularly decisive state trial. The point was to prove to the world that two British spies, Best and Stevens, had been responsible for organizing the Munich beerhall plot. He would then be expected to testify that in 1938 he had been called to the Hotel Baur-au-Lac in Zürich by Otto Strasser, a one-time associate and now an enemy of Hitler, who, after introducing him to Best, asked him to take part in the plot. Best was supposed to have given him an advance of 1,000 Swiss francs. Therefore, Elser was supposed to have become a British agent and, in October, 1939, after having met Best at Venlo and received payment of some 40,000 Swiss francs, promised to kill Hitler during his stay in Munich on the anniversary of the Putsch. It was these 40,000 Swiss francs that the customs men had found on him at the time of his unsuccessful attempt to sneak over the border.

All this may seem very contradictory. If the plot was really only a propaganda device, how did it happen that there were so many victims? It has been said that the Gestapo did not foresee that the participants would linger there so long. After all, a button had to be pressed to touch off the explosion. Did not whoever pressed the button realize that all those Nazis were still there? And besides, why the Swiss watch movement if the bomb was not preset for a specified time? It has been alleged that the explosion was really only an execution in disguise, Hitler wishing to get rid of some associates he no longer trusted. That seems unlikely. It is not possible, when a large crowd has gathered, to separate certain people and make sure they will go to a given point and stay there. A bomb kills haphazardly and there was nothing to guarantee that certain Gauleiters would be slain and others spared.

I refuse to accept the theory that Hitler, knowing there was a bomb in a column behind him as he spoke and imagining the ticking of that bomb, would have gone into the beerhall even for a moment. A Swiss alarm clock is not infallible and Hitler would have been relying too heavily on his conviction that no mistake was made and no malfunction was possible. And anyway, could one trust Elser, a KZ Haftling? He could very well just then, without anyone being the wiser, have set the timing of the explosion forward and rid the world of Hitler once and for all.

I prefer to think that Georg Elser, once freed in a routine manner—for at the time it was still fairly frequent that inmates of Dachau were released from captivity—had gone back to his subversive activities, established contact with British agents, and probably organized the assassination attempt with or without their knowledge.

Why, it may be asked, would Elser have made up a different version if that were the case? Would it not rather have been advantageous for him at the time of the Allied victory to be able to identify himself as the man who almost killed Hitler? Let us note that these stories of machinations are related to us only by those who are alleged to have been his accomplices: Best and Stevens; they might have persuaded him to make such statements. If the Intelligence Service had decided, even up to the present time, to deny its complicity in the Munich attempt, Captain Payne Best would have had no alternative but to comply and therefore give us the version which best suited his superiors.

One can well wonder why, if the plot was really organized by the British, the Gestapo which had so brilliantly infiltrated their ranks and therefore would have been informed of it, did not neutralize this bomb before the deadline. This, I repeat, effectively exposed Hitler to a great risk.

The answer may be that the British did not tell all to the disguised emissaries of the Gestapo. The latter were included in only part of the discussions. The first contacts between Payne Best and the German military were perfectly legitimate. It was only when the Gestapo arrested one of the plotters, a Major Solms, and tortured him, that they got wind of it. Then the Gestapo locked up the wife and daughter of Dr. Franz, the intermediary, at Dachau. Under such pressure, he accepted the substitution of Gestapo men for the original officers.

There remains the paradox of the favored treatment given

to Elser, Best, and Stevens. This could be explained by the desire to keep the principals in good shape for public display at the showcase trials which were to follow as soon as military operations warranted. Germans love vulgar farces, and this might have been enough to keep the populace amused for several months. This explanation fits in well with the Nazi mentality.

Then there is the unadmitted, but nevertheless real, solidarity between secret agents. They try not to cross-massacre each other. Best and Stevens were important personages who could come in handy at trading time. Also, during that period, Hitler still had an inferiority complex where the British were concerned. He did not dare be too hard on a pair of British subjects. There was still the possibility of a negotiated peace with England. Making two martyrs of them would not have made things easier. And, against the day when he might decide to invade England at last, it could be useful to call on two competent Englishmen with impressive titles and who were thoroughly conversant in German. In 1943, did not the Soviets in just that way gain the services of a German general taken prisoner at Stalingrad?

Certainly circumstances changed, and after 1941 there were probably no more cogent reasons for going light on Best and his associates. But there again one has to make allowances for the operating methods of the German hierarchy. Hitler had probably at first given specific orders concerning the way these prisoners were to be handled. After that, he became absorbed in other preoccupations and it is comprehensible that no one ever dared interrupt a discussion of the Leningrad retreat to ask him what was supposed to be done now with an Elser or a Best. And if no one dared disturb him for such a trifle, no one dared to go counter to one of the Fuehrers' standing orders, for he was given to ready rages and he could severely punish those who, even with the best intentions in the world, had taken it on themselves to disregard one of his directives.

The three prisoners therefore became in a way cogs in the administrative machinery of the Nazis and even at Dachau, for even when the very end had come, they were still treated with the greatest of care. It was only when Himmler at last began acting independently of Hitler that he ordered the "accidental" death of Elser. As for the other two, he decreed that they were to be evacuated to a tourist town in the Italian Alto-Adige.

Were these men, at that time, finally removed from Dachau because they were to be used as precious hostages, and he therefore wanted to spare them the final solution he had in store for the concentration camp and the rest of its inhabitants: total destruction by flame-thrower?

That is another of the many mysteries which the liberation of Dachau was not able to solve.

9

"They Are Worth More than a Whole Armored Division"

Toward the end of the afternoon, on April 4, 1945, a Black Maria stopped in front of the small prison of the Flossenburg Camp, not far from the German-Czech frontier. It was to pick up a strangely diversified group. The first of the prisoners, escorted by six SS men carrying submachine guns, was a man with graying hair, in Tyrolian attire, who came staggering out because he was so unaccustomed to walking.

This man has today been forgotten by history, but at the time, although continuously imprisoned since 1938, his sharp-featured face was still very familiar. He was the ex-chancellor of Austria, Kurt von Schuschnigg, the first head of a European government to oppose Hitler openly and therefore his first victim.

It was widely believed he was dead even though from time to time the Hitler propaganda machine produced vague versions of his idyllic stay in a fairy-tale castle somewhere in the

Alps. Adolf Hitler, during the fateful night of March 11, 1938, while his divisions were infiltrating Austrian territory, put Schuschnigg under house arrest at the "Berghof" at Berchtesgaden, to which he had invited him and where he was therefore his guest. The Fuehrer cared little for conventions when he was beside himself: Von Schuschnigg had dared say no to him, one of the rare Germans or Austrians who ever dared do so!

The premier was put into isolation in a sordid room at the Hotel Metropole in Vienna; then interned at the camp of Sachsenhausen. He was treated severely, even brutally, but thanks to Mussolini he was allowed to marry his fiancée by proxy, Countess Vera Czernin. (This was his second marriage, his first wife having died in an auto accident.) Countess Vera wanted to share her new husband's captivity. This courageous decision was to prove costly to her. As a result of the privations and humiliations, she contracted an incurable illness and died a few years after her liberation. In 1941, in the camp prison which had become the home of the ex-chancellor, was born Maria-Dolores, today a ravishing young woman of twenty-five.

Apart from this exception to the Nazi penal code, Schuschnigg's political isolation was complete. He received no news, was forbidden newspapers, and was allowed no contact with other prisoners. But now here he was, loaded into the police patrol wagon, anticipating the worst of fates for his wife, his daughter and himself. That very morning, had they not executed a fellow captive, Admiral Canaris, the notorious head of the German secret service?

The Black Maria was not empty. In the dim light, Schuschnigg could barely make out its other occupants on the benches. One of them got up and—but let us quote Dr. von

Schuschnigg, who personally gave me a vivid account of the events:

"A man gets up, stands at attention in a very Prussian manner, clicking his heels, and holds out his hand:

" 'General-Oberst von Halder,' he says.

"I had never met him before in my life so I didn't know what he looked like, but his name was familiar to me. He was the Fuehrer's famous chief of staff. I was so delighted to meet another human being, someone who could talk to me, listen to me, give me some news, a man who was neither an executioner nor a jailer, after so many years spent in a mental purgatory, that I warmly shook the extended hand without even thinking about the background of the man. Since this von Halder had taken an active part in the invasion of my country, he had long been the 'Monster's' right hand and therefore one of my worst enemies. And here we were now together in the same cart of the condemned. . . .

"The situation became even more ironic when I saw a tall man in a general's uniform, with epaulettes, decorations, the Pour le Mérite cross hanging around his neck, as if he were about to go on stage for the finale of *The Merry Widow*. He also introduced himself with a click of the boots: 'Von Falkenhausen.' He too was a famous general.

"My wife and daughter sat on the bench facing me. At this point another couple climbed into the van with difficulty. The woman was relatively young, but the man had stooped shoulders, long white hair which came down practically to his neck, and he was leaning on a rustic cane. He first sat down next to Falkenhausen and then, realizing that he was in a German uniform, he got up and came to sit near me. I had immediately recognized him although I had never in my life met him either: Leon Blum. We had been at opposite poles of the social spectrum, but I had always had a great admiration for the French premier, and under any other circumstances such a meeting would have given me enormous pleasure. At the time, however, I felt as if an icy gust had whipped across my face. Blum, the president of the Popular Front, the best-known Jew in all of Europe, with us? Then we must all be heading for our deaths!"

There were two other prisoners in the van: Colonel Bogislaw von Bonin of the Wehrmacht General Staff and Sigismund Payne Best, the British Intelligence agent whom Himmler had had abducted at Venlo.

"A lively conversation was struck up following the introductions," Schuschnigg told me. "Of all of them, I was the one who had been most completely isolated and they could not succeed in quenching my thirst for news. Von Halder was extremely talkative and outlined the military situation for us. 'Hitler is *kaputt!* Hitler is *kaputt!*' he repeated continually, and to him this was an inevitable conclusion. Falkenhausen, who was more discreet, spoke to us of the demoralization of the people and the disorganization of the army. Blum listened, and when he wanted to ask a question—he was particularly interested in what would happen to Pétain—he spoke to me in French as if he didn't want to have anything directly to do with the German generals.

"We arrived at Dachau very late at night. The car stopped in front of the Jourhaus, that unforgettably famous guard post, and like any other deportees we had to go through the wrought-iron grille between two rows of SS men holding flashlights, after which they sent us to a sort of refectory where we joined some other prisoners, including the steel magnate

Thyssen and his wife. The camp commandant, with an amia-
bility which must have been most unusual, especially for an SS
officer routed out of bed in the middle of the night, said a few
words to us. 'There is not much in the way of comfort here but
we will do our best. You must obey all the rules; you may
speak to each other but avoid any contact with the people of
other groups. You are forbidden to go out into the camp. You
will be severely punished if you disobey us.' "

The reader will find in the illustrations of this book a complete list of the 137 so-called *Ehren-Haftlige* prisoners—the
hostages of honor who were transferred into Dachau that
night. Among them, besides the Blum-Schuschnigg group,
were fourteen British subjects, including Peter Churchill,
supposedly a nephew of the Prime Minister; a nephew of
Molotov; Prince Xavier de Bourbon, whose son twenty years
later, by marrying Princess Irene, was to create excessive gossip
and very nearly bring about a dynastic upheaval in Holland;
General Papagos, the head of the Greek general staff, who
was to play a predominant role in the destiny of his country;
the Italian General Sante Garibaldi; the Hungarian Premier
von Kallay, with other members of the Magyar cabinet and
the son of the regent, Nicholas von Horty, Jr.; the Mayor of
Vienna, the hail-fellow Schmitz; the Prince of Hessen, married to the daughter of the King of Italy; the Protestant Pastor
Martin Niemöller; Canon Johannes Neuhaeusler of Munich;
Prince Leopold of Prussia, the Kaiser's nephew with his
secretary, valet and chauffeur; Hjalmar Schacht, the financial
wizard of the Third Reich, thanks to whom Hitler had gotten
the gold he needed for the conduct of the war; and especially
the members of the families of the conspirators of July 20,
1944, together with the brother of Burgmeister Goerdeler,
responsible for the plot; Countess Elizabeth Stauffenberg, wife

of the man who had placed the bomb under Hitler's desk, with his daughters, sisters and brothers, and his father and mother . . . the German people had been told that this accursed tribe had been executed, and one can only wonder why Himmler, perhaps without Hitler even knowing about it, had preferred to lock them up.

Although this group of privileged characters had never been allowed inside the enclosure of the camp proper, and any contact with the real prisoners was impossible for them, we had been rapidly informed of their arrival by the fellows working in the political office and those responsible for their supplies. Their registering at Dachau was met with a variety of interpretations. There were those who saw in it the harbinger of the collapse of the Gestapo colossus, and others prophesied a general massacre with flamethrowers, for if prisoners of this stripe, so deeply involved, were brought to Dachau, it must have meant that the place was going to be burned out or blown up.

I was particularly intrigued by the presence of the Hungarian prime minister, Nicholas von Kallay. I could think back to the day when German troops had occupied Budapest: having had a premonition of the misfortunes that lay ahead of me, I had gone to my ambassador to seek his protection. That diplomat, who made no secret of his admiration for the Hitlerites, ridiculed my "terrors."

"You've been paying too much attention to the London radio," he told me. "You see nothing but plots and crackdowns everywhere. . . . They won't touch a hair of your head. Anyway, I wouldn't have any place to put you up. The guest room is taken. Premier von Kallay has also asked for asylum here. He's like you. He's scared, too."

And so this Kallay, who had taken "my place," had now also turned up at Dachau.

The hostages were put up in some buildings which until then had been the lodgings of the camp prostitutes—ignominious perhaps, but comfortable!

"Life at Dachau was relatively agreeable for me," Schuschnigg confided. "I was together with my family in a small, almost bare room with two metal beds, stools, a water basin and a table. It was a common prison cell but the doors were open and almost all day long we could be in touch with our neighbors. For me, who for so many years had been locked away with only my wife, this was almost a foretaste of liberty.

"The food was horrid, but frankly we weren't very hungry. We were too excited. Nevertheless, I remember that Monsignor Neuhauesler, who had friends at the Munich bishopric, got some packages of bacon and he shared them with us, for in spite of the strictures and the threats we still had some contacts with the other groups. As I remember it now, our diet consisted of potato soup, ersatz sausages, and some kind of a brown liquid. We were never given any Red Cross packages. My daughter, then four years old, had no idea what milk was.

"Halder and the other generals got themselves involved in endless discussions of strategy. They even argued it out with the SS guards.

"I had lengthy conversations with Léon Blum. He was an exceptional man, and he gave me captivating accounts of French politics, from the Popular Front to the defeat. With him, the hours fled rapidly by. He was always full of pep, never complained about the lack of physical comforts and never showed the slightest fatigue. He had a guardian angel— his wife, who was many years younger than he. She took care of him, watched over him, foresaw his slightest wishes. She tried always to be gay, and her gaiety was contagious. She was greatly responsible for keeping up our spirits, for there were extremely painful moments, though we all tried hard not to show our fears and to make believe that, as Mme. Blum described it, we were on a tourist trip which could only end in a fine celebration.

"We had no more doubts now about the imminent end of the war: one of the prisoners, a German engineer, had succeeded, with parts picked up here and there, in building a short-wave radio set, and we could therefore listen in on all the Allied broadcasts. But what naturally obsessed us was why we were now here in the Dachau 'staging area.'

"Blum was highly pessimistic. He would say: 'I was ready to die from the day the first German soldier pointed his gun at me. So each day I remain alive is that much velvet.' Although General Delestraint's execution had been kept secret, Blum had somehow heard about it. After that, he was depressingly quiet.

"He always avoided the company of the German prisoners. On their side, the generals and the tycoons had nothing but contempt for the 'little old Jew.'

"But with me, he talked about almost anything. 'We will never agree in politics, your Excellency,' he would say, 'but that's what makes democracy, always to disagree and still be able to shake each other's hand.'

"He would speak about the future. 'We must all remain united, just as we were in our opposition to National-Socialist Germany. Tomorrow we will have to close ranks against the Communists. They too will be the enemy, I'm afraid.' But he never made the slightest allusion to General de Gaulle.

"There was only one subject he stubbornly avoided, although on several occasions I tried to bring it up. 'Monsieur

Chancellor, you belong to a country which is still backward on this score. As for me, I am the unshakable defender of the lay school. If we discussed religion and education, we would be carrying on a dialogue of deaf men.'

"Blum was a bit chary of everyone, and he imagined Gestapo informers to be everywhere. He was perhaps right on the score of a certain Dr. Rascher who was locked up with us and who each morning organized a sort of medical roll call. He asked all kinds of questions, on the pretext of looking after our health. We learned afterward that he had taken part in cruel experiments on the prostitutes, and that the authorities had decided to do away with him so as to silence him. He was executed in Innsbruck the day before we left."

In the early hours of the morning of April 27, a distant booming could be heard perhaps from American guns. The 137 guests-in-spite-of-themselves of "Hotel" Dachau were loaded into large vehicles—not police patrol wagons but simply postal trucks, all green and having the characteristic insignia of crossed hunting horns on the doors. The camouflage seemed necessary, for the convoy commander, *Obersturmfuehrer* Stiller, was afraid, without foundation as it turned out, that the inhabitants of the places through which the convoy had to pass might try to liberate the prisoners. Indeed, he had been put in charge of a precious cargo. "These prisoners are worth more to me than a whole armored division," Himmler had told him on the phone. "Your head will be answerable for their fate." Stiller had understood, and he had surrounded himself with eighty SS men who were among the most fanatical of the garrison. A small pickup truck followed the vans. The SS commander had told the driver, "Take good care of the crates of munitions and high explosives you're carrying. We're going to need them badly."

"We were very much upset," Schuschnigg went on, "for, as we pulled out of Dachau, we had seen many of the prisoners piled into railroad cars and others walking along the sides of the roads, and now and then we saw a corpse lying in the ditch. The SS men herding them were quick to use their weapons. This mass evacuation seemed to bode evil, and when at Innsbruck some SS men from Buchenwald and a committee of six Gestapo functionaries joined our escort, our anxiety almost turned into panic. One of our fellow prisoners had been able to identify the Gestapo team: they were special agents in charge of executions. Until then we had been lulling ourselves with the illusion that we were merely hostages and that we were going to be kept in the 'Alpes Fortress' to be exchanged for Nazi big shots held by the Allies."

What Schuschnigg did not know then was that in his brief case SS Commander Stiller had a formal order signed by Himmler, reading, "If you are unable to escape from the enemy or if there is danger of liberation of the prisoners by partisans, you are to execute them all without mercy. . . ."

This strange convoy spent the night in a small town in Bavaria and it was only on the evening of Saturday, April 28, that they reached their stop at the village of Niederdorf. The SS men, wielding their submachine guns, immediately surrounded the group, for according to von Schuschnigg the inhabitants had recognized some of the captives and had started conversations with them.

Pastor Niemöller recalls that one of the SS officers, a giant of a man, yelled in his face: "End Station. . . . This is the last stop before the end."

As a matter of fact, and this was to be confirmed at the trial of General Wolff, commander of all SS and police forces in Italy, held in Munich in the spring of 1945, *Obersturm-*

fuehrer Stiller had intended to transport his hostages to a mountain chalet romantically hidden away near an Alpine lake, where the massacre was to take place. The bodies were to be thrown into the water.

For Schuschnigg, "Our arrival at Niederdorf was like a liberation. Stiller, because of the breakdown of one of the trucks and also because he had been warned of partisan activities in the area, allowed us to get out and refresh ourselves at the village inn and in some of the surrounding houses. None of this had been organized: the Nazis were at the end of their rope. As a result, we were able to move about freely, to speak with the inhabitants, have a glass of beer, or even a glass of milk. A few of the prisoners, the younger ones, who could run and climb, even succeeded in getting away from the SS men and take refuge in the nearby woods where the partisans came to their assistance."

Niederdorf, now known as Villabassa, is a pretty little town, a skiers' paradise, north of Cortina d'Ampezzo and more than 70 kilometers from the Brenner Pass. Until the arrival of these VIPs, the village, surrounded by the crown of the Dolomites, had remained completely outside the war, even though both Italian and Yugoslavian partisans were active in the region. Its inhabitants had mostly been fanatic Nazis until they understood that catastrophe was no longer avoidable. Villabassa, like the Lake of Braies (called Pragserwildsee in German), is in the very heart of the Alto-Adige, the province annexed by the Italians in 1919, which the Gross-Reich reconquered in 1943, and which today the Austrians, who would never dream of recognizing Hitler as one of their countrymen, keep clamoring for on the basis that its people speak their language.

General Sante Garibaldi, the most important of the Italian

prisoners, immediately tried to get in touch with the Calvi Pier Fortunato partisan brigade. Then Garibaldi suggested to his German fellow captive, Colonel Horst Petersdorf, that they organize a revolt of the prisoners to be synchronized with the expected attack of the partisans. But the German officer was not ready to assume such a responsibility.

Moreover, the German captives were not especially anxious to be liberated by partisans. . . . There were those among them who did not have exactly pure consciences, and who therefore felt it still preferable to be in the hands of SS men rather than the underground.

Along these lines, Colonel Bogislaw von Bonin had also undertaken his own course of action. Eluding the surveillance of the SS men, he had reached the village's telephone exchange, and since he was still in uniform it had been easy for him to convince the soldier on duty to put him through to the military headquarters at Bolzano.

Here is how Schuschnigg tells it:

"Von Bonin had been General Heusinger's successor as chief of the army general staff, but he in turn had fallen from grace and been arrested by the SS. He was perhaps the only one among us who had not lost his head in the immense confusion at Niederdorf. So he got in touch by phone with the vice-commander of the German occupation forces, General Hans Roettiger. The latter did not want to get involved, but nevertheless he instructed one of his subordinates, Captain Gerhart von Alvensleben, to have a look-see. The captain happened to be in the area, at the head of a company of some hundred men.

"He came over by car, accompanied by several blond uniformed telephone girls, members of the women's auxiliary, as if he were off on a romantic outing, and arrived in the main square of the town. The place by then was quiet and dark, all the prisoners having been put up either at the inn or the nearby houses, under the surveillance of the SS. And then, as if by accident, the SS commander came out into the square to take a stroll. The two officers exchanged salutes and American cigarettes (confiscated from shot-down American flyers), and then went off to have a cup of real coffee, also part of the war booty.

" 'What are you doing way out here, comrade?' Alvensleben asked casually. The other one told him his story. The Wehrmacht officer could hardly believe his ears. People as important as this exiled in such a hole! Generals, prime ministers, a nephew of Molotov!

"But von Alvensleben did nothing to betray his interest. He talked about other things, asked whether his SS colleague might be needing a bottle of cognac, and finally said good-bye without any further allusion to the people in the convoy.

"The officer immediately went back to his post and organized a small expedition of fifteen subalterns to be ready to overcome any opposition, for he had decided to take our group away from the SS people. He came back at the first light of dawn on Sunday, April 29, and suddenly confronted Stiller while the latter was shaving.

" 'Turn your prisoners over to us,' he ordered.

" 'No, my mission will be over only when all the subjects have been executed,' was the reply.

" 'In that case, your mission no longer has any meaning. You are *my* prisoner!'

"The army men immediately invaded the village but did not try to disarm the SS contingent. Alvensleben simply phoned his superior, General Roettiger. But the latter still did not want to be involved!

" 'Have you gone completely crazy?' he shouted. 'How can

you possibly have done this? Are you trying to lose your head and mine?'

"Alvensleben, however, was unwilling to leave the captives to their fate. On his own initiative, he sent a call for reinforcements, and proposed to Stiller that, while awaiting developments, they take the whole crew to the luxury Hotel Pragserwildsee. And that was how we had our first real meal, a good split-pea soup Tyrolean style, just a few hours before the Dachau concentration camp was in its turn liberated by the Americans."

But Chancellor von Schuschnigg's memoirs are far from giving a complete picture of the situation. On one hand, the SS men had not yet renounced their claim to their victims, and on the other, General Roettiger might at any moment disavow his subordinate and instruct the Wehrmacht forces to withdraw.

General Garibaldi had foreseen this peril and was deeply concerned. He considered, no doubt correctly, that the German army was interested in getting the prisoners out of the clutches of the SS only to have these precious hostages in its own possession, to negotiate exchanges with the Allies or use them to extort better conditions in the event of surrender.

At one P.M. that Sunday, with amazing daring, Garibaldi simply presented himself to Stiller and invited him to lunch. He was accompanied by two armed partisans. Stiller did not dare turn him down. Their meeting took place in a festive atmosphere, accompanied by food and drink. Garibaldi explained: "The partisans already have the locality surrounded. Tomorrow we will have overwhelming strength. The Wehrmacht is undecided, and also powerless to do anything. If you promise not to harm a hair of the heads of your charges, we will allow you and your SS men to return to Bolzano," Stiller promised.

In the meantime, there was a dramatic development at

Bolzano. General Roettiger, who up to now had refused to send any reinforcements, without which von Alvensleben could not overcome the SS, was relieved, as was his immediate superior, General Viettinghoff, by a fanatic Nazi, General Scholtz. At this point, Roettiger decided to move. He had Scholtz put under arrest, as well as the Gauleiter of the region, Franz Hofer (who had been talking about going over and killing the 137 prisoners personally), and ordered Alvensleben to get rid of Stiller and cooperate with the partisan brigade. Alvensleben, in turn, phoned General Wolff who, at Caserta, near Naples, was getting ready to sign the surrender. Wolff told him to call Stiller to the phone, and he commanded him to return to Bolzano with his SS men but without the hostages. While Stiller was still on the phone, von Alvensleben gave urgent orders to move all the prisoners to a hotel high up in the Dolomites, the Wildsee, which was easier to defend.

The SS escort was loaded into trucks and driven off toward Bolzano, but they were never to arrive at their destination, preferring to take off on their own into the countryside. Stiller and a few other guards decided to stay where they were and meekly put themselves under the command of Captain von Alvensleben.

The prisoners were informed that they were now free and that the Wehrmacht was there only for their protection. The local population, trying to ingratiate itself, sent them a whole pig, quantities of sausages, vegetables, butter, cigarettes, wine, and clothing.

"It was from the radio that very night," Schuschnigg told me, "that I learned of Mussolini's horrible death. This news threw a shadow over my joy. Mussolini had been a fair-weather friend and he had betrayed me when the going got tough, but to know that he had been hanged by the heels from a meathook did something to me."

In spite of all the celebrations, the fate of the prisoners was still precarious: at any moment the SS men might come back and take over, or the Wehrmacht might transport them elsewhere. It was only the next morning, May 1st, that the Italian partisans turned up in force. They obtained permission to talk to the hostages. "If you want, you can come with us," they offered. Garibaldi and Ferrero, as well as the Soviet Lieutenant Basili Kokorin Nedotowsk, Molotov's nephew, accepted the invitation. The others preferred to stay where they were.

Why? Schuschnigg explains it to us:

"All of us at Niederdorf had voted to put ourselves under the orders of the British Wing Commander Harry Day, whom we considered the ranking man and the one best qualified to represent us. He decided for us."

In fact, Day was working on his own liberation plot. Helped by Stevens and Sigismund Payne Best, the Intelligence men, he had been able, right after leaving Dachau, to make contact with the Allied armies. Somewhere, there was a clandestine radio operating. He knew that the Anglo-Americans had a brigade of parachutists all ready to come in and liberate them. He preferred to gamble on their arrival rather than to allow the captives to disband. Yet one of the Englishmen, Thomas Cushing, taking advantage of the general confusion, had succeeded in escaping out of one of the rear windows of the hotel and, helped by a member of the Resistance, joined up with the American army.

A battalion commanded by Captain Bodo was cautiously approaching the hotel. It was now May 4th. The German soldiers, on seeing them, promptly threw their hands up. This was the end of the nightmare for the 137 "prisoners of honor."

The caution shown by the American captain proved justified. When his men had traversed the village of Braies, right at the end of it, an SS man, *Oberscharfuehrer* Fritz, threw a grenade at the liberators. The Americans were furious and shot down all the guards posted around the village. The Resistance, during this time, had not sat on its hands. The six Gestapo functionaries, the professional killers who had joined the convoy at Innsbruck, were hanging from the trees in the village square.

"On May 6th," Schuschnigg says, "we were taken to Bologna, where I was put up at the famous Albergo della Colomba d'Oro. We were then asked what our plans were.

" 'I would like to return to my home in Vienna,' I said.

" 'That just isn't possible,' an American general told me. 'You all are in need of rest and sunshine. We would be very happy if you agreed to go to Capri.'

"We had no other choice. A special fleet of sixteen planes soon dropped us at the Naples airport, and there was a good lunch, spaghetti alle vongole, waiting for us at the Zita Teresa Restaurant. Then a U.S. Navy torpedo boat took us aboard and conveyed us to Capri, where we were installed at the Eden-Paradise Hotel. The name was appropriate. For my daughter, Maria-Dolores, this was a paradise indeed."

It would take too long to detail what happened later to each of these famous hostages.

For Kurt von Schuschnigg, Chancellor of the Austrian Republic, liberation was not, as for so many of us, merely a changing of the guard.

A return to his mother country was for a long time made impossible. After publishing a successful book and giving some lectures, he was to lose himself in anonymity.

I found him again in St. Louis, Missouri, teaching history and politics in a Catholic university. His students were completely unaware of the eminence of their professor. This was true to such a degree that Schuschnigg asked me if I had any pictures of Dachau that he might show to his classes to prove to them that the camps had really existed. He was living modestly with his daughter, a student herself—so modestly, in fact, that he confided to me that he was really cutting corners in order to be able to buy a hi-fi record player; he, who in the days of his glory, had been able any night to sit in the Imperial box and watch the performances of the Vienna Opera. Since then, his situation has improved. He has a small secondhand car and even a television set. He has been traveling, and is talking now about retiring to Switzerland.

"But why doesn't Austria, now free, democratic, and prosperous—Austria which never, but really never, cheered Hitler in the streets and squares of Vienna—call you back? Why does it not honor the man who, in order to preserve the independence of his country, spent seven years in jail with his wife and his daughter, and came so close to being fed to the fishes in a tiny lake up in the Dolomites?" These are the questions I asked him while pointing out that, whatever one may think, it is surprising that the present Austrian ambassador to Washington should be a man I had often seen carrying on in the corridors of the Wilhelmstrasse as servile assistant to one of the most fanatic Nazis of the Ribbentrop gang. . . .

"Oh, my dear friend," Schuschnigg replied, "there are many things worse than that. They just don't want me back there any more. I remain Austria's guilty conscience."

10

The Girl on the Balcony

A hideous legend was associated with the building where prisoners' clothing and other possessions were kept.

While it was being built, a worker, a Jewish internee who had aroused the ire of one of the guards, was shoved into the layer of fresh cement that had just been poured in the foundation. The Jew screamed and struggled, but the SS man was so delighted with his feat that he had a second load of concrete dumped in, and the Jew was buried in it, petrified forever.

I had gone there at the very first chance, hoping to get back my civilian clothing. Normally, everything confiscated from the new arrivals was turned over once a month to the sorting centers within the SS enclosure, but the upheaval of the last months had interrupted the routine and it was just possible that some of my things might still have been there.

Alas, the very evening of the liberation, some German internees had forced the locks of the warehouse, skirted around the American sentinels, and made off with everything that they could use as civilian disguises and thereby escape. They had carried off the rest to sell on the black market. I never again saw my mink-collared coat with the fox lining, which I had bought for three gold pieces in Budapest and which since had several times saved my life by protecting me against the freezing nights on the stone floors of the jails at Foe Utca and Vienna. The coat had so impressed police patrols that, when they saw me so luxuriously bundled, after my concentration-camp escape, and were checking my identity in the trains leading to the Swiss frontier, they readily believed I was really the Hungarian diplomat on leave that I pretended to be.

It was not the loss of the coat that upset me so much as the loss of what was in its pockets—my passport, some pictures, some notes, some friends' addresses and especially the address of Perrette.

"You won't need my address, *chéri*," she had said to me the last time we saw each other. "Just go to the village, ask for Perrette, everybody knows me, and by the time your apéritif is served at the Café du Commerce, I'll be there. . . ."

We had made a date to meet on September 5th, her twentieth birthday.

"Just go to the village," she had said. But what village? A village with a very simple name, a village in Burgundy, or rather in Franche-Comté—or no, on the Loire, somewhere near Blois. . . . After leaving camp, my memory had perceptibly weakened and just a few days after liberation it was already difficult for me to remember the names of comrades who only yesterday had shared my bunk. It was even difficult for me to recognize the faces of some of the SS bullies. And I could no longer remember the name of the village of Perrette, that charming, adorable, little Perrette with whom I had been in love for a few short, endless weeks.

It was in Vienna, in the central prison which lies alongside that gray, dirty, and turbulent Danube that at the time was so repulsive to us. I was locked in a cell on the first floor, usually intended for two occupants, into which a dozen of us had been crowded. They had brought me there from Dachau for some kind of interrogation. The penitentiary staff was not made up of SS men. They were professional turnkeys, but that was no reason to think that they behaved any less brutally. As good Austrians, they had no use for those foreign "good-for-nothings" who were all enemies of their new greater fatherland.

"Don't expect any pity from a professional policeman. They serve any regime, in any country. For them, there are no innocent ones or guilty ones, there are only whipping-boys. In a year or two they'll be just as scornful to the Gestapo guys whose orders they are now carrying out so servilely, when it comes their turn in prison. If they had any brains or any hearts they never would have become cops."

It was one of my cellmates who spoke thus, and he must have known what he was talking about, for he had been a district attorney in Graz. He had been arrested for not being harsh enough in pressing the cases against anti-Nazis.

Another prisoner in my cell was a violinist from the Hotel Sacher. His crime was not playing enough waltzes by Strauss, who with Wagner was a favorite of Hitler, and for playing too much Dvořák.

There was also a young Iranian diplomat whom we all suspected of being a Gestapo stool pigeon; he claimed to have been caught between two rival factions which had both been trying to become Quislings.

There was also a Hungarian who had quite simply tried to carry off by truck, through two battlefronts, all the equipment used in the oilfields of the Carpathians in order to resell it in

Liechtenstein. He had been arrested at Bratislava and his drills stored on riverboats under the Reichsbruecke near the Prater.

One night, they brought us a fat peasant with red cheeks and nose, a Burgmeister of a village in the Salzkammergut. He was accused of having slaughtered a pig without authorization. He was our favorite comrade in spite of his stupidity, for his wife regularly brought him huge baskets stuffed with victuals, which he had no choice but to share with us. Unfortunately, his stay among us was short. His wife, a shrewd woman, got the idea of presenting similar baskets to the Gestapo functionaries in charge of his case. The Burgmeister was soon released.

Another inmate, corpulent as a Falstaff, was brought in to us one evening. Before even introducing himself, he disappeared behind the screen which hid the toilet bowl, for in Vienna they observe niceties of this sort. For two hours we heard nothing but stormy sounds, pulling of chains, and gushing of water, and of course there were the smells. He explained later: "The Gestapo put such a scare into me, it upset my stomach!"

He was a weird character, who spoke some twenty languages and fifteen dialects fluently. He spoke to me in Latin, was able to answer me in Turkish, wrote Arabic, and recited poetry in Hungarian. He had been in the Gestapo service as a postal censor. It was he who read and sorted all letters going abroad; but, at the same time he had decided to join a Resistance group. He relayed compromising messages directly from his censorship office, convinced that no one would open any letters officially stamped with the Gestapo seal. But one day, absent-mindedly, he had put a letter intended for one of his fellow plotters on the pile of envelopes "for censorship," which meant they were to be carefully examined by the police.

This was what gave the show away. Fortunately his accomplices, being prudent, had told very little to this fathead. He might easily have been turned over to the headsman, but the Gestapo did not want to make anything of it so as not to appear ridiculous. As for us, we did hear about it and it gave us a chance to laugh at them for once. Such occasions were not frequent.

There was also a Berlin engineer who proudly proclaimed that he held the high Nazi honor of being a Golden Party Member. It seemed he had been arrested for having gone too far in his pillow-talk with his Mitzi. He worked on an ultrasecret project for the Hermann Goering factories. I figured it more likely that he had put his hand in the till. No doubt in the hope that the walls had ears, he was constantly singing the praises of National-Socialism and, in spite of the advice of my cellmates to hold back, I could not keep myself from contradicting him. We held heated debates each evening when the Wehrmacht communiqué was read out of the paper that the waltz-player was privileged to receive. Naturally, we had to interpret this public-relations handout in our own way, and usually we pushed the Germans back some twenty to thirty miles beyond what they admitted having lost. This was a precious moment in our lives, for to us every yard and every mile the Germans gave up meant that many fewer hours or days from freedom.

The engineer sneered at us and announced that all these retreats were only provisional and there would soon be a dramatic turnabout. One evening, we came to grips over it.

"How can you dare to think you'll win this war?" I demanded. "You're surrounded."

"With new weapons," he replied.

"But your V1s and V2s are practically useless," I said.

"What weapon could change the situation all at once in the air, at sea, in Warsaw, at Budapest, on the Rhine, in Italy—"

But the German excitedly contended that he was working with many others to build a "weapon that would destroy entire armies on the battlefield in a matter of seconds."

We had to stop the discussion right there, as it had become ridiculous. This Nazi locked up by his fellow Nazis had obviously now lost his marbles. A bomb that would wipe out armies—indeed! What a joker that Hitler was, getting them to swallow such nonsense!

Apart from our discussions of strategy, the daytime hours went by slowly, there being nothing to break the monotony except perhaps for the visits from the doctor, who had the build of an Ichabod. We were sure he was a mute. He would open the door, put one hand on the padlock and the other to his ear, listening to the detailed, colorful and dramatic recital of their ills by those who had put themselves down for sick call. He made various faces according to the descriptions, nodded or smiled, whichever the reaction called for. Then, when the patient had finished, he would give him one, two, or three aspirins. We had it figured out that the number of aspirins was in proportion to the length of the recital.

But at night, as in a Walt Disney animated cartoon, the prison underwent a transformation. The jailers had either gone to their homes or were looking for *Gemütlichkeit* in some distant wing of the prison. Their rounds were few and far between. Then we would all go to the barred windows looking out on a rectangular courtyard some twenty yards wide and almost a hundred yards long. Inevitably, a voice called out in French, *"Bon soir, les copains."* That started off a bizarre concert which would go on sometimes till after midnight. There would be answers in French, followed by

*Guten . . . Abend . . . servus . . . kalisperas . . . ciao, dobre
. . . buenas tardes*—the language depending upon the arrivals and departures. And then—this usually also from the
French—there would be an announcement of the latest military news. This was an uncensored news service, and I must
admit highly imaginative—a mixture of items plucked from
the German papers; tips from Radio London brought in by
new prisoners; prison grapevine; and a good dose of the
optimistic fancy of the anonymous reporter. Oh, if Eisenhower would only have known that this very evening he was at
the doors of Leipzig, and Marshal Zhukov that he was sunning
himself on the outskirts of Vienna!

This broadcast on world news was then followed by local
news. Such and such a French collaborationist had been
executed; Tito's partisans had blown up a bridge near Zagreb;
there had been another attempted murder in Prague; someone
had shot at the mayor of Vienna; three Nazi generals had been
hanged on Hitler's orders; and the Fuehrer's health was once
again faltering. When the news was big enough, it would be
followed by the singing of the *Marseillaise, Garibaldi's Hymn,*
or *The Internationale.* It did not really matter whether the
news was true or false—or even unlikely. We still wanted to
believe in it; it was good for our morale; and it took the place
of the cigarettes that were hard to come by and the Schnapps
we could not get.

There were also personal messages, as cryptic as the ones
broadcast by the BBC. We always took delight in their mystery. There would be an announcement of the day's departures, followed by a moment of silence. You wondered
whether such and such a friend, or a comrade who had just
passed through, or this unknown one whose name you were
hearing for the first time had gone off to freedom or to the
execution wall. . . . Then we would sing. Sad songs, nos-

talgic songs, sentimental songs, anything that reminded us of back home and the good old days. *"J'attendrai";* Cavaradossi's aria from *La Tosca;* a Zarah Leander song; *"Heimat deine Sterne"* ("My country, where are your stars?") which almost always brought tears to our eyes; the solo from "The Czarevitch"; the Russians humming "Volga-Volga" or "The Red Army March"; and all these voices coming from behind the darkened bars at the four corners of the courtyard, yet finding a way to harmonize, had something magical about them. Sometimes there was applause. Choruses were repeated. There were requests for an encore and there were shouts of *bravo.* . . .

And then there were the conversations between men and women. The latter were all in the part of the building that was along the Danube. The men would call out, *"Bon soir,* Yvonne. . . . *Gute nacht,* Isolde. . . . Maria, *vieni.* . . ." And the women would answer, "I'm here, *chou* . . . good night, *chéri.* . . . *Schatz.* . . . *T'agapo.* . . ." If their windows were too far away, we would relay the messages from bar to bar. Some of them were husbands and wives who had been arrested together but whom the prison had separated; some were betrothed; lovers; young people who had met on the outside, where they lived on the same street or worked in the same factory; but most of the times the acquaintance had started here in prison. They talked without modesty or effort at privacy, for after all, weren't we just one big family? They shared their loves or their affections with those who had none and who listened in, just as they would share a slice of bread or a cigarette.

On the other side of the courtyard, directly opposite us, two floors higher, was a cell without windows but with a kind of perpendicular transom. One morning I heard a feminine voice pouring a stream of French slang at the matron, calling her every species of *grue* or *vache* and of *vieille bourrique*. When the storm had settled, I called out a few words of encouragement to the unknown French girl. She seemed delighted to hear someone speaking her language and told me that she had just arrived. Her name was Perrette, she said, and she had been turned in for laziness by the farmer for whom she worked as a stable girl.

For a few days, these exchanges of civilities were fine for us. Now I too had someone to whom I could call out, "Good morning, Perrette, did you sleep well?" One day, while her cellmate stood guard, Perrette moved the table to the wall and climbed up to the ledge of the transom. The view was not exactly favorable: first I saw prison shoes, then two legs, the black fabric of a dress, and finally a cute little round face with Bebe Daniels bangs covering the forehead. She was very pretty. Actually, I would be unable today to describe her any better than that or even to recognize her. But at that time all was illusion, dreamlike, and for a few moments we could believe in our mirage.

Perrette came often to her barred-in balcony, and our talks became progressively more intimate. I must admit that they were not very loud colloquies, which would have caught the ear of the matron, and besides, you can't very well express your love while three hundred windows full of prisoners listened in. We communicated by signs; a language you inevitably learn in prison but which is not quite the same as that of deaf-mutes. You outline the letters; you pinch the palm of your hand; and, to make a comma, for instance, there's a gesture as of chasing a fly away. It does take quite some time to spell out "You're a very pretty girl," but that only makes the build-up more effective, and you try to guess each letter in advance. And in that way we were able to say things to each other, things that a fellow and a girl would usually be saying on the banks of the Seine or sitting behind the wheel of a convertible. She sent me kisses; promised to wait for me, that she would remain faithful. . . .

We could barely see each other; we conversed in monkey language; we could not touch each other, yet I fell madly in love with Perrette and I hoped she had fallen in love with me, for she was the sun to me in this cold gray courtyard; her voice was music in this place as sad as a tomb; and I no longer feared the start of each new day, for now I could wake up to Perrette's bird call of "Good morning, Nerin. I love you. Here's a kiss. . . ."

One afternoon, feeling particularly amorous, I asked Perrette to raise her skirt, because I wanted to see her legs. Perrette thought this was very flattering and lent herself willingly to the unique strip act. "I couldn't raise it very high, darling," she apologized later, "because I didn't have anything on under my dress. I traded away all my underwear on the black market."

It is not love if you don't feel you want to make a present to your loved one. So I "borrowed" some handkerchiefs from the oil smuggler. And I made an arrangement with Perrette: men and women, separately of course, used the same shower room, and so I said I would leave the hankies behind a certain cabin. Then, by the use of a few pins, Perrette was able to make herself a pair of bikini panties out of two squares of material. As for brassières, it was more complicated. I knew a trick for making one by folding the handkerchief in a certain way. It took a lot of sign language to explain it to her, and I finally had to resign myself to demonstrating it on my own person behind the bars of my window. The other women prisoners, who all watched this strange show, thought it was a very ingenious method. So I had to repeat my do-it-yourself brassière course for their benefit. For a few days there was an active exchange of handkerchiefs around the shower room.

Perrette was terrified of air raids. Our Viennese turnkeys would take to their heels and hide, but they left the prisoners in their cells. If a bomb were to hit the prison, our fate was sealed. We would be roasted like chickens on a skewer. Nevertheless, the American air excursions filled us with joy. During the raids, we could yell at the tops of our voices, there being no one around to punish us—"Murderers! Cowards! Monsters!"—all meant for our guards, of course. We were delighted to see the sky streaked by those metal pencils known as Liberators, which sparkled in the sun like diamonds set in platinum. Each bomb that fell, spreading ruin and flames, seemed to us a personal gift.

Perrette, however, less sophisticated, preferred to hide under her bed. Afterward it took a lot of talking to reassure her.

"I'll teach you a prayer to say when the planes come over," I told Perrette. "It will calm you down:

Our godfather Churchill who art in London,
Acclaimèd be thy name,
Thy planes return safe.
Thy will be done in Berlin as it is in Rome.
Give us today our daily bombardment.
Forgive not the Germans, as we will never forgive them.
Try not to hit us,
But, especially, deliver us, deliver us."

Every morning at dawn came the hardest part of our waiting period. A guard called out the roll of those who were to leave by convoy. Our hearts, gripped with panic, stopped beating, as with pain and distress we saw one among us leave. But at the same time a selfish, violent, endless joy took hold of me; joy at knowing that *I* was not the one to have to leave. Our good-byes were touching and hypocritical. One morning the world crumbled for me, as I had often dreaded. My name was on the awful list. Dachau, once again. My friends got my things together for me. The Iranian diplomat took possession of my bunk (there was a seniority system for this). Everyone wanted to shake my hand, to hug me, and I barely had time to let Perrette know.

"I'm heartbroken," she called out. "Heaven protect us! Don't forget—in September after the victory, in my village. Everyone knows me; all you have to do is ask for Perrette."

That was how I saw her for the last time, one hand throwing kisses, the other repeating the signal, *"Au revoir, chéri,"* her frail little body cut up into jigsaw pieces by the window bars against which she was pressing.

It was sad not to be able to find at the clothing storeroom the little piece of paper on which I had written Perrette's address. I just hope the overcoat brought no good luck to the comrade who stole it, and with it stole one of the dearest wishes I had for the liberation.

Perhaps Perrette never returned to her village. Who knows? Perhaps her little body was turned into ashes, or perhaps she just never went to keep our rendezvous, having forgotten all about that nightmare. . . . I would just like to think she is aware that often, very often, I have intoxicated myself with the memory of our silent little talks, and that I can still see her as she was then, with her round face, her short hair, clinging to the window bars with one hand and with the other pulling up her skirt, the timid reflections of the September sun embroidering arabesques of light on her naked legs.

INTERLUDE
III

Responsibility

. . . During the months following the libera-
tion, I had occasion to visit the Munich prison cells occupied
by some of the Gestapo employees who had been responsible
for our misfortunes. During our long months of incarceration,
we had sworn that we would make these monsters pay dearly
for their arrogance and their mistreatment of us. However,
when I entered the cells, I was horribly embarrassed and, out
of pity, I gave them cigarettes. Many of my comrades, and
most recently Geurisse, the president of the International
Committee, told me of having had similar reactions.

We were not models of generosity. We had not yet stopped
hating, but we realized that it was unfair to try to wreak
vengeance on a few wretched individuals for the crimes of a
whole nation.

I am not one of those who have carefully preserved the
prison garb and boastfully wear it on all occasions to make a
political or economic weapon of it, as if to trade on a horror-
filled past. I do not feel that, because I was a deportee, I
should have a special right to a seat in the subway as does a
pregnant woman. I have never joined any political associations, much less demonstrated before the windows of any

German consulate. To me, Dachau and all the rest was for a long time a name to be forgotten, and I have always tried as much as possible to avoid recalling the atrocities.

I have no hatred for the Germans. I still consider Berlin one of the most beautiful cities in the world, and it remains to me the golden city of my youth. Whenever I have a moment of leisure, I go for a glass of beer in the German section of New York. I love movies with a Bavarian atmosphere. I am sure the Mercedes-Benz is the best car in the world, and my dream is to own a villa on the shores of Lake Constance.

However, I refuse to grant that anything at all should be changed in the history of the Third Reich, even if the reason for it is to put the Moscow government in one devil of a spot.

If you go to the city of Dachau and order a good beer in the *brasserie* of the Church Square, there will be a fat waiter in leather pants who will tell you: "The camp is all right to tell the tourists about, but between you and me it never really existed. It's just an invention of Communist propaganda."

I am not one of those who want to see the German people publicly whipped. I could not care less whether the statute of limitations is further extended on war criminals. Most of these trials are demanded only by the State of Israel, which wants to get political, financial and propaganda advantages from them and does not give a hoot about the fate of a few toothless old SS men. Beyond that, all the laws in the world will not force the German people to punish men whose guilt it won't admit.

I was reading an article in the Paris *Figaro* deploring all these trials of nameless underlings and denouncing this as a new witch hunt. In that writer's view, these men did nothing but carry out orders. The ones who deserved to be punished were the leaders: the Bormanns, Goerings, Eichmanns, Kaltenbrunners, Megerles. I go even further than the *Figaro*; even Bormann, Eichmann, and the rest should not be held responsible. They too were only obeying orders. Had they not carried out Hitler's instructions, they too would have been executed. Did not the Fuehrer arrest Goering, and did he not intend to have Himmler shot? Did he not do away with Fegelein, Eva Braun's brother-in-law and Himmler's own right-hand man, in his bunker a few days before the end? Only one man, therefore, was responsible—only one deserved a trial: Adolf Hitler.

Yet if I were a member of a jury sitting in judgment on the Fuehrer, I would vote "Not guilty."

Hitler was not a supernatural monster, emerging from hell with lightning in his hand, who supposedly took some magic hold over the lives and souls of the Germans, as the present president of Federal Germany, Mr. Lubke, would have us believe. Hitler was not a tyrant in an ivory tower, surrounded by robots, who secretly achieved power by conspiring with a few gregarious aides in a beer hall, as we might be asked to believe by Dean Rusk, Secretary of State of the United States, who seems to learn his history in comic books. Hitler was called to power by a decisive majority of the German people, after years and years of struggle, in an excessively democratic country, where the opposition, the Communist party, was exceedingly strong. Hitler won majority after majority, swept election after election, and he, the simple World War I corporal, came very close, in a national plebiscite, to being elected president of the republic in place of the venerable, respected and sanctified Hindenburg, the hero of Tannenberg.

Hitler did not come to power thanks to his janissaries fighting their way to the Wilhelmstrasse with machine guns, but was invited there by Franz von Papen, the representative of high finance, supported by Fritsch, Blomberg, and von Schleicher, that is to say the army; and deliriously acclaimed by millions of Germans. You can make people stay at home, but you cannot force them to go out into the streets and scream their enthusiasm. Hitler became Chancellor because Hindenburg shook his hand. He could not have remained in power more than three weeks without the approbation of all strata of the population. He would not have been able to conquer Paris and Tobruk without the help of the generals and the sacrifices of the soldiers. He was not betrayed: youths were still dying for him in the streets of Berlin when he, with his mistress and his dog, were lying dead in the bunker.

And don't talk to me about plots and attempts on his life. The people, the soldiers, the hierarchy were so faithful to him that all the attempts, all the conspiracies, failed miserably. As for Mussolini—all it took was a few *carabinieri* to make a ridiculous, upside-down effigy of him.

Hitler and Germany are one indivisible unit. If Germany fails to accept its responsibility, then Hitler too must be innocent in the eyes of history.

The eminent British historian, H. R. Trevor-Roper, wrote in *The New York Times* of June 6, 1965: ". . . The Germans put [Hitler] into power, not because he promised revolution but because he promised to fulfill old ambitions, ambitions which had been pursued, by various means, in peace and in war, for fifty years.

"In 1918 these ambitions had been disastrously frustrated. But they had not been abandoned. Hitler revived them; and in 1940 it seemed that, at last, he was about to fulfill them.

"Today," he goes on to say, "it is the fashion in Germany

to try to disassociate Hitler from Germany and paint the Germans as the victims of, rather than the participants in, his crimes. But history is patient and will not accept this version. Hitler is the continuation of Wilhelm II and Bismarck, the third head of the three-headed monster. *Mein Kampf* was not a work of the imagination, it was the application of Bismarck's concepts. Hitler conquered Paris by studying his Clausewitz.

"In that perspective, 1940 is the continuation of 1914, the revenge for 1918."

Hitler was neither a madman nor a clown. He was an extremely intelligent man who was superior to his ministers, his generals, and his diplomats. If he lost the war, it was because the German people were incapable of winning it.

Hitler did not invent anti-Semitism. It existed before him and was as ingrained in German life as today the hatred of Negroes is within the white supremacists of Alabama. An SS functionary told me one day, as he was taking me to the Feldkirch prison, that they would never have been able to arrest so great a number of Jews without the denunciations by their neighbors, their enemies and even their friends. The Gestapo did not have lists of the Jewish population. It would have been able to do almost nothing without the active collaboration of the populace.

Hitler would not have been able to build the concentration camps with the help of just a few ignorant mercenaries. He required organizers, engineers, doctors for the experiments, executives to make the forced laborers work, officers and soldiers to arrest the victims, and railwaymen to transport them. And don't tell us that the man in the street did not know what was going on in the camps.

From 1939 on, one could see the KZ Haftling working at

the intersection of Kurfurstendamm and Kaiserallee; the prisoners were already plowing the fields of the farmers, helping the petty artisans, clearing away the wreckage after the bombardments, and one had only to be in a railway station to see the convoys of deportees.

I will never forget that parade through Vienna. We were herded down the Maria-Hilfestrasse from the station to the very heart of the Kartnerstrasse, St. Stephenplatz, in handcuffs, while the SS men alongside us brandished their whips. And the man in the street merely laughed. . . .

Do not claim, as does Willy Brandt of West Berlin, that "the sons are not responsible for the crimes of their fathers." If that is so, why are they demanding the return of the provinces conquered by their fathers? Why are they asking for East Berlin? East Berlin was German only in their fathers' time. Why do they speak of unity? The unity was what their fathers created.

And do not bring up the Communist threat. Yes, the Communist hydra exists; it is present, dangerous and terrifying. But does that justify Dachau?

If we arm Germany in order to frighten our former Russian allies; if we try to justify the Nazi crimes in order to embarrass the Soviets; if we encourage the Bundestag to sit in the Reichstag building which was burned at Hitler's behest, merely to provoke Moscow—then our policy is blind and petty and we will be its first victims. For, how can one be sure that a Federal Germany, once powerfully armed, will not join with Democratic East Germany to march on Paris or to conquer London? This time, you can be sure, the new Fuehrer will not repeat the mistakes of the former.

Ask my friend Kerensky, who was responsible for the failure of the only democratic government in Russia, who sent

Lenin through the lines in an armored train, and who financed the Communist revolt of 1917. In 1917, I was not yet born, but I most clearly remember the Molotov-Ribbentrop handshake in 1939, and the partition of Poland.

But for the war Hitler started, Soviet Russia today would have remained the secondary power it was in 1938; the European balance would not have been upset in its favor. Germany threatens the world with the Communist menace, but it is she, above all, who is responsible for it.

Is the question then of unity? By what right? Less than a hundred years ago, Germany was not united, and a hundred years is very little in the life of a nation. So why not be satisfied with going back to the situation as it was before 1866—weren't those the good old days?

But what if unity to the Germans really meant revenge? Do they want reunion with relatives or reconquest of lost provinces? And what if anti-Communism were only a pretext for fighting over again the lost battles and trying to take Moscow and Stalingrad for good?

We are told that the youth of today is carefree and peace-loving. So what? Youth prior to 1933 were just as flighty, as free of constraint, and as frolicking. They danced the Charleston; they indulged in orgies; they were romantic, adventurous, eccentric. All you have to do is read Remarque or Fallada. The youth of the thirties was against Hitler. Thousands of those young people were fighting then in the ranks of the Socialist, Communist, Nationalist, or Catholic organizations! Those were the ones who, almost to a man, became the most devoted of the SS troops.

We are told that German youth today has changed. Travel in Germany, talk to the Germans, read the German press (with a few rare exceptions, such as the truly admirable *Der Spiegel*). Question those who remember the years before Hitler—1928, '29, '30. They will tell you nothing has changed.

We are told to look at the sorry spectacle of the Berlin Wall. It is awful, inhuman. But the Communists were not the first to think of such a wall. Remember the Warsaw Ghetto.

And what about the people on the other side of the wall—aren't they Germans? Are they not obeying blindly, goosestepping to the new orders, and denouncing their neighbors and friends? Are these not German police standing guard at the wall? Why, then, have *those* Germans not changed? Do not tell me they are living under a reign of terror. You cannot force a man to denounce his nextdoor neighbor; you cannot force policemen to see everything that takes place along the whole length of a wall. You cannot force young people to scream their enthusiasm at the sight of Ulbricht.

There is one solution that would be so simple, fair, convenient for Berlin, East as well as West. Let us transform that capital into a vast museum of the horrors of war, a refuge for its victims!

I do not wish to see the German people punished, nor do I want them to live in shame. I do not ask that they incessantly repeat their *mea culpa*. I ask only that they do not deny their past, the past of Dachau, for only then could I regain confidence in them.

All I ask of my German friends and enemies is not to spit upon our graves, and then we will not spit upon theirs.

*   *   *   *

I quote the conclusion of the volume *Die Letzte Hundert*

Tagen (The Last Hundred Days), by Franz Werfel, published in Munich by Kurt Dasch, 1965:

"Men of Germany, in order to save your soul you must acknowledge your guilt. It was you German men and women who were responsible for the terrible years of 1933 to 1945. It was you Germans who were accomplices in the murder of millions and millions of peaceful, innocent Europeans who were not threatening anyone. It was you, men of Germany, who encouraged acts of cruelty which would have made the Devil blush. . . .

"You hear these atrocities described and you say, 'But I did nothing myself . . .' It is exactly because you did nothing, nothing to stop them, that you are guilty. Were you not proud of your unity—'one people, one Reich, one Fuehrer'? Did you not dance with joy when you were told of the bombings of London? Did you not sing, too, 'Deutschland, Deutschland, über alles'?"

A general view of the Dachau camp.

The prisoners celebrate their liberation, May 1, 1945.

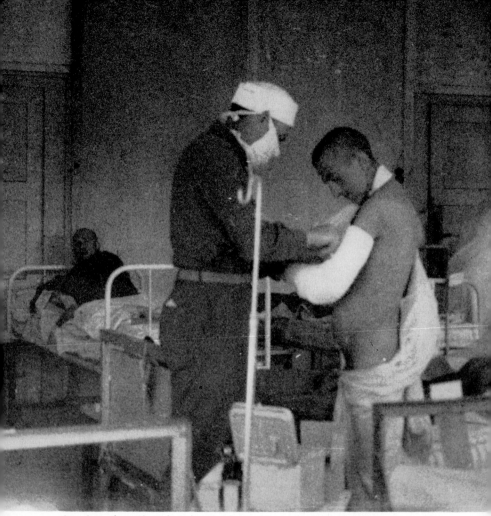

An American hospital in Dachau. Photographed by Gun from his hospital bed.

The marvelous G.I., James Ortoleva, sitting next to the very sick Gun in the Dachau hospital.

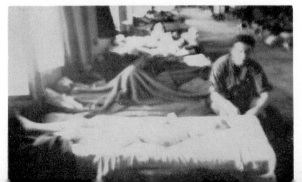

Gun and the famous American correspondent, Louis Lochner.

The home-made flags in Dachau after the liberation.

Berlin SW 11, den 5. April 19 45
Prinz-Albrecht-Str. 8
Sammelnummer 12 00 40

Schnellbrief

Geheime
Reichssache!

An den

Kommandanten des KL.

D a c h a u

SS-Obersturmbannführer W e i t e r

Persönlich!

Auf Befehl des RFSS und nach Einholung höchster
Entscheidung sind die nachstehend aufgeführten Häftlinge sofort dem KL. Dachau zu überstellen:

Ehem. Generaloberst H a l d e r ,
General T h o m a s .
Hjalmar S c h a c h t ,
S c h u s c h n i g g mit Frau u.Kind,
Ehem. General v. F a l k e n h a u s e
der Engländer B e s t (W o l f),
der Neffe Molotow's K o k o r i n ,
der Oberst i.G. v. B o n i n .

Da ich weiss, dass Sie in dem Zellenbau
einen sehr beschränkten Raum zur Verfügung haben,
bitte ich, nach Prüfung Zusammenlegung vorzunehmen.
Jedenfalls bitte ich Sie, dafür Sorge zu tragen, dass
der Häftling S c h u s c h n i g g , der den Decknamen A u s t e r führt - ich bitte, ihn unter diesem Decknamen einzutragen - , eine grössere Wohnzelle
zur Verfügung hat. Die Frau hat sich freiwillig in
die Internierung ihres Mannes begeben, ist daher an
sich nicht Schutzhäftling. Ich bitte, ihr dieselbe
Freiheit zu belassen wie bisher.

Ss

Order to kill Elser.

From left to right: George Elser, Major H. R. Stevens, and S. Payne Best, as their photos were published in the German Press after their arrest.

Payne Best, at the moment of his liberation.

Chancellor Kurt von Schuschnigg, at the moment of his liberation, with Dutch Cabinet Minister Van Dyk.

Zur Erinnerung an gemeinsame
Sippenhaft in Stutthof auf der Hindenburg
Baude, in Buchenwald in Dachau (K.Z.)

1944 – 1945

1. Otto Philipp Graf Schenk v. Stauffenberg
2. Clemens Graf Schenk v. Stauffenberg
3. Alexander Graf Schenk von Stauffenberg
4. Markwart Graf Schenk von Stauffenberg
5. Markwart Graf Schenk v. Stauffenberg
6. Lini Lindemann geb. von Friedeburg
7. Else-Lotte von Hofacker geb. Pastor
8. Anna-Luise von Hofacker
9. Maria Gräfin Schenk von Stauffenberg geb. Klein
10. Maria Freifrau v. Hammerstein-Equord geb.
11. Frei... v. Lüttwitz,
12. Hildur von ...
13. Franz Trilon v. Hammerstein
14. ...
15. Hildegard Maria ...
16. ...
17. Annelise ...
18. ...
19. Josef ...
20. ...
21. ...
22. ...

The 137 Dachau honor prisoners liberated in the Italian section left
an interesting memo: they all signed the table napkins at their first
meal in liberty.

23 Ingeborg Schröder mit 3 Kindern Harring, Hans-dietrich und Sibylle Maria

24 Dr. Gustav Goerdeler

25 Ulrich Goerdeler

26 Irma Goerdeler geb Reuter

27 [illegible] geb. [illegible]

28 Elisabeth Kaiser

29 Mika Gräfin Schenk von Stauffenberg

30 Elisabeth Gräfin Schenk von Stauffenberg geb. Freiin von und zu Guttenberg †

31 Walther Graf von Plettenberg

32 Gräfin Gisela Plettenberg-Lenhausen

33 [illegible]

34 Eberhard von Hofacker

35 Major [illegible] Schatz

36 Gertrud Halder

37 Käte Gudzent

38 Alexandra Gräfin Schenk von Stauffenberg

39 Marie-Gabriele Gräfin Schenk von Stauffenberg

40 Léon Blum 41 J. L. Blum

42 Dr. Erich Heberlein 43 Margot Heberlein

44 Лейтенант армии Красной армии В. Кокорин

45 [illegible]

46 [illegible]

47 [illegible] 48 Hatz Endre

49 [illegible] 50 [illegible] 51 [illegible]

[illegible] 52 Friedrich Leopold Prinz von Preussen

53 v. [illegible] Géza

kgl. ung. Generalleutnant [illegible] 54 [illegible]

55 [illegible]

The liberation of the Dachau honor prisoners in Alto-Adige by the Americans: From left to right, one sees Premier von Kallay, the Greek General Staff Chief, Marshall Papagos, Sissy von Schuschnigg, Prinz Leopold von Hohenzollern, the nephew of Molotov, and General Garibaldi, and others.

Kurt von Schuschnigg and his daughter, Maria Dolores (Sissy), in St. Louis, Missouri, today.

11

The Pseudo-Republic

It was in front of the crematorium, during the first days of May, 1945. With cynical, impudent sacrilegious nonchalance, I was raising the heads or limbs of the piled-up corpses, the better to photograph them. It was there I first met James Ortoleva.

The adjectives I just used are inappropriate. My nonchalance was commonplace. We had become used to dead bodies; they were to be seen everywhere in the camp—at the doors, in the streets, in the hospital, the showers, the canal. The only thing that bothered us was the irritating, upsetting odor of the chemical which the Americans had sprinkled on the bodies to retard their putrefaction. They seemed powdered with sugar, like so many Neapolitan popovers.

I was quietly taking pictures, assisted by my inseparable Ivan, who constantly guarded my camera and films—and who, occasionally when I was not looking, tried to loot the bodies.

An American soldier came up to me. He was tall and thin, with dark, curly hair, and I immediately took a liking to him.

193

He mumbled a few words of German, made outsized gestures, and tried in every way to communicate. I guessed right away that he was an Italian-American, or, more specifically, of Sicilian descent, and I started to talk to him in that language.

At first I thought that, like all the other GIs, he wanted to get hold of my camera. It is difficult to imagine how priceless that camera seemed in those crazy liberation days. The Americans offered to buy it for its weight in gold, because the spectacle they were seeing was so incredible to them, so inconceivable, so unimaginable, they wanted to get it on film there and then, failing which they felt baffled and frustrated, like a fisherman who has hooked a monster with no one there to vouch for his catch. Ivan thought I should sell it. He promised he would get me another during his plunders, and I imagine he did pull this off two or three times for his own benefit; but in spite of the time spent in Dachau I was an inveterate newspaperman, unwilling to part with my precious camera. I must say that I finally did sell it, disposing of it the evening before I left for Paris, to a doctor at the hospital, whose check for $50, a small fortune to me, was the first deposit in my new account at the Chase National Bank of New York.

All this American private wanted was to be photographed alongside the mountain of corpses, so that he could show them to his family. I took the picture and we went on talking in Italian, and then he invited me to join him in a cup of coffee.

I remember every detail vividly because that soldier was James Ortoleva, my Jim, my friend now for twenty years; the only friend I have left from the Dachau days. He liberated me; he later saved my life by getting me out of the painful atmosphere of the inmates' compound and then watching over me when I was hospitalized. It is because of him particularly that I now have a new, a real country.

It was strictly forbidden, from the very first hours of deliverance, for prisoners to leave the Lager or even their barracks. Liberation, admittedly, was merely a changing of the guard. They did not open the doors wide to us, happily proclaiming, "You are free. Free. Go home!" The bars were still down and the GIs in uniform closed the doors and locked the gates that first night, just as the Germans had done the night before. To the great majority of the prisoners then, the International Committee which, under the protection of the liberating army, was supposed to become the government of the Provisional Fraternal Republic of Dachau, was nothing but a fresh group of Kapos who had taken over from the others.

By the same token, American soldiers were forbidden to come inside the compound. Nor, probably because of the stench, did they want to. Just a few members of the military ventured inside in the line of duty, or to guide and protect the visitors—a veritable wave of generals, senators, newspapermen,* doctors, sociologists, judges, who had come to see at

---

* Among these guests was Louis Lochner, bureau chief for the Associated Press in Berlin. One of the most brilliant journalists of the day, he later was to publish *The Goebbels Diaries* in Berlin. Lochner had nicknamed me the "enfant terrible" of the Wilhelmstrasse, not only because of the impudence of some of the questions I would ask during press conferences at the Wilhelmstrasse, but because I was a source of grief to him and his colleagues. In fact, every time I scored a scoop these important correspondents were flooded with tart queries from their bosses about how they had let a cub reporter get the story while they were asleep at the switch.

When Lochner saw me at Dachau in a prison uniform, his first reaction was one of indignation: "Gun," he exclaimed, "this time you've gone too far! How dare you masquerade as a prisoner just to get a story! It's positively indecent!"

"But Lochner, I *am* a prisoner," I replied.

He then did everything he could to help me. He was the first one to advise the American authorities and my own embassy about me and to press consistently for my liberation. I owe much to him.

first-hand this extraordinary, inadmissible, savage, out-of-this-world peepshow of men and women who went right on dying, outdying each other.

But the ordinary GIs were not at a loss: they could watch it all from afar, without fear of being mobbed by prisoners begging for cigarettes or candy, or they could go and see the corpses in the trains, at the station, or piled up in front of the crematorium.

At first, among the prisoners, only the members of the International Committee were allowed to cross the line drawn around our prison, and since, albeit in a very humble capacity, I was one of these "new officials," I had the privilege of going unhindered into the SS base, which had been taken over by the American troops guarding the camp, the sanitary personnel, and the administrative machinery.

"You attracted attention because you walked upright; snooped around with your camera; took an interest in everyone and everything. In spite of your skinniness and your slow pace, you looked alive, effervescent, human. All the others were like zombies." That was the way Jim Ortoleva described me later. But I think it was simply that he was happy to have found someone he could talk to about Italy, in Italian.

He was in charge of the medical supplies. "I have enough penicillin here," he would say, "to make a million bucks on the black market." Later, he gave me free access to his bailiwick, but he was always careful to keep the supply of the precious drug under lock and key. Since then I have often twitted him about his suspicions of me, and each time he has apologized. The truth of the matter is I gave more than a little thought to the idea of pulling a raid on that drug cache, with the help of Ivan and a few of the others, and then making a lightning escape.

Jim did not let me want for anything. I rarely asked him for handouts but he had a way of knowing what I needed. He got his commanding officer to give me a certificate making me his handyman, which allowed me to sleep outside the prisoners' compound, have my own room and be *persona grata* at the GIs' mess. He took me to the movies, to ball games. We went for walks together. He introduced me to his friends, including a delightful nurse, as if I were his adopted son or brother. He had set up a rather luxurious apartment for his sergeant and himself in one of the SS barracks, with a record-player and a small bar. I looked forward to these quarters' being the setting for orgiastic parties, what with all the beautiful Red Cross girls and the alcohol available at the drug depot, but Jim spent the better share of his time there sleeping under the watchful picture of his wife and daughters. It was my first contact with American puritanism.

We used to talk—or rather he used to talk—about America. What he told me was like a fairytale: it was the country where orange trees bloomed, where men were born equal and died equal; where you could register in a hotel without showing your passport; where you were allowed to shout from the housetops that the President was a moron; where kids went to school in cars; and where men lived, like Jim Ortoleva, with no taste for war, asking for nothing, needing no conquests. It was the country where the hungry were fed and the thirsty might drink. . . .

What impressed me even more was his manner toward the officers: not only did he remain seated with his feet perched comfortably when they entered, but he talked to them with a familiarity that bordered on impertinence. He had no qualms about contradicting them. At times he even issued friendly orders to them. It was then that I decided that I too had to live in that marvelous country where an enlisted man could be an individual.

Since then, I must admit, the harsh truth has all too often dispelled this image I had created: but when I get too discouraged, when I feel too weary, I go back to see my friend Jim at the little hotel he runs in Connecticut, near West Haven. His presence wipes out my disillusionment, and our memories give the world around me the rosy hues it used to have.

Maybe it was because of Jim and his optimistic outlook that, right after the freeing of the camp, I failed to realize the tragic situation it was in. The new commandant, Lieutenant Colonel Martin W. Joyce, had certainly not been properly prepared for the herculean job facing him. Some thirty thousand prisoners—underfed, sickly, indolent and thieving— were wandering up and down the pathways in their ragged uniforms, lice-ridden, their noses broken, and he still had no food, vitamins, or medicines for them. The legless, one-legged, one-armed victims made good newsreel shots—but what could Joyce do with them? And what about the thousands of sick inside the barracks—those who had not yet seen the sun, who didn't even know they were free? The ones who each morning, just as before the liberation, were carried outside and laid out between the buildings? And the cases of madness—the hundreds of cases of madness? Or those who died of overeating because they had gorged on the cans of Spam the generous American soldiers had—open-handedly but unwisely—given them, even depriving themselves?

People went on dying in Dachau—at an even higher rate than in the days before liberation. It is hard to quote accurate figures, for the military avoid statistics about those who die while in their care. I estimate that more than three hundred prisoners a day must have died during the actual occupation of the camp by the Americans.

O'Leary, the chairman of the Committee, had set himself up regally in the little château that had belonged to SS General Pohl, where the horticultural nursery was, and had established the nucleus of a governing organization. There had even been a plenary session attended by Colonel Fellenz, the American liaison man, during which it was decided that discipline must be maintained; that the same German Kapo would run the inside section; that the camp police would remain on duty—but now they would be answerable to the Committee. Regimes may change, but the police stay! And it was also decided that work would continue as usual. . . .

It is not hard to imagine how unpopular these decisions were. Picture our consternation when a bulletin was issued warning us about the dangers of typhus: "In the blocks, there are more and more unidentified dead. Those responsible for them must, insofar as possible, identify the corpses. This must be done whatever their nationalities. The names of all known dead and comatose are to be written in ink on their chests."

The drastic measures taken by the Americans to arrest the epidemic seemed unfair to us at the time. Even today it is hard to justify them. As the whole place had been put under quarantine, not only could we not leave the camp but we were restricted to our own barracks, the healthy along with the sick. We were still sleeping two or three to a pallet or on the ground; the food was still horrible and, as Professor Moviglia put it, "White death was still hovering over us."

Feeding this dying mass must have been a complex job. Nevertheless, it would have been relatively simple to go to the local population and requisition their milk, their fresh vege-tables, their chickens for the making of broth, for around the camp the farmers lived prosperously. Such a move, however, with its overtones of illegality, was unacceptable to the American command. They continued to lump together the internees in the camp with the Germans on the outside. In fact, I have always suspected, and not alone, that to these American bureaucrats who took the camp over after the fighting men had left, we were really in the final analysis some sort of criminals: because if you were to admit that prisons could be full of innocent people, it would make an awful mess out of certain preconceived ideas. And besides, how could they feel sympathy for deformed, ugly, filthy creatures who acted like so many savages?

The camp remained closed to avoid risk of epidemic. It was an idiotic precaution, because any number of prisoners, with or without official permission, succeeded in getting out. There was an average of about five hundred escapes a week. Even if we had spread a few germs among those good, kind, handsome Germans, would that have been such a catastrophe?

Had not the American commandant himself given an order to the inhabitants of the city of Dachau to come into the camp and bury the dead? It was a grandstand play and it made fine news shots, but it did not mean a thing, for the Germans of the area knew very well about the dead in the camp; they had known all about them since 1933, and this gravedigging job was very minor punishment indeed.

The only way to end the epidemic entirely would have been to move at once all the patients into the hospitals and clinics of Munich and into private German homes; to draft every doctor in the area; and to see to it that the sick were in a clean and peaceful atmosphere. For, what was killing them was not really the lice but the discouragement—the horror and the closeness of life in the camp.

In that way, not only could many of the sick have been saved, but those who were well might not have had to fall sick in their turn. Many who danced with joy in the twilight of April 29 were to face the supreme ordeal shortly afterward— at the very time when the hope of seeing their homes and loved ones had been given to them.

I admit that letting the prisoners loose on the countryside would have entailed a certain amount of danger for the people, but if it had been a matter of sacrificing the lives of half the Bavarian population to save a fellow prisoner, I would not have batted an eye.

Some say that the American administrators could not have had proper experience, for, after all, Dachau was a unique phenomenon in the history of our century. The War Department in Washington must have known that there were extermination camps in Germany and that someday it would be necessary to liberate them. What did they teach in the schools in which whole armies of "occupation specialists" were trained?

And why, incidentally, were all the Oflags and Stalags containing American prisoners of war evacuated in such perfect order, without the least difficulty? General Eisenhower, from the very moment of victory, had given orders for the immediate repatriation of all American prisoners. Why was this order not extended to us? We were allies too. Why this discrimination? Was our contribution to the mutual effort any less essential?

Even after the typhus epidemic was controlled, actual liberation was painfully slow in coming. It was said that the roads were bad, transport unavailable, the authorities overwhelmed with logistic detail. No one wanted to unleash on the local population this ill-clothed, penniless, unemployed mob so long out of contact with society, which would probably have looted and raped. How worried the American authorities were over the chastity of the Gretchens!

It just would not do, the American commandant himself explained to me, to allow the prisoners to go as they pleased. That would make a farce of liberty. Why, they were the liberators, and they had come to re-establish order in Europe. No, the prisoners would have to go back to their countries of origin, even if their families lived elsewhere; even if they had been apprehended elsewhere; even if they expressed a desire to go elsewhere!

It was hard for us to conceive that the wonderful American war machine, which could fill the skies above us with thousands of bombers day after day, night after night, was unable to move a few thousand prisoners quickly from Dachau into civilized country. On the other hand, as the Committee was to find out, there was an amazing similarity between American administrative methods and those of old Europe. It was summed up in two words: red tape.

There was nothing but orders, counter-orders, requisitions, lists, documents, plans, ordinances, regulations, counter-regulations, orders of the day, of the week, of the month, statistics, inventories, recaps of all kinds. You needed a pass to eat; another to go out, another to get back in; a special pass to visit a friend, one for going to the doctor.

We were treated to the pleasures of making out a form, which afterward had to be translated into English, that merely asked:

Name of camp:	Place of birth:	Date of Birth:
Date of arrest:	Reason for arrest:	Religion:
Race:	Nationality:	Judgment of court:
Profession:	Name of judge:	Details of imprisonment:

Cruelty, excesses:	Were you a Nazi?	
Are you married?	Engaged?	Military service:
Children?	Legitimate?	Illegitimate?
Residences for last		Where do you
five years:		wish to go?
Supplementary		
Remarks:		

Looting, despite all disciplinary restrictions, was the order of the day. In the part of the camp that had been reserved to the SS men, there were huge warehouses containing enormous quantities of French perfumes, hardware, ladies' bags, optical instruments, medical accessories. I myself found a large supply of false teeth, much needed at the time, Germany having been a heavy producer of them. There was everything the SS men had confiscated from the enemies of National-Socialism. Beyond that, there were the porcelain works, the military sheds, the motor pools and the canning plant.

Ivan was in heaven; he helped me supply the less privileged friends who had to remain inside the camp. Sometimes, when the impressiveness of an American uniform seemed advisable, Jim Ortoleva would accompany me on these forays. I succeeded in getting an SS officer's uniform, minus insignia, and put it on in place of my striped suit, of which I had had my fill. I had also found an Afrika Korps summer outfit, with khaki shorts and a tropical helmet of the same color to strut around in. Jim had got hold of a whole case of Jean-Maria-Farina toilet water, and I still behold with admiration, when I visit him, the exquisite Nymphenburg porcelain statuettes that he simply picked off the ground. For the Russian deserters of Vlassov's army had been there before us, and they had swiped everything that seemed valuable to them. With what may have been Slavic peculiarity, they threw down or smashed everything else. The rubble soon became little mountains which we had to climb to reach the upper shelves of the warehouses and then work our way down carefully, booty in hand. Sometimes the prisoners fought over it and the soldiers had to fire at them to break them up. These thousands of broken bottles of Chanel, 4711, Coty, Houbigant, Molyneux lent a strangely rich fragrance to the looters, and for days we moved around in clouds of perfume that contrasted sharply with the stink of the corpses about us.

The wives and children of the SS men continued to live in their comfortable pink-and-white bungalows. They were even allowed to keep their servants. O'Leary, nevertheless, made a little speech to them: "Do not hide any SS men. Do not help any fugitives from justice." This did not eliminate nighttime visits to those bungalows and Ivan always came back with fascinating things. Poor Ivan! He disappeared one night while I was sick in the hospital. I never heard of him again.

Summary executions continued to take place but the prisoners had no part in them: the Americans were using firing squads right and left, having under their orders some gangs of Montenegrins who took advantage of the occasion to eliminate their own rivals, the partisans of Mihailovich. The International Committee took steps, with the commandant, to see that these avengers were disarmed. For now there were batches of SS men being turned in mainly by the local population, who had at last understood which way the wind was blowing. They arrived at the camp by the hundreds. The prisoners would point out the most guilty among them, and sometimes they took the law into their own hands, but this rarely went beyond a severe beating. That was how we finally discovered the sinister *Rapportfuehrer* (disciplinary director) of the camp, *Hauptscharfuehrer* Boettiger, disguised as a prisoner, trying to ride unnoticed into Switzerland on a bicycle.

We wanted to lynch him at first, but we settled for making him spend a few hours doing the disciplinary exercise, *Mutze ab, Mutze zu* (Cap off, cap on); salute each prisoner with a "Heil Hitler" while standing at attention; and then parade around with a large sign on his chest that read: "I am a big Nazi pig. I killed thousands of prisoners, personally executed 92 officers, and have no right to live."

The SS commandant of the camp, Weiter, for having disobeyed Hitler's orders, was executed by a fanatic SS sergeant, Ruppert, in the countryside while trying to escape. Weiter died with a bullet in the neck, clutching a picture of Hitler.

Each night we heard gunshots. It was the sentries firing at hidden SS men or at prisoners trying to escape, or at looters. At times, it was only Negro soldiers squabbling among themselves. We were intrigued by these Negroes, who were curiosities to us and also to be feared, for we had so long been brainwashed and told that the colored troops were brutal, stupid, and irresponsible. Actually all that we noticed was that these good black men simply seemed happy to be able to sing, or else, firing a few shots in the air, to be able to speed through the camp piled into a black Mercedes that had belonged to Goering or to Hitler.

I must admit I was a bit amazed at seeing American soldiers practicing golfing drives in the SS sheds, for I had thought that golf was a millionaire's sport, and was equally astonished at seeing them spend entire days playing catch, monotonously, tirelessly, and, I thought then, just like girls. They were everywhere; in the square, before the Kommandantur, even at the Jourhaus. Always doing the same thing, throwing a ball back and forth. At first I assumed it was some sort of therapy for the feeble-minded. Ortoleva told me that was baseball, the American national pastime.

There were also some girls, usually going about in pairs, always smiling, always saying a few chopped-off words like "Hi!" or "See you!" Apparently they were incapable of normal conversation. There were some with curlers in their hair. All wore wide uniform trousers, with heavy boots, and blouses too large for them. They didn't have a dime's worth of femininity. And you could not convince yourself, even after years of camp isolation, that they were pretty. We had expected Dorothy Lamours, Betty Grables, the Bathing Beauties out of the musical movies we had loved. What a disappointment! Yet some lovely French nurses arrived from Paris.

Carloads of food and medicine were sent by the Vatican. And soon the first lucky ones were finally able to leave. Once again the camp was split between the haves—whose who were being helped, who had found a way out, who were going home—and the have-nots—the poor, abandoned, forgotten ones. There were still prisoners who could not get it through their heads that things had changed, who hid in terror at sight of a uniform.

The American authorities were probably guilty of trusting too much to the International Committee. It played a precious moral role in the liberation, but its importance should not be exaggerated. The single revolver that the infatuated German woman warder had got us evidently would not have allowed us to wipe out the SS garrison. The members of the Committee were simply prisoners like the others, with no mandate whatsoever, and for good reason. They were totally unprepared for and incapable of solving the crushing problems of post-liberation. Because of that, they had to maintain the SS structure of the camp—accept the cooperation of the German Kapos whom the mass of prisoners so detested, turn over to them a good share of their responsibilities; but, above all, they had neither the authority nor the courage to oppose certain ill-advised decisions of the American command. The Committee therefore became a servile instrument of the new masters, just as its predecessors, the Kapos, had been for the SS.

O'Leary, before the liberation, had claimed he was English or Canadian because he thought it safe to do so. Afterward, he continued the impersonation, strutting around ostentatiously in a paratrooper's outfit, holding court in his little château, with his field telephones, his motorcycle dispatch rider, and his general staff.

Every honor carries with it a responsibility. However, I will refrain from asking whether the International Committee should have answered to us for the three hundred who died daily and whose deaths it was unable to prevent. But I remain perplexed by the reasons that prompted O'Leary to leave the camp by plane on May 6th. He was one of the first ones liberated. Couldn't British Intelligence have done without his presence just a few days more?

No question about it, fate was not kind to that Fraternal Republic of Dachau. Only a week after it was set up, its president ran out on it. . . .

12

An American Hospital

Everywhere in the world, even at Dachau, Americans like to feel at home, so they had set up a cafeteria in the former Nazi officers' mess hall. I had never seen this kind of restaurant where, tray in hand, you could select from such marvels displayed along the buffet counter and where you could even ask for almost anything that entered your mind. The place was strictly off limits to civilians. I moved heaven and earth to be allowed to eat there. Our new American masters would have been very naïve to think that they could keep out men who, in the tough school of the camps, the prisons and the underground, had learned to get around the most rigid orders.

There was always a way. You were "entitled" because you worked in a certain office, or you were interpreter for a certain colonel, assistant to such and such a commission; or you could claim you were a journalist, a researcher on war crimes, or a captured commissar of the Red Army, not to mention those who by some miracle had gotten hold of an Allied officer's uniform and marched right in, saluted by the MPs on duty. I also knew that a tunnel had been dug from the neighboring barracks right up into the latrine of the building. The trouble there was that those responsible for that underground access demanded a passage fee. Not all of us could afford it.

I had several passes that attested to my belonging to the International Committee as well as to my job as principal helper in the drug depot of the 116th Evacuation Hospital of the American Army. I probably would have had no difficulty in getting into this gastronomic sanctuary legally, but nobody ever bothered to ask to see my credentials. The MPs at the door were my pals. I had taken pictures of them the day before, in front of a pile of corpses at the crematorium, and they were all clamoring for the negative so that they could send prints home. They opened the doors wide for me, with a jovial, "Have a good healthy breakfast, Mac!"

Pantagruel, suddenly unleashed after a Lent of total fasting, could not have displayed a better appetite than I did that morning. My tray was so overloaded that it looked like a magician's after he finishes his act. There were slices of buttered bread, rolls, toast, roast beef, bacon; I had ordered American pancakes and eggs, all kinds of jams, juices— orange, tomato, grapefruit—and mysterious and extraordinary things like the gooey stuff they called peanut butter and the little multicolored boxes filled with grains of rice or wheat they pleasantly termed breakfast food. I could no longer count the times I had been up to the counter, and I think this first American breakfast of mine must have lasted as long as four normal meals. I can even remember that I somehow got hold of a copy of *Stars and Stripes* which I read while stuffing myself.

For us prisoners it would have been unthinkable to get

up from the table while a scrap of food remained. My gluttony was to take its toll, yet I never learned my lesson. Even today, I can never leave anything on my plate. At home, I finish anything my wife and daughter leave on their dishes. I will never get used to the American way of considering it polite to let half of one's portion be taken away untouched, and I am sure my hostesses consider me a boor. I absolutely refuse to go on vacation when there is food in the refrigerator which is going to be left to spoil, and more than once I have gone off a reducing diet rather than see a slice of sausage or a plateful of noodles go down into the garbage disposal. I even sweep up bread crumbs. Anything else would be sacrilegious to me, for hunger is the stepmother of death.

For two days I went to that unbelievable American fountain of food, but on the third evening I felt a kind of seasickness coming on. All I could get down was a cup of tea and the next day I started to feel cramps. At the camp, we had all become medical experts, and I diagnosed my trouble as acute indigestion. Unfortunately, my diarrhea got worse, my fever rose, and at night I shivered with cold while my blankets were soaked with perspiration. Someone called in Dr. Bohn, a French deportee who had shown magnificent devotion in continuing to take care of his fellow prisoners. He was not long in making up his mind.

"You can't stay here, *mon vieux,*" he said. "I'll alert the boys at the American hospital."

An hour later, a Pole wearing a Red Cross armband, dressed in a newly pressed striped prison outfit, asked me to follow him. I had already wrapped my few possessions in a blanket which I had turned over for safekeeping to my roommate, the French major, but I kept my camera, which hung from my neck.

The Pole, after many a detour, took me to one of the old SS buildings which had been turned into the first-aid station. An American corporal with a Southern accent, complete with chewing gum and overseas cap, made me wait in line behind a dozen or more other sick-bay candidates, several of whom had fainted. But there was method in what he did. He gave us each a thermometer, each thermometer carrying a numbered label with it, with a square of cardboard and the corresponding number pinned on the patient's shirt. Then he took each pulse and wrote the figures down into a large notebook. After that, he went to wash his hands. My turn came.

He told me to lie down on the ground on a cloth stretcher which had been placed there. I had a half hour's wait. Eventually two prisoners, also Poles, wearing Red Cross armbands, picked up the litter and crossed the little company street between the two buildings, not more than ten or fifteen yards across, to a room which previously had been the infirmary of the SS noncoms. I made a mental note that it would have made more sense to carry the patient directly from barracks to hospital bed rather than expect him to walk halfway around the camp, but I could not feel that this detail was too important. This was my first contact with the impressive American sanitary machine, and my faith in American methods was then unshakable.

The sick bay was quite a contrast to the pesthole which had been the camp infirmary. The medicated odor of the place seemed like perfume. There were a hundred beds or so, all with clean sheets, blankets, and, that most unbelievable of luxuries, pillows. A nurse in khaki trousers, but pretty nonetheless, gave orders to aides who, marvel of marvels, served meals to the patients in their beds, just as in Hollywood movies.

The nurse told me in English to strip, and went to get me a

pair of American army pajamas. One of the aides rubbed me down with a towel soaked in alcohol and then directed me to an empty bed along the wall. On my left, between the window and me, a Russian sat propped calmly against his pillow, devouring a copious meal. On my right, a patient who scarcely seemed to be breathing lay with his covers pulled up to his nose and one arm sticking out. From the ceiling a glucose machine, like a hungry spider, sent its rubber fang down to bite into the patient's arm.

The Russian, the one who was eating, looked at me disdainfully and, in German with an accent which bespoke service in General Vlassov's anti-Red legions, informed me by way of introduction: "Three of 'em died in your bed this week. It's a transit bed. They come and go. The one on the other side doesn't have long to go. Tonight he'll be kaputt."

This delightful character was named Boris. He came from a village in the Baku region. He said that he had been captured as a partisan, and then that he had served in the regular Soviet army. Once, he forgot himself and admitted that he had only been deported into forced labor, but I was sure that he had fought on the side of the Nazis and that he had ended at Dachau, as had so many like him.

He seemd to be in excellent health, although he continually complained of unbearable pains and undiagnosable ailments. When the doctors came through, he would launch into interminable harangues in Caucasian dialect. They probably thought it easier to let him stay where he was than try to get him to admit that there was really nothing wrong with him.

For Boris this was the life. He was allowed four meals a day and I daresay this was the first time in his life that he had ever been so well fed or so well housed. "In our country, Soviets," he would confide haltingly to me, "work fifteen hours and eat only potatoes; potatoes morning, potatoes noon, potatoes night. Sunday, potatoes; wedding, potatoes; funeral, potatoes."

Because of that, he gave me to understand, he was resolved not to go home. There was probably also another reason: either Siberia or the firing squad awaited him.

For him, the hospital was like a show. He watched the comings and goings of the patients, made fun of them, and barked out his predictions somewhat like that African prince at the Epsom Derby: this one has three days to go, that one will last a week, another will make it out of here. Like a circling buzzard, as soon as one of his neighbors breathed his last, he went over to finish up the remains of his meal. Sometimes he was bold enough to go into the kitchen and claim a tray that had been prepared for a patient who had just died. He even finished up the prescriptions that were left on the night tables. He would try to take over any meager possessions the dead ones left: a handkerchief, a pair of slippers, or a pocket knife.

He also looked convetously at the camera I always carried around my neck and which at night I hid under my covers.

The head doctor, a tall, blond, very nice major, came on his rounds with two assistants. For the ward call, they all put white aprons over their sand-colored summer uniforms. They wore masks over their mouths and noses, just as in the movies. The head doctor affably asked me a few questions, as if we had met over a cocktail in a Madison Avenue bar. He talked about the weather and about the war, but he made it a point never to get near me. As a matter of fact, he impressed me as being the least inquisitive medico I had ever met.

The nurse, to whom I expressed my surprise, explained that we first had to wait for the results of the laboratory tests. They had examined my blood, my urine, my sputum; recorded my blood pressure; counted my heart beats; and entered the data on the chart at the foot of my bed. The nurse, with the skill of an industrial designer, traced lines on it which went up and down like the graphs of Wall Street quotations: those were the variations of my fever; and beyond this there were symbols in red, green, and yellow ink, crosses, and even Greek letters.

Each morning, the head doctor examined these diagrams with the greatest care, added a few more marks to them, consulted his assistants, then talked to me some more about the weather and the war. During my entire stay in the hospital he never once touched me. No tapping on my chest, no listening with his ear next to it, no palpating. He wore his stethoscope around his neck as an ornament, as if it were a ribbon of the Order of Malta.

At first I was hypnotized by this American method of healing a patient simply by inspecting charts, as if the duel between life and death were merely the up-and-down of a roller-coaster.

Then I started to get upset, irritated, furious, and finally convinced that these doctors and nurses were nothing more than big kids playing make-believe. I know this judgment was unwarranted, but I still get somewhat the same impression from the foreign policy of Washington.

The head M.D., however, had already made his diagnosis: typhus. However, he wanted to wait for the appearance of all the symptoms "according to the book." Exanthematic typhus was the fashionable illness at Dachau. It would have been madness to expect to get out of there without it. It was only normal that the American doctors, valiantly fighting against an epidemic under conditions unfamiliar to them and help-lessly watching the death statistics mount, should think of nothing else.

Yes, we had all become medical experts at Dachau, and I was sure that I didn't have typhus but was suffering from a combination of double pneumonia and dysentery. A fellow prisoner who had studied medicine and had succeeded in slipping into the hospital to look me over, as well as the Polish aides, all felt the same way. My increasing violent colic—they had to change my bedding several times a day, for I was no longer able to get up—was in all likelihood a result of my gluttony. I expressed these views each morning during the doctor's round, but the medical staff undoubtedly thought I was delirious. One afternoon, when all was quiet, I asked the Polish ward attendant to get me some suction cups. He swiped a half-dozen of the small glasses the Americans drank their whiskey from, put sheets of paper into them that he had torn out of magazines, lit them, stuck the glasses onto my back. After a quarter of an hour there was improvement. I had stopped coughing.

But my neighbor Boris informed the medical officer of the day of this unscheduled treatment, for Boris was also the stool pigeon of the ward. The American was outraged. He called us ignorant asses out of the Middle Ages, heretics, superstitious idiots. The Pole was transferred to a different assignment and I had to promise not to resort again to old wives' remedies.

However, I was to repeat myself soon afterward. I suddenly remembered the French Communist Germain Auboiroux, who went about the camp in his "fart-shaver"—all the Communist prisoners made a fetish of these short coats that came halfway down to the knees and were almost a distinguishing uniform—the pockets of which he stuffed with bits of charcoal to distribute to the diarrhea victims. Michelet swore that they had cured his. So I asked the Marquis Pallavicini, who had come to see me, to get some for me; and I swallowed them slowly, distastefully but obstinately.

The American nurse, a delightful blonde from Vermont with cheeks red as apples, who smiled from morning till night and gave us a glimpse of her breasts when she bent over us, for her shirt did not button very securely, continued to bring me all my meals, as if she had not noticed that my intestines had sprung a leak and in spite of the stench around me. During the first days, those omelets, sausages, the pure white bread, the jams, the corned beef, seemed to me like something straight out of Horcher's, the famous Berlin prewar luxury restaurant. As my fever went up, as my lips dried out and I threw up more and more, I began to feel a growing disgust for the food. Seeing Boris devour all those treasures that I could not stomach only made me feel worse.

"Is that all you can bring me?" I would snap irritably at the poor girl, who looked at me as if I were slightly mad.

Jim Ortoleva, the GI, came to see me several times, bringing me chocolate, vitamins, cigarettes. Often, during the ensuing twenty years of our friendship, he was to tell me how the odor in our ward used to turn his stomach.

"You must have been suffocating in there," he says now. "And to tell the truth, you looked to me as if you were one of the corpses that we photographed together in front of the crematoria."

Jim was very much concerned about what might happen to my camera. He suggested I let him keep it for me, but I would not hear of it. I must admit that I didn't fully trust his motives—we had seen so many Machiavellis around us in the camp. In later years I felt a bit ashamed about it, because Jim was really interested only in the pictures of him that I had taken, and he was simply, and not unjustifiably, afraid that a neighbor might get hold of the camera. Jim was really magnificent! He left the camp sometime before I was well, but he sacrificed several hours of his precious first furlough in Paris to go to the Turkish ambassador, Numan Menemencioglu, in order to tell him what had happened to me.

I was dying of thirst. I had a mad craving for orange juice, and every time Jim came to see me, I begged him to get me some cans of it. Jim tried to find it everywhere in the camp. For some mysterious reason—even the American supply system could foul up sometimes—the PX had all the tomato juice you could want but not a drop of orange, lemon, or grapefruit juice. He would sheepishly set the cans of tomato juice on my bed and promise that next time he would do better.

"Tomato juice is very good for your health," he would assure me. "Very American."

But I was dying for citrus juice, and the red-labeled tomato juice cans were completely repellent. Boris, on the other hand, made away with them as soon as Jim left. He seemed to be making a collection of them.

Jim had also got me several copies of *Life* magazine, with stories and layouts about the war fronts, and also about the camps, all written in comfortable, air-conditioned offices in New York, and they gave me an unflattering idea of American journalistic abilities. That, incidentally, has not changed in the last twenty years. This pseudo-reporting was not what mattered. The magazines went from hand to hand around the ward. What fascinated us were the pages of advertising.

Could such a world still exist? A world without ruins; where you could buy automobiles, washing machines, soap, candy; where not only were articles like these for sale, but the dealers felt it necessary to boast of their qualities to induce you to buy! In our barracks in the hell hole, sitting on our dirty beds, we the anemic ones, the stinking ones, the slobs, could see a new world through these technicolor ads. We could see a land of plenty, a Shangri-La, and we realized that the American soldiers' yarns were more than tall tales. A lot of the men in our dormitory died before getting out, but before they breathed their last they had at least had a chance, through the magazines that Jim brought in, to share the optimistic vision, to make contact, if only for the briefest time, with the America of their dreams. . . .

As the Russian had predicted, my right-hand neighbor did not last the night. His bed remained empty for several days. But men were also dying elsewhere: near the door, along the wall, in the operating room. I had photographed hundreds of corpses piled up near the crematorium and had even propped up heads whose features had already begun to decompose, in order to get a better shot; but now, seeing the white sheets covering the faces of the dead like shrouds in the hospital ward filled me with horror. With each of these, a part of myself was dying; a ray of my hope for a rapid cure, a shred of assurance. . . .

Finally a young red-headed fellow was put into the bed on my right. He was just a boy, a little Jew from Warsaw. His name was Moses, or more accurately Moishe, and I believe he had no identity other than an Auschwitz number tattooed on his left forearm. He was in a pitiful condition, not with typhus, which he had already had, but with general organic exhaustion, tuberculosis, asthma, various malfunctions, a weak heart. He spoke to me only briefly, as the rest of the time he was either asleep or unconscious. He refused to take any nourishment whatsoever. He had to be fed through the nose.

He had grown up in the ghetto, surviving by some miracle when a Polish family gave him shelter. During the battle of Warsaw, he had fallen into the hands of the German army, and had been turned over to the Gestapo. Then it was Auschwitz, Maidanek, but because of the pressure of the advancing Soviet forces he had escaped the gas chamber which had not spared his parents, three sisters, and two brothers.

After being shunted around, he had landed in a camp of the Dachau network. The cage cars had been thirty days on the way. For thirty days he had been without water or food, practically buried under the corpses of his companions. Miraculously he had been discovered alive, treated on the spot, and, as soon as it was feasible he had been sent to our American hospital.

Boris predicted he would not live to see the end of the week, but the little Jew had amazing stamina. It must also be said that the whole hospital team—doctors, nurses, and aides —had decided that, come what may, they were going to save this survivor of three gehennas. For them, it was a matter of principle, the kind of thing that decides the outcome of a war. They took turns watching at his bedside; they requisitioned special medicines from Munich; they gave him all kinds of injections; and they even brought in a surgeon from headquarters on a consultation. One of the interns, a fellow built like a star athlete, had been particularly devoted to the job. You would have thought Moishe was his younger brother. He watched over him constantly, examining the instruments, studying the rhythm of his respiration, trying to get him to swallow a bit of bouillon. They had even found some ice somewhere and used it to cool his temples.

And the little Jew was going out slowly like the wick of a candle when all the wax has been consumed. He finally started to chant in a hoarse voice. The melody was monotonous, but the words told an epic tale. It was in Yiddish, but I could understand almost all of it and could guess the rest. He told of his childhood, his first days at school, the holiday of Purim, the cakes his mother baked; he spoke of the ghetto, and how he had stolen bread for his people; the raids; the hiding. He tried to imitate the sound of the machine guns, the shouts of the SS men; then he yelled, "Watch out! Here come the bombs!"

He weakened gradually. The nurse had to check him every half hour, otherwise he would pull out the tubes that were feeding him glucose. Because of his heart, they could no longer give him morphine.

Finally he started to cry "Mamushka," the Yiddish or Polish word for mother. He called at regular intervals, first in a low moan, then louder, and still louder, until it died down again to a murmur. After a long silence he would start again, the rhythm of the "Mamushkas" becoming more frequent, until he whined a "Mamushka" with each fetid breath of air he exhaled. He continued for hours, except when he fell asleep out of utter exhaustion, but his rest did not last long.

This went on for two days and two nights. At night it was especially terrifying. I don't know whether the patients in the beds farther away from him were able to sleep, but those of us who were his neighbors could scarcely close an eye. Even when he was quiet for a while, we could still hear his "Mamushkas" floating through the air and tearing at our hearts. The nurse would try to soothe him and make him believe she was the mother he was calling. Each "Mamushka" made my skin crawl, for I could see his mother being shoved naked into the reinforced concrete cell, her head, armpits and pubic hair shaven clean, a towel and a bar of soap in her hands. I could smell the odor of the *Zyklon* bomb, hear the whistling of the gas as it escaped slowly through the slits in the ceiling. I could see his "Mamushka," who was not even a number any more, not even a tattoo mark, piled up on the stack of corpses before the oven.

The second night, I was afflicted with fear. I hid under the covers to try to escape those "Mamushkas," so persistent, so piercing, so tyrannical, which lacerated our nerves. Boris, the Russian, cursed loudly:

"Won't that goddamned Yid either croak or shut up?"

And it may be that, deep down, I too was wishing for what Boris voiced in his blasphemy. For it was not so much the lamentations that terrified me as the haunting idea that Death stood next to me, between our two beds, come to take the little Jew away. But Death might lose patience and decide to settle for someone else.

As dawn approached, Moishe stopped calling out. He was drooling, and from time to time, in his delirium, he would speak a word, calmly, quietly: "Hunger," then "train," then "hunger" again. He even tried to raise himself as if he were about to get up. . . .

On her last round of the night the nurse had put a thermometer into his mouth. A few seconds later I heard the crunch of glass. The little Jew, imagining perhaps that he was getting his first mouthful of bread after thirty days of starvation in the accursed train, had chewed the thermometer up as if it were a peppermint stick. Bits of glass, caught in the blood that was running from his mouth, stuck to his lips. But he just kept on chewing, and the glass fragments were being crunched in his teeth.

I signaled the nurse, who ran to get the doctor. The big fellow arrived—the athletic-looking one who had toiled so hard to save Moishe. He still had on his pajama coat. He immediately gave him a shot and wiped his face with cotton, but could not get him to open his mouth. He sat down on a chair and waited for the shot to take effect.

Then he saw that it was too late. He tried massaging the

Jew's heart, made a few other desperate attempts; then, losing control of himself, like a madman, grabbed the chart from the foot of the bed and, punctuating his actions with curses, tore it into bits and threw them to the floor, along with the needle he had used, the cotton batting he still held in his hand. . . .

I was to witness, much later, a similar display of frustration. It was after a football game at Yale. The coach of the team that had lost the game in the final seconds took out his rage in the same way, on his pipe and his sport coat.

But the young doctor at Dachau wept. . . .

* * * * *

A young doctor, fresh out of medical school, getting his first experience at Dachau, was madly in love with one of the nurses, a captivating blonde named Carol who often came to speak to me because of her endless curiosity about Parisian women. I had taken a picture of her, and the young doctor, who followed Carol around like her shadow, kept after me for the film. He had slipped a ten-dollar bill under my pillow, and each morning and evening came by to make sure that the film was still in my camera. He wanted to develop it himself in the X-ray laboratory, but I made him wait. He was a nice fellow; innocent and romantic as a schoolboy. He would get down on his knees in front of everyone to make his lovesick speeches to Carol, or else to sing her "South of the Border" or "Parlez-moi d'amour," in his Brooklyn accent. She was delighted with all this attention but was not eager to get herself involved. After all, there was only one girl for every thousand American soldiers at Dachau, and she preferred to play the field.

There was also a tech-sergeant in charge of personnel and the mess. For him, war, Dachau, the hospital were one continual fiesta. He would break into the ward at 6 A.M., waking everyone with a gong, spreading the latest news reports, and informing us whether he had won or lost in last night's crap game. One morning he had an inspired idea. He woke us by shooting off all six cartridges of his service revolver. He was so delighted with the result that he repeated it next morning. We were all stunned: you can imagine what it was like, after years of indescribable captivity, to be awakened by a salvo of pistol shots, even if they are fired over your head. But we didn't complain. For all we knew, this was an old American custom.

My condition worsened. My fever hovered between 102 and 106 degrees, and I had become so weak I could hardly raise my body. Thirst kept driving me crazy. Penicillin had arrived at the camp and I was given an injection of it; then, because of my heart, I received other shots which I believe were camphor oil.

Everything became blurred and vague around me—Boris, the nurse, the doctors, the aides, all were only shadows in my nightmare.

Then came a fall, maddening, as from the top of a skyscraper. I tried to hold on to the walls but couldn't. I fell and bounced up off the pavement, floated away into darkness again—then came a buzzing, a faraway singing in my ears, and I was thinking of my mother, my father, a girl who perhaps was waiting for me in Budapest. . . .

I returned to reality. It must have been almost midnight, for here was the nurse on her round. Everyone seemed to be asleep. I insisted that she call the doctor on duty. When he arrived I recognized my friend, the lovesick Lothario.

"Doctor, I promise you I'll make a hundred pictures of your girl, just for you alone, as soon as I'm able to get up. But you must help me, because my heart is failing. If you won't help me, I'm done for."

The young man tried to reassure me. He came back with a needle. "It's not called for on your chart, but that doesn't matter. I'm going to give you another shot of penicillin anyway."

I was counting my heartbeats. If this was death, it was a funny thing, because they seemed like merry-go-around horses gyrating. The carousel was azure and white. I could see a lady—was it a Madonna, or a girl I had loved, dreamed of, calling to me, smiling at me, bidding me farewell. . . . At last I fell asleep.

Next morning the sun warmed me through the dirty windowpanes. I had perspired a great deal. That was a good sign. My fever was down and I had an appetite. To the despair of neighbor Boris, who could hardly believe his eyes, I devoured the powdered eggs and guzzled the powdered milk. They tasted delicious. I felt that I was saved.

Six years later, passing through the Montreal airport, I heard the loudspeaker paging Sir Alexander Fleming. I recognized the famous scientist. He took his call, then went to sit alone at a table near the bar.

I knew I would probably sound like an idiot but I plucked up my courage and approached him. I introduced myself hurriedly, and then told him the story of that pencillin shot in the American military infirmary at Dachau. He listened distractedly at first, then began to take interest, and finally was plainly fascinated.

I have been told that the discoverer of pencillin collected virtually no part of the millions his drug earned for the pharmaceutical industry. I like to think that my little story and my few words of gratitude made Sir Alexander Fleming as happy as if I had given him a million dollars.

13

The flag

Everybody knows how Western cowboys brand their cattle.

Hitler used the same system on his concentration-camp prisoners. The serial number was not enough. The prisoners had to be divided into separate categories, to keep them from getting into the wrong corrals.

We each wore a colored triangle, the color showing the nature of our crime and the letter, the initial of our country of origin. This identification device was also symbolic. To Hitler we were a nonhuman mass, just as to the cowboy a steer is a steer, whatever its brand.

The Fuehrer was making a point. We must understand that we were no longer Europeans; we no longer had a homeland, flag, nationality, for there no longer was any Europe other than Hitler's. On one side, the Germans, *his* Germans; on the other, the rest of the world, including us.

If Hitler were successful with some of his technical undertakings—his Autobahnen, his Volkswagen, the airport at Tempelhof which even today is a marvel of modernity—his social and political teachings made no more lasting impression than his military victories.

Yet we had sworn before liberation that we would never give up this enforced leveling, and that we would make of a free Dachau a phalanstery—an immense experiment in fraternization. There were to be no more differences between us, no chauvinistic clashes; we were not going to squabble about the respective merits of our armies, the tastiness of our national cuisines, the amorousness of our girls. We would all have but one birthplace: Dachau; and only one passport: our deportees' card; only one password: "KZ." Our flag would be the white flag; the flag of shame of our murderers, and only the star-spangled banner of our American liberators would be allowed to wave over the camp.

Alas, the first few days of that fraternal republic of Dachau under U.S. protectorate swept away these naïve illusions like the *lodos* wind blowing down from Russia carrying the last dead leaves to the Bosphorus. The International Prisoners' Committee, which had set itself up as the "government" and promised to bring to fruition this utopian dream, almost immediately had to face internal dissension beside which the quarrels in the U.N. Security Council were like angels' dialogues. The Soviet general saw class enemies everywhere, which was of course to be expected, but surprisingly it was the Austrians who made the most trouble by demanding perpetual exclusion of all Germans, a position the Committee refused to take. This was a mistake on its part.

The American general who was temporary commander of the camp, surrounded by his own interpreters, transmitted all his directives in German. As Edmond Michelet put it, it was intolerable to us that the liberator should continue to use a language which at the time was the very symbol of the slavery we had just escaped. He gave in, and promised henceforth to use only English and French—a small point, perhaps, but as Michelet again points out, at the same time, in San Francisco, the delegates were having the same kind of childish disagreements in discussing the United Nations Charter.

The Lithuanians, Letts, and Esthonians wanted to be represented on the Committee, as was everybody else. In fact, I would not have been much surprised if a representative of the SS asked to sit on the Committee, for it was ready to accept the German Oskar Mueller, an old camp trusty who had been good to many of the Committee members and had done them special favors, but who to a large number of the other prisoners was nothing but a *Kapo*. The Russian general bitterly opposed the admission of the Esthonians and other Balts.

"These countries no longer exist," he argued. "There is only one country, the Soviet Union, united and indivisible."

Since his arguments did not seem to convince the other members, he took it up with the American general who, either because this was still a time when the U.S. was doing anything the Soviets asked or else because he had not the slightest idea of what Lithuania and Esthonia were anyway, sided with him.

The very day after the liberation a livid Michelet came into the meeting of the International Committee. With sweeping gestures, he complained that everywhere in the camp the "flags of the four Great Powers" had been run up.

"And what do I see? American, British, Russian—and Chinese flags! I won't take exception to the British, even though there is not a single *real* British prisoner in the Lager, but what the devil is the Chinese flag doing there?" And Michelet, as a good disciple of General de Gaulle, one of whose ministers he was later to become, insisted there could only be a fourth Great Power—France.

Ali Kuci, our "minister of propaganda," got his, too. There

were too many pamphlets being circulated around the camp, Communist mostly, I agree, and each group made no bones of the fact that its country or its party was the one that had really won the war, while all the others were to blame for the misdeeds of the Nazis. The American general found this too much to take. All these scribblings had to be censored. Thus we learned the general had brought us the gift of freedom; the freedom to say and write what the American army thought for us.

The French tricolor got is own prominent place alongside the flags of the four others, but that was only the first little skirmish in the war of the flags. The Poles, who were in control of virtually all the sewing shops in the camp, had secretly manufactured hundreds of flags with their national colors, and soon the camp was a forest of banners, standards, and pennants in Polish red and white. But this did not appease the Poles, for there were those among them who wanted the traditional Imperial Eagle and those who wanted a Red Star in the emblem. The same kind of disagreements split the Yugoslavs who were for Tito from those who were for Mihailovich. Among the Italians it was even more complicated: they were rooting for the *bandiera rossa,* the *tricolore republicano, lo stemma dei Savoia,* or the yellow-and-white Vatican flag with the keys of St. Peter.

Naturally, on May 1st, the red flags had the place all to themselves—this being the first holiday to be celebrated after liberation. Everyone paraded out of solidarity with the Communists but it was not at all to the liking of the American general who, feeling that the Fourth of July was too far off, decided to make legal holidays of every American advance, of the German surrender at Reims, Fathers' Day, the birthdays of his staff officers, and even the anniversary of Lafayette's meeting with Washington.

My faithful and inseparable Ivan had got together some thirty Russian prisoners from the Caucasus or Turkestan, as well as some Levantines, and two or three Rumanians and Bulgarians, all obsessed with the idea that the Americans might force them to return to Soviet territory or to the lands occupied by the Red Army. Why, then, should we not make of them a Turkish committee—for they were all Turks by assent, if not by race or religion? Then we could ask for representation on the Committee and maybe get them "repatriated." Ivan had gone so far, after bartering the loot he had acquired during the night, as to have shimmering silk armbands made up for them.

Turkey suddenly became well represented at Dachau. Morally, she was nowhere to be seen, inasmuch as I, the only really Turkish prisoner, was mortally ashamed that my country had broken its word and obligations and abandoned its allies to play up to the Nazis.

Atatürk would never have stood for that. He was one of the fathers of the Balkan Pact and a champion of collective security. His aversion to dictatorships was well known. It was equally noted that, wanting to reduce the influence of the army, he, though he was a victorious field marshal, never appeared anywhere in military garb. Only one day, when Mussolini made a speech that was just too bellicose, he had summoned the Italian ambassador and received him in his dress uniform, bedecked with braid, medals, pistol at his belt and helmet on his head.

"Go tell your master," he told him, "that if this is the way he wants to see me, all he has to do is go on making speeches like that."

Atatürk could not conceive of a normal man swearing off tobacco and alcohol. He characterized Hitler as "the Charlie Chaplin of the asylum." Atatürk would have declared war even more readily than Daladier or Chamberlain, but his successors preferred to stall. Turkey was governed, from the end of the Ottoman dynasty's despotism on, by generals, the only exception being the time when Celal Bayar was president, with Menderes as Prime Minister. Breaking the rules this way cost them dear. Menderes was hanged, and Bayar escaped the gallows only because he was old and ailing.

And because the military was still influenced by the training of Prussian cadres, their admiration for the Reich knew no bounds. So it happened that when I was a Berlin correspondent for the Turkish government wire service, I had many more quarrels with my own Turkish ambassador, General Gerede, who got up in the morning making obeisance toward the place where Hitler lived, like a good Mohammedan bowing toward Mecca, than I did with Goebbels.

Even in camp the guards felt that I had been turned over to the Gestapo by a Turkish government anxious to get rid of a journalist who opposed its policy of servility to the Reich. The Gestapo itself tried to convince me I had been turned in by another member of the Turkish wire service. They showed me documents to prove it. I never followed up on this, for I had vowed not to denounce a political adversary. Besides, it didn't matter. This former wire-service man was killed in a plane crash while covering a trip of Premier Menderes. Some coincidences in life seem so like miracles. . . .

Ambassador Gerede had forwarded to the Turkish government the personal request of Adolf Hitler to have me recalled from Berlin and had enthusiastically added his own endorsement to it. Luckily for me, old Marshal Fevzi Cakmak, then chief of staff and a faithful companion of Ataturk, did not share his colleagues' adoration for everything that pertained to the German army. In fact, he told me that my cables used to amuse him greatly, especially the one in which I told how Ambassador Gerede had been unable to get a hotel room in Breslau during a trip in June, 1941, despite his distinguished titles, because the town was full of soldiers. Gerede had protested vehemently that the boy newspaperman was trying to ridicule him. The Marshal had understood what I was trying to say. Seeing in it only the misadventure of a foreign diplomat, the censors had let my wire through, but the Marshal undertood that it meant Hitler was about to invade Russia, since he had moved whole divisions back form Calais to Breslau.

I think the Marshal even used some of my cables in discussing the situation in Germany with his general staff. That was more than enough to make a twenty-year-old fledgling journalist dizzy.

He was the one responsible for my getting a private meeting with Prime Minister Sarajoglou (which just missed being canceled because I obstinately refused to agree to kiss his hand, as is the custom. "Try to imagine he's a pretty girl," my father told me) who, after having congratulated me on my daring, assured me that one day I would become the most famous Turkish journalist in the world. He was not a good prophet.

However, since he had to play both sides against the middle, he refused to let me go abroad again. "We cannot take the risk of offending Hitler." Marshal Cakmak* got around the diffi-

* He had been a great friend of my grandfather, Emrullah Effendi, whom I never saw except in a photograph, but who, according to what everyone tells me, was one of the legendary figures among the revolutionary Young Turks. It was he who reorganized the public education system and was the author of the first modern Turkish encyclopedia. Which explains with indisputable logic why his only wife, my grandmother Halide, did not know how to read or write.

The stories about my grandfather Emrullah Effendi's absent-mindedness

culty by having another passport issued to me with my name spelled backward. Even Ambassador von Papen, who gave me a diplomatic visa, failed to see through the ruse, and the Marshal had me escorted to the border by his own orderly.

Perhaps all of Marshal Cakmak's assistance was in gratitude for my having warned him in time of an incident which avoided a disastrous military adventure for Turkey. It was during the battle of Stalingrad. I was in the office of the wire-service head Menemencioglu, who was phoning his brother, the Minister of Foreign Affairs. "A cable from Berlin has announced the fall of Stalingrad," he told him. "Now is the time to issue our mobilization orders."

Was Turkey really going to get into the war alongside Hitler, whose soldiers were now only a few miles from our Caucasian frontier? I went to the old Marshal and pointed out to him that the Berlin dispatch has been sent by a Rumanian correspondent who was notoriously untrustworthy. The outcome of the battle might be quite different. Cakmak induced his young military colleagues to be a little more patient . . .

Also, this business about setting up a Turkish prisoners' committee did not strike me as all that amusing. Ali Kuci helped me out of the jam by undertaking to look after my people—for the more there were of them, the more imporant

---

were widespread, and the Marshal once told me how a few weeks after having moved into his summer house at San Stefano, my grandfather one day walked into the police station and calmly announced: "You'll have to tell me where I live because I can't remember either the street or the number."

Another time, my grandfather submitted for signature at the Cabinet meeting at which he presided his butcher's, grocer's and milkman's bills; whereas, earlier the same morning he had torn up and burned a whole sheaf of secret state documents while screaming at his valet that everything was getting too expensive and from now on they'd have to be more economical—penny thrifty.

Alas, I inherited neither his good humor nor his fatalism.

his own miscellaneous committee became, and besides, I had enough to do as his propaganda assistant.

Nevertheless, we needed a flag. Even if it were only to remind the honorable Turkish army that it might do better to be marching on Dachau than to be staying home and keeping its own peasants in check. During the night it was child's play for Ivan to steal the newest of the Soviet flags, all fringed with gold. With the help of another, we left the star and sickle, but we cut out the hammer and lengthened the sickle a little and we then had something resembling the Turkish star and half moon. It was very fuzzy and blurry. However, nobody else in the camp could criticize it.

Come morning, my thirty-odd candidates for Turkish citizenship queued up in a well-dressed line. We had asked for help from the Polish band which, not knowing better, played Mozart's "Marche Turque," and we formally raised our flag. The other prisoners, delighted with the occasion, applauded and saluted, as did a few American soldiers passing through. Just then the Soviet general was crossing the street. He too, unaware of the source of the materials for the flag, stopped and stood respectfully at attention. . . .

I asked the American newspaperman, Louis Lochner, on his way back to Paris after having a visit to the liberated camp, to send a long wire in my name to the Turkish President Inönu. I no longer remember the exact wording of the telegram, but the original must still be in the archives of his former residence at Cankaya. This is what I said, approximately:

"Turkish flag now flying over Dachau concentration camp, where I still am; being vanguard of glorious Turkish army which you command and which courageously, ignoring all dangers, took part in universal struggle against Hitler tyranny. Our flag flying alongside others. . . ."

Inönu was known as the deaf man of Ankara because, every time a diplomat or politician asked a question, he pretended he could not hear so as to avoid answering, or at least to have time to think up a reply. This time, however, he was not deaf to my appeal. He sent a request to General Eisenhower to have a U.S. Air Force plane dispatched from Paris to Dachau to take me out of the camp immediately. But before leaving I took one long last look behind me, at the red flag with the half moon flapping ironically in the breeze, as if it were laughing at finding itself there.

INTERLUDE IV

Dialogue

. . . if the Dachau concentration camp no longer offers its visitors the original buildings of the Lager, on the other hand you now find, scattered throughout the enclosure, a variety of commemorative religious monuments which did not exist before. There is even a large and elegant Carmelite convent, the Convent of Repentance. I tried in vain to find out whether it was the repentance of the Church for its inability to prevent the crimes committed on this spot or the repentance of the Germans who had committed them.

Anyway, every major religion is now, or soon will be, represented in the camp by a statue, an altar, or a symbol.

Sometimes in the night I imagine that the rival gods thus forcibly placed face to face in the camp, having little to do now, with no more victims to pray for their aid, must surely become bored in this deserted area of stones and yellow-green grass; I imagine their nocturnal dialogues:

GOD OF THE JEWS (who is abreast of international affairs) lamenting: "I see the God of the Moslems has just taken his place at Dachau. What a scandal!"

GOD OF THE MOSLEMS: "What do you mean—scandal?

236 / The Day of the Americans

why, among the prisoners there were Croatians, Azerbaid-
janis, Mongols, Albanians. I am their God! And besides, I am
a God of strength. Thanks to me, to my soldiers fighting in
the ranks of the Soviet armies, the camps were liberated.
Whereas you, God of the Jews, are powerless. You were
unable to do anything when your flock was whipped, gassed,
burned. Hitler wiped out 75 per cent of your people and in
time he would have destroyed them all. You, God of the Jews,
did not lift a finger. You ought to go and hide instead of
trying to remind posterity of your pitiful impotence."

GOD OF THE JEWS: "It is not for me to prevent martyrdom.
Rather, I reward it. Today, my people have triumphed. They
are in Jerusalem, in my land. Your people are the ones who
have fled. But we are not at Dachau to discuss what is going
on elsewhere. I am here representing those of my people who
were unjustly cut down. But you, God of the Moslems, you
represent the executioners. You threw your lot in with the
murderers."

GOD OF THE PROTESTANTS: "I like clear ideas, well-reasoned
logic. Do not allow yourselves to be swept away by passion!
How can any one among us be accused of complicity in these
horrors? Allah did not declare a holy war for the victory of the
Germans as he did in 1914."

GOD OF THE JEWS: "Not Allah, perhaps, but his representative on earth, Hadji Amin El-Husseini, the Grand Mufti of
Jerusalem.

"Yes, the Grand Mufti, the friend of Eichmann, the honored guest of Hitler, the man who embraced Goebbels in
public and was financed by Mussolini. The man who in 1944
used the microphones of the Italian Radio to ask 'Moslems of
the whole world to pray for the success of Hitler's armies.' It
was he who for three years begged Hitler not to permit any

further emigration of European Jews who would thereby have 'overpopulated Palestine,' and he who demanded a 'final solution.' That final solution was the gas chamber, and just to make doubly sure the Mufti encouraged and at times financed the formation of special SS divisions of Moslem volunteers. There was the Croatian division, the one of Soviet deserters, made up of Kalmucks, Mongols, Caucasians, and these were units which distinguished themselves particularly through their pitilessness toward the civilian populations and at times served as garrisons in several concentration camps. The Mufti himself inspected these death camps and congratulated the Moslem soldiers for cooperating so efficiently in the elimination of Jews and other infidels."*

GOD OF THE MOSLEMS: "That is libelous, for if it were not, the Mufti would have been tried as a war criminal at Nuremberg. And the fact is, he lived out his life very peacefully in an outlying section of Paris as guest of a Resistance government."

GOD OF THE CATHOLICS: "All of which does not change the fact that the Mohammedans imprisoned at Dachau were merely former SS criminals who had deserted and were locked up here because they were no longer loyal to Hitler. Whereas my children, the priests, the Catholic prelates, were covered with honors when liberation came. There were 1,240 men of the cloth at Dachau at the time of liberation and of those, 95 per cent were Catholic. Look, almost every book ever written about this camp was by a Catholic priest!"

GOD OF THE PROTESTANTS: "Don't try juggling with figures. If there were so many Catholic priests at Dachau when it was

---

* The role played by Hadji Amin El-Husseini has been covered in detail in the excellent historical study, *The Mufti and the Fuehrer*, Joseph B. Schectman. (New York: Thomas Yoseloff, 1965.)

liberated it was only because they were not systematically massacred like the rest of the prisoners. They lived comfortably in their block and refused, with a few rare exceptions, to let any other prisoners take refuge there. They did not work, they were not mistreated, and therefore they were able at their leisure to observe everything that went on about them and then write fine books. Meanwhile, the others were dying.

"Dachau is not far from Munich, and in Munich there was your Cardinal Faulhaber. But your Cardinal did not rebel, and he never read out in all his churches a pastoral letter asking the faithful to rise as one and march on Dachau to break down its gates. Nor did he come to present himself to share the fate of those who were thus being tortured within his own archbishopric. And don't tell me he didn't know what was going on or that he had no influence! He was not unaware, since his own assistant Canon Dr. Johann Neuhaeusler, a prisoner in the camp himself, kept him posted and since he had sent ecclesiastical vestments to be used at the ordination of Karl Leisner, a deacon of Munster. And just a few days before the liberation, thanks to the sausages and rolls that the Cardinal, despite the chaos and disorder, was still sending through to Neuhaeusler, the people imprisoned in the 'Honor Bunker' were getting enough to eat. Neuhaeusler and the Bishop of Clermont-Ferrand had been transferred out of the Lager so as to take advantage of the privileged treatment in the 'Honor Bunker.' The Gestapo had made those concessions to the Cardinal.

"For behind the Cardinal there was your Pope, who had never made a secret of his sympathies for Germany and authoritarian regimes. In 1917 when he was the nuncio in Munich, he had tried to favor the Central Powers and gain for them a favorable peace, because it was necessary to save

Austria-Hungary, that great Catholic nation, and to preserve Germany, that bastion against the new menace of Bolshevism.* He had not changed his views for this war. He made Fascism respectable by signing a concordat with the Socialist Mussolini, and even in 1942 the unspeakable Ribbentrop was received with honors at the Vatican.

"The Pope's sympathies for Hitler are understandable. Hitler was born a Catholic, raised a Catholic, and it would have been embarrassing to have to explain how such a solid Catholic education could turn a normal baby into a mad sadist. That is why he was never excommunicated, as today excommunication is pronounced against the most obscure Neapolitan cobbler who happens to vote Communist at the elections. Hitler—his secretary vouched for it—paid his religious dues to the German Catholic Church until the day of his death. He never apostasized."

GOD OF THE CATHOLICS: "You all use the same underhanded attacks which disregard historical truth. I refuse to answer them. And as for you Protestants, how dare you throw anything up to us? Hitler may well have been born a Catholic, but his concept of Germanism, the men who brought him to power, the institutions, the traditions, the clerical support he used, the wave of anti-Semitism—all that was Protestant, as the German soul is Protestant. Hitler was only following in the path of Martin Luther and of Bismarck, who before him had already become an enemy of our religion. You chose him, you elected him, you loved him, you fought for him, you died for him, even after his death."

GOD OF THE ATHEISTS (for at Dachau there must be also a God for those who believed in none of the other gods, or who

* Secrets diplomatiques 1914–1918, by Jacques de Launay (Paris, 1963, Brépois.)

because of Dachau refused to believe in them any longer):
"But none of you has the right to be here. What are you all
boasting about? Having liberated Dachau? Well, if you are
the ones who saved the 33,000 prisoners the Americans found
here when they arrived, if those 33,000 are supposed to thank
you for having saved their lives, that miracle, then you must
also be responsible for the fact that they were in Dachau in
the first place. And what about the others, the 370,000 who
were not saved? Don't they have you to thank for their suffer-
ings and for their deaths? For you cannot very well boast of
the gains without assuming responsibility for the losses. And
the balance—370,000 lost against 33,000 saved—is hardly in
your favor.

"You say you are not responsible for the madness of a
Hitler? But did your priests not serve as chaplains in his
armies, with a swastika embroidered on their uniforms? Did
your bells not toll to announce the German victories? Did you
not sing the *Te Deum* in your churches to celebrate the fall of
Warsaw, Paris, Athens?

"Sure, you did not take sides completely. There were also
chaplains in the French army, and the Sacred Heart was
embroidered on the flags of the Breton regiments just as it
was on those of the Bavarian. Reynaud called on that same
Sacred Heart when the Nazis were invading France, those
very Nazis who had received the benediction from their own
priests in their own churches. In *Is Paris Burning?* we can read
that the church bells of France stopped ringing from the time
Paris was taken and that they never rang again until the
liberation. But the church bells of Germany and Austria
started ringing when Paris was taken, and became silent only
when Paris was freed. There was a *Te Deum* for the armistice

dictated by Hitler in the Forest of Compiègne. And then, when General de Gaulle entered Paris unleashed with joy, he went to Notre Dame for a *Te Deum*. I guess you people have the divine gift of ubiquity. Or else, maybe it's just that you lay off your bets on both sides at the same time."

GHOST OF A PRISONER HAUNTING THE CREMATORIUM: "And you, God of the Atheists, what did you do for us? The others at least left us some hope, some illusion that all was not lost. Sometimes they even gave us a bit of pity, a bit of human solidarity. But your people were the most cruel, the most unflinching, the most bestial. Gas can only be the work of godless people. Crematoria can only be the work of godless people, as are the massacres, the horrific experiments, the holocausts—those of Dachau and Auschwitz, and also those of Karaganda and the other Siberian camps; those of Katyn Forest, of Leningrad, and now those of Red China. All that is the doing of those who accused religion of exploiting the human race and who now decimate and tyrannize it in your name."

*   *   *   *   *

Like everyone else, I have seen Rolf Hochhuth's excellent play *The Deputy*. Yes, the author tells the truth. No, I am not in full agreement with the author, because I believe that a German writer, before setting himself to deal with the Pope, with Oppenheimer, or with the bombing of Dresden, ought first to denounce the misdeeds and explain the motivations of the men of his own country. Hochhuth's admirable talent would better have served Germany and humanity if he had tried to make us understand why a Hindenburg called on a Hitler to assume power; why a Marshal Keitel served him blindly; why a von Papen became his valet. For Hochhuth to point the finger at Pius XII and the Vatican is only a ruse to set up extenuating circumstances for the crimes of Hitler and his Germany.

As a good Catholic, raised by the Brothers and educated in part at the Catholic University of Paris, I have always felt that even if the policies of His Holiness Pius XII were bad, the reproaches that have been made and will continue to be made to him cannot attain the Catholic Church as an institution, and they even may well increase her prestige. For what is being brought out against the Pope? That he did not oppose Hitler; did not denounce his crimes; did not risk his own person? But no one is making such accusations against spiritual leaders of other religious faiths, much less against the heads of certain neutral states. No one has written a *Deputy* to denounce the neutrality of Inonu or the attitude of the King of Denmark. And General Franco, that friend of Hitler and Mussolini, still remains in power, honored and admired. The fact is that the world expected a denunciation from the Vatican, seeing it as a symbol of justice, peace and security. It was a beacon. It matters little if through the fault of the guardian its light went out. Another will light it again.

That is why Catholics are wrong to become indignant and take offense when Pius XII is criticized. They are wrong to try to snuff out any free discussion of the part played by the Pope. They are wrong to call for riots or official suppression to keep the public from going to see *The Deputy*. His Holiness Pius XII was perfectly aware of what was going on in the camps. He could have intervened. He should have intervened. To deny that is to deny that the earth turns. And I believe it would be preferable for the Vatican not to get itself embroiled in another Galileo case.

In November, 1945, I was in Rome. Thanks to the recommendation of a cardinal who was perhaps impressed by my

American captain's uniform and won over by my arguing that an interview between the Pope and a deportee would find good acceptance in the press, I obtained an audience with the Holy Father. Pope Pacelli was somewhat in need of good publicity. The story making the rounds was that Stalin, at the conference table at Potsdam, had snapped: "The Pope? How many divisions does he have?" And the quip had given President Truman a good laugh. . . .

I am reproducing herewith the essential text of my interview, the first one given by this Pope to any journalist. I am taking it from the documentation offered by the French writer Jacques Nobecourt in his book *Le Vicaire et l'histoire* (*The Deputy before History*). I am referring to the version carried in this pro-Vatican book, for my interview was published at the same time in a number of leading newspapers, and it is well-known that managing editors are in the habit of rearranging articles and presenting them according to their own tastes.

DECLARATIONS OF PIUS XII

The Pope immediately took up the subject which was closest to me and asked to hear details of my internment in concentration camps. I acceded to his request, while expressing frankly to the Holy Father the inability of us deportees to understand the fact that the Vatican had not organized any kind of help during the period of our imprisonment—which it seemed to us would have been its duty—and that it did not unequivocally condemn the Nazi criminals responsible for the atrocities committed nor the German people who were their accomplices through their attitude of passivity.

The Pope registered both surprise and unhappiness at my question.

He answered quickly:

"We knew that for political reasons violent persecutions were taking place in Germany, but we were never informed of the inhuman character of the Nazi repression. We were never permitted to make the slightest intervention nor send the least assistance. As soon as, after the Liberation, we were apprised of the true situation, the continual reports which we receive brought desolation and sadness to our heart. We organized missions which did everything possible to succor the deportees. Only yesterday, we sent another delegation charged with bringing relief and helping in every way possible, materially and morally, those deportees who are still in Germany."

"Nevertheless," I pressed on, "thousands of priests were tortured and killed in the camps. How could your representatives in Germany have left Your Holiness ignorant of this?"

"The information they had must have been incomplete," was the reply, "and it was difficult for them to get it to us."

The Pope was silent, my question appearing to have touched on a delicate point.

"Your Holiness will permit me to say that not only my comrades from all the camps in Germany but all of world opinion would like to know how far you go in condemning those directly and indirectly, actively and passively responsible for the crimes committed in Germany."

The Pope answered directly:

"I have pronounced a great many speeches and each of them contained passages which left no doubt about my intention of putting blame on those responsible for such acts, anti-Christian in their very essence and contrary to all human concepts. But if you wish a formal condemnation, I am making such a condemnation now."

"Does Your Holiness approve the principles of the Nuremberg trials?"

"Yes. Not only do we approve of the principles of these trials, but we wish to see those who are guilty punished quickly and without exception. They are responsible not only for the material evil they have done, but also for their spiritual crimes, since they refused religious assistance to so many dead. It is necessary that they be punished so that the others, the Germans who 'have nothing against their records' may go back to normal living conditions and be helped to rehabilitation."

I can still remember that this conversation about the camps was not quite casual. I had been informed that the audience was to be considered terminated when the Pope gave me his benediction. But, after each benediction, I got up but continued to talk about the camps. The Pope could not do otherwise than answer me.

For the greatest part of the interview revolved mainly around the situation in those regions of Europe occupied by the Russians. For the first time, Pius XII denounced in truly unequivocal terms "the cruelties and abuses of the Soviets in the countries of Eastern Europe." These declarations were widely responded to, and can be looked upon as the forerunner of the break between East and West.

The Holy Father accorded me a special benediction, the fourth one, and promised that he would pray especially for the thousands of my comrades who had been murdered by the Germans. The audience was finished. I had the authorization to publish "the spirit of our conversation."

*　　*　　*　　*　　*

This interview constituted the most brilliant success of my career. I was only twenty-five years old. I had barely escaped from the camp, and here now was my piece on the front pages of newspapers the world over, from America to Australia. I was proud of having gotten the Pope solemnly to condemn the German people, to give his approval of the Nuremberg trials, and especially to his open accusation of Soviet Russia, at that time the ally of the victors, whose Communist comrades were powerfully influencing the political life of France, Italy, and Germany, to mention only those three countries.

The question of papal responsibility was really secondary, for at the time everyone was convinced that the Pope had been wrong to remain neutral and no interview was needed to assure them of that.

Pius XII was the head of the Holy Roman and Apostolic Church, and for the Church the incidents of history lose their importance. It thinks in terms of centuries, of millennia. To it, Hitler was only a passing phenomenon. What counts is the eternity of the Church. Just as in 1917 the future Pius XII wanted mainly to eliminate the Bolsheviks from Europe, so—undoubtedly against his better judgment—did he tolerate Hitler. He had a political justification for it and an excellent one. None can deny that Emilio Pacelli had remarkable qualities as a statesman.

But to me the life of some poor innocent child burned in a crematorium carried more weight than all the political future of all the churches and all their popes. Did I not read somewhere in the Gospel the parable of the good shepherd who left his flock to look for one lost sheep?

What could the Pope do? He could at the least have abstained. He might have refused to sign concordats with Fascist Italy, with Hitlerite Germany. He could have excommunicated both of their dictators as in olden times he had excommunicated emperors (remember Canossa).

It has been said that the Catholic clergy suffered tremendously. This is true—but to exactly what proportions? For each anti-Nazi Catholic priest, how many were there who collaborated with the regime or tolerated it? Was not Monsignor Tiso in Slovakia a friend of Hitler? And the Cardinal

Archbishop of Zagreb? And the highly Catholic government
of Marshal Pétain and Premier Laval? The Pope could have
used his influence and restrained them.

And what about the Catholic Franco? And Prince-Cardinal
Mindszenty who for nearly ten years now has been hiding out
at the U.S. Embassy in Budapest? I spoke to him there. He
told me, "My voluntary imprisonment is intended to denounce Communist tyranny to the world." But was he in
prison or did he take sanctuary in a foreign embassy when the
Nazis were terrorizing and massacring the population of
Budapest?

It is said that the Pope could have had no influence on
Hitler. Directly, probably not, but indirectly his influence
could have been great. If not, Ribbentrop would not have
bothered to go to the Vatican at the height of the war. Hitler
was not as stupid as some would have us believe. He did not
underestimate the value of a diplomatic action by the Vatican, and he knew that any open hostility by the Church could
cause enormous difficulties for him, for a good share of the
peoples of the Axis were Catholic. Let us not even mention
Italy, which would certainly have revolted against the dic-
tatorship of the Black Shirts from the very start if the Pope
had only wanted that.

It is said that the Supreme Pontiff, by unequivocally oppos-
ing Hitler, would only have provoked more cruel repressions.
That is not proved by any means. It would have been difficult
for Hitler to be any more pitiless than he was. What could he
have done? Burned the corpses of the Jews a second time?
And besides, fear of reprisals has never been a valid excuse for
not doing one's duty. After all, if all of us had kept our arms
crossed so as not to expose our families, our friends, our
possessions, there would have been no Resistance, no parti-

sans, no counteraction of any sort. The camps would not have had any prisoners. Chancellor Schuschnigg would not have opposed Hitler; de Gaulle would have stayed quietly at home; and, very humbly, the author of this book would have continued to live in the comfort and tranquillity of the Berlin suburbs, letting his salary accumulate in Swiss banks, instead of bothering to write articles about the Jews being hunted down in the ghettoes.

Well, it is said that the Pope saved a great many Jews who lived in Rome. Certainly no one denies this. But did not the Jews of Lodz or of Minsk have the same right to stay alive? Did they not love their children just as much? Did they not have the same need for sunshine as those who happened to live within a stone's throw of St. Peter's?

Finally, it is said that the Pope must always remain neutral. If so, then why did Pius XII—and on that very day I happened to be in Rome—go down into the streets of the capital to protest against a few unfortunate British bombs dropped on some old church? Why did he remain quiet in his room when Warsaw, Rotterdam, and Coventry were bombed into extinction?

I admit that the Pope is not responsible for the material acts of people killing each other off like savages. But, as head of a universal religion, he does have a moral responsibility; we are taught that in our catechism. How many, alas, how many Catholics died at Dachau, to mention only Dachau, cursing their own religion? How many died with blasphemy on their lips, eternally damned because they had rebelled at the idea that their Pope did not care about their fate?

Perhaps the corpses of the gas-chamber victims do not

count, but certainly the loss of a soul must weigh heavily on the scales. . . .

One legend—and isn't all religion made up of legends?—made a deep impression on my childish imagination. Saint Peter, fleeing from Rome where Nero was putting Christians to death in his circus, was on the Appian Way when he met Our Lord Jesus Christ, who was going in the opposite direction, carrying an immense cross.

"Quo Vadis, Domine?" Saint Peter is said to have asked.

And the Lord answered him: "I am going to Rome to be crucified in your stead, Peter. . . ." And Peter then turned back. . . .

His Holiness Pius XII revealed during his lifetime that he had had several supernatural visitations. I often wonder whether Our Lord did not appear to him just once, carrying his cross, and say to him, "I am going to Dachau to be crucified in your stead. . . ."

But then, perhaps Pope Emilio Pacelli was no Saint Peter.

14

Epitaph at Taishad-Lak

Marquis George Edward Pallavicini, Prisoner No. 32352, was without a doubt the strongest and most sincere person in the whole International Prisoners' Committee. He had been brought to Dachau toward the month of December, 1944, directly from Budapest. On the basis that he had once been a seminarian, a Hungarian prelate had got him admitted to the clerical block, thus avoiding for him the mortal terrors which haunted other new arrivals. In spite of this relatively safe assignment, his health was failing, and when I met him for the first time I thought he was an old man. He was wrapped up in a dirty old blanket, a rag twisted around his head like a turban, sitting on his hands as if the better to keep them warm. However, within the block, he commanded real respect; even the bishops were deferential toward him. It was generally believed that he was a close personal friend of Emperor Otto of Hapsburg, which was true.

We hit it off well, brought together by our respective prestige; his due to his impressive name, mine to my having been in contact at Mauthausen with the elite of the Hungarian

250

blue aristocracy, among them the real head of the Monarchist party, Count Shigrai.

The name of Pallavicini meant something at that time. The marquis was the last of the line of the Hungarian branch of the family that had emigrated there from Genoa in the eighteenth century, one of its younger sons at the time having married a Magyar princess and inherited castles in Hungary. The Pallavicinis go back into history as far as nobility itself and their family is spread throughout Europe. In the spring of 1965, they held a reunion in Rome to celebrate the thousandth anniversary of the death of their earliest ancestor.

George Pallavicini, whom I affectionately called Juri and sometimes, to tease him, *Il marchesino,* was the firstborn of four children, one of them a girl, and saw the light of day in 1912 at Andrassy Castle at Tissadob. His mother had been a Countess Andrassy, another prestigious name, Andrassy Avenue having been the most beautiful in Budapest, even though the Communists have since renamed it, first Stalin Boulevard and then Red Avenue. His father, noble but poor, had entered politics, thereby perhaps giving an unfortunate example to his son, and he was a member of Parliament.

George Pallavicini, Sr., had had the courage to make a speech in Parliament, at the very time Hitler's janissaries were terrorizing all of Hungary, in which he forcefully denounced the inhuman and revolting Jew hunt that was taking place. I would like to know why Messrs. Adenauer, Erhard, Lubke, to name only those few, never found occasion to show equal courage.

Juri went to school with the Jesuits, and then to the University of Louvain, where he was a classmate of Otto of Hapsburg, who, to him, has always been The Emperor. After that, he worked for the Hitel Bank, supervising a factory which that financial institution controlled. But that was only a front, for he scurried in all directions throughout the Budapest area, alerting the Jewish families who stood in the way of falling into the hands of the Gestapo. Very often his villa served as hiding place for Jews or for left-wing politicians, among them Minister Sokachic. He was anti-Boche to the point that some days he would wear the Star of David prominently on his coat when he attended high-society gatherings in Buda. His political ideas were confused: on the one hand, he was a liberal who talked about reforming the feudal institutions which were still characteristic of the Hungary of before 1945, and on the other hand he argued for the restoration of the Hapsburgs as the only solution capable of guaranteeing the simultaneous elimination of Hitler and Bolsheviks. Then, he decided he would become a priest, which shocked his relatives and friends, especially his mother, who found it difficult to conceive of her exuberant, happy, girl-chasing and prankster son as a prelate in a cassock.

The Nazis, having traced an underground Polish radio transmitter to one of the houses where the Resistance people were hiding, trailed and arrested him on August 15, 1944. His mother did everything she could to get him released (she knew everybody who was anybody in Budapest) but it was all fruitless. She was able to see him twice before his departure for Dachau, only to learn that the Gestapo had brutally beaten him.

Most of the Hungarians in the camps were mere serfs from the countryside, or rootless ghetto-dwellers. Pallavicini the magnate was therefore logically the obvious man to represent his countrymen within the International Committee, the more so since the Catholic priests of the block, while they would never admit this, were in mortal fear that at the time of liberation Pope Pius XII's too-great understanding toward Hitler might be held against them. Therefore they also saw Pallavicini as their best spokesman on the Committee.

His new position transformed him completely. He suddenly discovered that he had marvelous energy and boundless vigor; he had already conceived the idea of a huge organization, an "international corporation of all the Dachau deportees," which would become a guarantee of peace and an inspiration of human solidarity; he wanted to see a court of honor, a prisoner's passport, and for the present he felt it necessary to resist with whatever arms at hand any attempt at a general massacre by our Nazi jailers.

He was on almost all occasions on the side of General Mikhailov, the vice-president of the Committee. The Russian asked for more understanding for the Russian captives. Then, as the Red Army got closer and closer to Berlin, he started to make tougher demands, and a diplomatic battle was waged at Dachau comparable to the one there would soon be at Potsdam. He accused the other members of the Committee of playing into the hands of the Americans at the expense of the true interests of the Russian prisoners.

"The general is right," Pallavicini on one occasion exclaimed to a flabbergasted Patrick O'Leary. "You parade around here in a British uniform which is not even yours, but don't forget that your people aren't the ones who liberated us. Without the Red Army and its campaigns, we would not have been freed by 1950, if then. . . ."

Because he loved making speeches and was interested only in ideas, he had asked for me, as a favor to me or because he wanted near him someone who would not be involved in the thousand intrigues which the imminent liberation was already setting off within the Hungarian clique. He knew I could handle the problems of paperwork, statistics, repatriation slips, identification verifications, and all of that sort of detail which was distasteful to him. As soon as one of the internees came to see him, addressing him as "Marquis" and "Excellency," he would, in spite of himself, launch into a terrifying Hungarian harangue.

Then, his good nature getting the upper hand, he would embrace his compatriot or pat him affectionately on the shoulder and, turning to me, assure him: "He will take care of everything, Servus," and thereby sending him away convinced that everything was going to be even better than ever. Forgetting all about the Committee, the Soviets, the Emperor, and the future of the turbulent Magyar nation, he would seriously ask me to lay out the schedule for our first tour of the Paris night spots, the "Grand Duke's Tour," as it is called, or the "Grand Marquis' Tour," as he dubbed it; all this to occur when we got back to that City of Light in our striped prisoners' uniforms, looking like two Charlie Chaplins.

Despite our illnesses and the red tape of the Americans, we did get to Paris, almost together. He caught up with me at the Colisée Café, at the corner of the Rue de Berri and the Champs Elysées, not in a striped prison suit but in a sports outfit, rather elegantly tailored, with his mustache already back to normal and his lordly airs of old, announcing: "I have a surprise for you. In exchange, you'll treat us to a really good meal; I've had the menu all picked out since last Christmas."

The surprise was the presence of three of my former Mauthausen prisonmates: three Spanish Reds who had been in jail more or less continuously since the end of their Civil War. Our feudal Margraf, champion of the restoration of the Holy Roman Empire, in this Paris crawling with concentration-

camp returnees, had picked out three hard-core revolution-
aries who had not even been in Dachau, and had made them
into his bosom pals. That was Juri Pallavicini all over!

"Did you wire your parents?" I asked.

"No," he answered, "I haven't had time yet. I'm in the
middle of organizing a league of displaced Hungarians, but I
just made a broadcast on the radio and I'm sure my mother
picked it up."

"Look, Budapest is far away. Maybe she doesn't have a
radio any more. Maybe the Russians confiscated it."

"You always see the dark side of everything," he complained. "Everyone at home will be fine. Our villa wasn't even
grazed by a single bullet. And tonight all Budapest will be
phoning her to say they heard Pallavicini's broadcast from
Paris."

Of course, he was right. His interview had been heard and
his parents were advised about it. Nevertheless, I did succeed
in convincing him to write them right away, and I mailed the
letter myself through the press office.

One day he came to the headquarters in the Hotel Scribe to
tell me he was returning to Hungary.

"My country needs me," he said. "I can't go on marking
time here in Paris, doing nothing. You'll see. We'll get what
the Americans promised us: a new Hungary, free, democratic,
a beacon of progress. Dachau was a school to me, and now I
have to put to use the lessons I learned there." He got home,
thanks to a British colonel who had a military vehicle put at
his disposal.

His admirable, courageous mother, who is now living
humbly in a ground-floor apartment on the outskirts of Montreal, tells me that immediately upon his return, without even

taking a breather, Juri threw himself into a crushing schedule of work. He wanted to set up a liberal legitimist youth organization and also create a Deportees' Bureau. He appeared before Parliament; wrote in the papers; and was already being mentioned as the next ambassador to the Vatican.

There was a brief interlude caused by the death of his father and then Juri was sent abroad on "official business." He was seen in Paris, London, Germany. In Paris, he had conversations with Otto of Hapsburg, who gave him a message to take back. Juri told me about it when we had dinner together in Munich at the American Third Army mess.

"Wake up, Juri!" I countered. "Hungary is practically in the hands of the Communists. I've just come back from Berlin. I was at the Potsdam Conference and I know what is going on in the Russian zone. And you expect to go back to Budapest as Otto's ambassador? The days of Viennese operettas are over. You'd do better to stay in Paris and watch how things go and prepare an apartment for the day when your family must take refuge there."

Juri only laughed at me. "We've overcome so many invaders; we'll know how to handle the Russians. Don't believe all those stories you hear about Moscow ogres. You still have Goebbels on the brain."

He said "Servus," and hopped into a jeep, to turn away on the road leading to the Autobahn.

I had not been alone in advising him against returning to Budapest. Many of his other friends did the same, and Geza von Bede, in 1943 who once was Press Minister and is today a director of Radio Free Europe, recalls that he spent an entire night trying to convince Pallavicini not to play with matches inside the Communist powderkeg. Bede knew what he was talking about, for at that time he was ambassador to London,

The Marquis, Georges of Pallavicini, photographed after his liberation from Dachau.

"As soon as I arrived in the United States for the first time, my visit was in West Haven, to the Ortoleva family (Jim, Del, his wife, his daughters—Joy and Gayle, and his son, Jimmy, Jr.)."

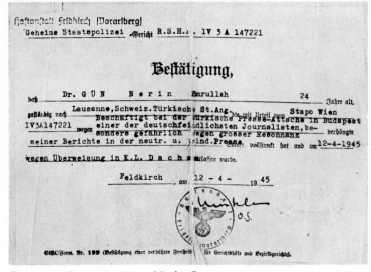

Gestapo order to transport Nerin Gun after his escape. It reads: Nerin Gun, Dr. from Lausanne, assistant of the Turkish press attache in Budapest, one of the most anti-German journalists, especially dangerous because of the repercussions of his reports in the neutral and enemy press.

The Turkish daily, AKSAM, announces the liberation of their correspondent, Nerin Gun, on front page, and shows photo of Gun before arrest and immediately after liberation. The newspaper, after informing readers of Gun's heroic actions, announced that he would soon print his memoirs from Dachau and that Gun would be a permanent correspondent in Paris. Shortly afterward, by order of the Turkish government, the newspaper stopped the publication of the memoirs of Gun and terminated him as a correspondent. In addition, his passport was denied.

Dechau toplanma kampını ziyaret

Burada 15 ay kalan ve Naziler tarafından türlü işkencelere maruz tutulan muhabirimizin hatıralarını yakında neşredeceğiz

Muhabirimiz şimdi içinde S. S. lerin mevkuf bulunduğu kampta neler gördü?

Harbin son senelerinde Akşam'ın Budapeşte muhabirliğini yapan N. Gün gazetemize çok mühim ve dikkate şayan telgraflar göndermişti. Bu telgraflar Almanların hiç de hoşuna gitmediğinden Almanya Budapeşteyi işgal ederek Macar hükümetini ele alınca Naziler kendisini yakalamışlar ve meşhur Dechau toplanma kampına göndermişlerdi. Muhabirimiz Dechau kampında tamam 15 ay kalmış ve tifüse yakalanmıştır. N. Gün bütün nüfuz ve işkencelere tulü tifüse yenerek rinayet burasını işgal eden Amerikan kuvvetleri tarafından kurtarılmıştır. Genç muharrir Alman zulmünden kurtulur kurtulmaz derhal gazetemizle muhabere temin etmiş ve müşterik kararğāhında Akşam'ın harb muhabiri olarak çalışmağa başlamıştır. Muhabirimiz Paris'ten ve Potsdam konferansı esnasında Berlin'den çektiği telgraflarda günün vekayiine dair kıymetli malümat vermiştir.

Merkezi Paris olarak çalışmasına devam eden muhabirimize Dechau kampını ziyaretle burasını bugünkü haline dair telgrafla enteresan bir yazı göndermiştir. Bu yazıyı aşağıda neşrediyoruz:

Bu münasebetle karilerimize şunu da haber verelim ki muhabirimiz, Dechau temerküz kampına ne surette düştüğünü, burada geçirdiği hayata dair meraklı yazı serisi hazırlamıştır. Bu serisi yakında neşretmeye başlıyacağız.

Dechau kampında

Muhabirimiz N. Gün

Muhabirimizin kamptan kurtulduğu gün çekilen resmi

After the liberation, Russian prisoners in Dachau revolted against the Americans by destroying their quarters. The liberated Russians did not want to be forced to return to Russia, as the Americans wanted them to.

German soldiers, unconcerned with the bombing by the enemy, drag Jewish children, women and old men through the streets.

16. Juli 1933
10. Jahrgang / Nr. 28
Verlag Knorr & Hirth,
G. m. b. H., München

Münchner
Illustrierte Presse

Preis: 20 Pfennig

Frühappell im Erziehungslager

Were the good Germans unaware of the existence of the Dachau concentration camp? Here is the front page, dated July 16, 1933, of the Munchen Illustrierte Presse, the equivalent of *Life* in the U.S.A., showing the Dachau inmates.

Dachau today. Visitors put flowers on the crematorium oven.

Dachau today. Visitors take photos of themselves in front of the crematorium, as if they were at the zoo.

Dachau today. Some of these blocks were inhabited by the German refugees.

Religious monuments in Dachau . . . but not a single reminder that the camp was liberated by the Americans.

A view of the city of Dachau today.

representing the pro-Communist coalition government, the dangers of which he knew better than anyone else.

So Pallavicini went back home "happy," as the French poet says, "as he who like Ulysses has had a wonderful voyage." It was the day before Easter, 1946. His alarmed mother warned him immediately that the political police, the AVO, were looking for him.

"Please hide, Juri," she urged him. "I'm so nervous I jump every time the doorbell rings."

In order to reassure her, he took up lodgings with a British friend, one Mr. Sidney, while calmly going back to his political contacts, taking part in meetings, transmitting messages from Emperor Otto, and appearing more and more often at the British Military Mission. In fact, his British friends were afraid the Bolsheviks might kidnap him, and put a soldier to guard him, with an official jeep to use. He must have thought they were being funny.

On August 10th, he got a note from the Central Office of the Hungarian Communist party. His presence was required at the offices in the Andrassy Ut, the name of which they had not yet changed. To go there meant sticking his hand into the wolf's maw, but Juri did not care. Nevertheless, when he came out he was most upset, nervous and irritated. The interrogation had been exceedingly disagreeable, and to top it he had been told that the Soviet secret police, the MVD, had been making inquiries about him. He was instructed to come back the next day.

"I was anxious to know how things had gone," his mother told me. "I had asked my son to meet me at the apartment of my mother, Countess Andrassy, for I was afraid to have him come to my house. He got there at about three in the afternoon.

" 'You're not going back into that bandits' den again to-morrow, Juri,' I said to him. 'That would be madness—'

" 'But Mother, if I did not go back, they would think I had something to hide. My conscience is clear.'

" 'Juri,' I insisted, 'when you were in Dachau there was at least something of you left with us: hope. The war was coming to an end and we could see that the liberation had to come. But if the Bolsheviks take you away, who will ever liberate you? It'll take ten, twenty, fifty years before it's their turn to be driven out.'

" 'I'm not afraid, Mother. You have a grotesque idea of the Russians. They're not monsters and they're not bogeymen. They fought on our side; they were with me at Dachau, and they'll never do a thing to one of their fellow deportees.' "

And George Pallavicini bent over his mother's hand, brush-ing it lightly with his mustache. He skipped down the stairs of the Andrassy Palace and jumped into his jeep gracefully but with care not to spot or rumple his blue striped suit, as the British soldier who was awaiting him saluted.

As ordered, he went back to the headquarters of the Com-munist party. Out of simple precaution, the British soldier had been instructed to wait for him before the door. He was armed, and the jeep had the flag of the Military Mission on the right-hand side of the windshield. The soldier saw Pallavicini finally come out of the building and, relaxing, started to turn on the ignition of his vehicle, but just then the survivor of Dachau was brutally shoved into a black limousine that sped off immediately in the direction of St. Margareten Island where the headquarters of the Soviet authorities were located.

Three days later, a strange party dropped a note off at Marquise Pallavicini's home. "I've been arrested. Help me," it said.

But even the Communist Prime Minister Rakozy, to whom the Marquise appealed for help, could not do much for a prisoner, who was in the hands of the MVD.

A second note brought the information that he was being held in the military prison of Conti Utca. He was allowed to receive packages. Then news came more often. Almost every day a Russian soldier would come to see the Marquise, sent by "Tovarich Pallavicini."

The Marquise always tipped them munificently, giving them clothing and food for her son, even though she was sure that many of these Russians had little or no real connection with him and that they were selling the packages she gave them on the black market, using her concern for her son merely as a dodge for their racket.

She was finally given permission to see him. When she got there the Soviet officer of the day looked at her and exclaimed:

"Why, that prisoner can't be your son! He's too old for that. He's your husband and you're just pretending he's your son to make us feel sorry for you."

Yes, Juri looked fifteen years older after fifteen weeks of imprisonment. He had lost his hair and his teeth, was skinny as a rail, and told her that life in the prison was unbearable, as he had to sleep on bare stones. The prisoners continually fought among themselves; everything was stolen, and interrogations went on without a let up days and nights on end, to mention nothing of beatings and other mistreatments.

"Mother," he told her, "there is only one thing I want and that is to be shot right away. Dachau was a paradise compared to what it is like here."

At Christmas the Marquise went to see him, bringing him some cakes and a turkey wing, but her pass was of no avail. George Pallavicini was no longer in Budapest.

Just as in 1944, they had come to tell him he was going to be freed and, just as in 1944, they told him he had to take the train to Vienna to sign his release papers. In 1944, the Gestapo was in Vienna. In 1946, the headquarters of the Soviet Mission were in Baden-Baden. So, just as in 1944, he went to the station to await the same train to freedom. Once in the train, the blinds were drawn tight, and for a long time George Pallavicini did not realize that the train was going in the opposite direction, toward the east—toward Russia. Lemberg first, then Moscow, and then on beyond the Urals, into Siberia.

For years there was complete silence. Of course, we knew that Pallavicini had been taken away by the Russians. Many of his friends had tried to intercede; there had been protests; there had been articles in the papers; and George's aunt, Countess Karoly, had even gone to see Marshal Voroshilov and asked him to transmit a petition to Stalin.

Ten years later—that is right, ten long years—we were to find out what had happened.

It was during the heroic Budapest uprising in the fall of 1956. His mother, now the widow Pallavicini, had finally succeeded in getting an exit visa a few weeks earlier and she was getting ready to go to her married daughter's home in Rome. But then the revolution broke out, and the delighted Marquise decided to postpone her departure.

My country is going to be liberated, she thought. How can I leave it now?

Then the Red tanks came, the collapse and the darkness, and she had to take advantage of the chaos to flee from the country she loved so dearly. She thought that in Rome she would find peace and quiet, for she was unaware that her younger son, Anthony, a career officer whom she thought safely tucked away in an outlying garrison, had taken an active part in the uprising. At first, he had been stationed in the little town near the château where József Cardinal Mindszenty was under house arrest. It was Captain Anti Pallavicini, Juri's brother, who at the head of his company liberated the Cardinal and escorted him triumphantly to Budapest. When the fate of the revolt was sealed, Anthony was still the one to escort Mindszenty to his sanctuary in the American Embassy. For this, he was executed by the Soviets in the courtyard of the Foe Utca prison.

A few weeks later in Rome, Marquise Pallavicini received another tragic message. It was postmarked Vienna and came from the information bureau dealing with prisoners who had disappeared into Russia.

"George Pallavicini," it said briefly, "political prisoner, accused of being a British agent, died at the concentration camp of Taishad-Lak, Siberia, in 1948."

I refuse to believe, even today, that any important government, especially the government of a world power, could honestly have entertained for a moment the ridiculous idea that Pallavicini was a spy. I was not in Budapest in 1946, so I do not know exactly what he was doing there, but it could have been harmless. You just don't kill men for things like that. Especially not a man who had been at Dachau; who had sat at the same table with a Soviet general; who had shared the intolerable hunger and hardships of the thousands of other Russian prisoners. No, even today, I cannot believe that Red Army General Nikolai Petrovich Mikhailov, together with those hundreds of thousands of Soviet returnees from deportation, could have accepted the idea that his fellow member of the International Committee, his brother, his friend, the one who voted on his side, was wasting away in a Siberian hell. They must remember and must be living with the shame that they never tried to save the life of George Pallavicini.

It was from another Hungarian political exile, Sandor Nemeth, that I found out what Juri's last days had been like.

After his arrival in Siberia, he was incarcerated in a punitive camp, one where the strictest discipline prevailed. He was not allowed to communicate with the other Hungarians, for he had been sentenced as an agent of the British Intelligence. On only one occasion was he allowed to dictate a letter to a Soviet jailer, which by devious means finally got to Szekfu, the Hungarian ambassador in Moscow. All the letter gave was a list of the clothing and medical supplies the prisoner urgently needed.

In the spring of 1948, after having labored hard at the construction of barracks in the forest, Juri took ill. It was no specific sickness, but total exhaustion. He simply refused to touch any food, and asked the doctor, also a prisoner, to do nothing for him.

"I don't want to live any longer," he told him. "There is no point to it. Life is just one big swindle. . . ."

He sent a last kiss to his mother; asked that she have a mass said for him; requested that a certain British Captain Redwood be advised of his death; that someone in his name kiss the hand of His Majesty King-Emperor Otto of Hapsburg. At four o'clock in the morning, Siberian time, on July 21, 1948, he sighed his last. He was buried in the camp cemetery, his grave marked neither by a cross nor an epitaph.

Who would dare write it?

"Here lies Marquis Georges de Pallavicini, bastard of liberty, who believed in freedom and who was a prisoner of the Germans at Dachau, and whom the Russians, allies of the Americans, murdered at Taishad-Lak."

15

Wasted Words in Barracks No. 14

All you had to do was sit on the terrace of a Parisian café, wearing your washed and ironed deportee's uniform with the serial number clearly showing—although some gilded the lily by wearing their berets with the red triangle on them—and immediately you were approached. Everybody wanted to shake your hand, to speak words of encouragement. Blushing girls would kiss you and sometimes wink at you. Children would bring you flowers, while the more timid simply stared. Often—in fact, very often—women generously invited you to have lunch at their homes, and even if you had just had a meal it would have done no good to refuse. They would not take no for an answer.

The food, of course, tasted unbelievably marvelous: this was what we had dreamed of during all the years when we gnawed at our stale crusts of bread. It was all the more

exquisite because we could well imagine the sacrifices that
went into it: the money that had miraculously been hoarded,
the ration tickets that for a whole week had been squandered
on this one meal, the mad extravagances on the black market.

Sometimes these luncheon invitations led to more romantic
consequences. The intimate atmosphere of a Parisian apartment, a few significant smiles, a woman dressed in something
less than necessary—that was all that was needed for us to be
seduced. And for the women, it was their way of saying thanks
to us, their way of helping us forget. Naturally, they wanted to
know whether this was the first time we had made love since
we got out of camp, and when they were told yes, they
swooned with delight. Those were the little lies over which I
will never feel guilty.

Nevertheless, I quickly shed this outfit with its vertical
stripes. I think I had already started to have nightmares in
which a puppet wearing that uniform danced on the ceiling.
Anyway, fabrics being hard to come by in Paris of 1945, my
aunt was able to cut it up to make pajamas for her children.
They lasted a long time.

I preferred my gray SS uniform with its Afrika Korps
blouse, which gave fits to the Turkish ambassador. "They'll
stone us; they'll set fire to the embassy," he would say to me,
"if they think we're harboring an SS man." But I was pig-
headed. I would not give up my handsome uniform, in spite of
the ambassador's entreaties.

From the very first days back in Paris I was able, at least
physically, to resume some sort of normalcy. I had been
royally received at the refugees' center in the Hotel Lutetia. Its
cooks knocked themselves out to please us. The French government had awarded me an 8,000-franc repatriation bonus.

It was really a token sum. Depending on luck, it might or might not pay for a bottle of champagne in a Montmartre nightclub. Anyway, I donated it to the Dachau Benevolent Association, which was already being formed. Later the government changed its mind because I had not been arrested by the Gestapo in Paris, and they asked for the 8,000 francs back, which goes to show how short-lived glory can be.

I wanted for nothing. Ambassador Menemencioglu, his counselors, and all his staff did all they could to keep me happy. I was invited to the best restaurants in Paris. Parties were held in my honor and a car was put at my disposal. On the other hand, in order to satisfy the ambassador, who sometimes awakened me in the middle of the night to give me the benefit of his ideas, I was writing editorials, which the *Gazette de Lausanne* carried on its front page, to call the Great Powers' attention to the desperate plight of little Turkey, then under the immediate threat of Soviet imperialism. I like to think that some of them were read and that perhaps they paved the way for the Truman doctrine that was to come.

I had immediately gone back to newspapering, which is not really a profession but a passion. Thanks to the understanding of Messrs. Laguerre and Vosges, who headed the French information section at the Hotel Scribe, and who by chance are now New Yorkers like me, I was allowed into the press headquarters. A remarkable American newspaperman, Dana Adams Schmidt of *The New York Times,* whom I had known in Ankara (where I secretly sent him unpublished items from Germany), not only put me up but he outdid St. Martin: he gave me his only overcoat. It rained often in Paris and I had no other protection against the weather.

The ambassador wrote another letter, again flattering me,

to General Eisenhower, asking that I be accredited to his headquarters as a war correspondent. In that way, just a few days after liberation, I was attired in an American officer's uniform, with an assimilated rank of captain; living in a luxurious room at the Scribe; surrounded by a small fortune in clothes, toilet articles, cigarettes, candy, and everything else available at the PX. It was simply fantastic. Every time I met a former fellow prisoner on the street, I asked him up to my room, as people take guests to see the imperial treasures in the Hapsburg Palace in Vienna. They came away dumfounded.

And at last I was sleeping peacefully. At first, my aunt, Countess d'Auvers, who was living in one of her châteaux in Normandy, close by the landing beaches, had begged me to take over her apartment on the Boulevard St. Germain. My aunt was a saintly woman, but the drawback was that she thought she was still living under the reign of Louis XVIII. The apartment was a maze of knickknacks, further encumbered by all kinds of religious pictures and statuettes. In a dark corner, she had hidden away her priceless Renoirs and Degas! And at night, in my imagination, these paintings would come out of their frames and dance a mad saraband around me, grinning luridly while doors opened which I knew I had bolted before going to bed, and a morbid death-knell ceaselessly tolled. I was quite relieved to be able to spend my nights elsewhere.

The Potsdam Conference and other stories which I reported delayed my return to Dachau. Nevertheless, what satisfaction it was to circulate in triumph through a completely demolished Germany! I, who had covered the length and breadth of it in other years, was peculiarly well suited to appreciate the enormity of the destruction and to see how its people, so aggressive and so self-righteous, were now reduced to abject poverty.

What a sensation it was to go back now through the gate of the Jourhaus, not only in the uniform of the conquerors but in a jeep driven by an orderly, its pennant flying in the breeze, no longer to be bullied but to be saluted by the sentries!

Dachau seemed deserted to me, somewhat like a theater in which the players have decided to interrupt the play and go out for a bite to eat. However, the barracks, our barracks, were not empty. The Americans were using them to house SS men picked up here and there, as well as some Hungarian POWs, the ones who had continued to fight until the last for the Nazis and whose fate had not yet been decided.

I went to visit my old barracks. It was miraculously transformed. Everything was so clean. There were only a dozen or so SS prisoners to a chamber. Some of them were out napping in the sun, while others played cards, mended their uniforms or wrote letters. It was a veritable rest home. All of the inmates had pink cheeks; they smoked and joked. Not one of them got up when they saw me come in with the American commandant. I was furious about it and I started to yell at them just as the SS officers two months earlier had yelled at me.

After voicing my best curse words at them, and completely forgetting my vow never to talk German again, I threatened them with immediate death by hanging if henceforth they ever failed to stand at attention in the presence of an American officer. It must have sounded very familiar to them; for hours they had barked the commands at the prisoners, "Cap off, cap on!" The American commandant watched me with amazement. He could not understand my rage, but he did not interfere.

I wanted to keep going in and out of the barracks to make the SS men jump up, salute, and stand at attention. The third time I did it, it was no longer fun.

At the end of August, there were still about five thousand internees left at Dachau, of our people. They did not know where to go; rather, they did not want to go where the Americans planned to send them. A few days before my visit, several hundred Russian prisoners rioted: they were from General Vlasov's army and had at first fought on the side of the Germans, then were interned in the camps when they refused to go on fighting. These poor fellows had, of course, been liberated by the Americans, but they saw no future in being turned over by them to their Communist allies, who would have made short work of them. The rebellion had been a serious one: men had died, some had committed suicide, furniture had been smashed, several barracks wrecked; and there were still some who carried on hunger strikes.

The Poles, less troublesome, awaited their fate. There was talk of sending them to England. Many had found jobs with the American army: in the kitchens, serving at the officers' mess, handling office detail; and some of them in this way were to remain in Dachau for ten or twelve years more. The remainder were a mosaic of nationalities and of individual tragedies: no papers, no money, no place to go, their families wiped out. They preferred to choose the comfort, security, and perhaps familiar atmosphere of the camp—now that it was in American hands.

I had a long conversation in Barracks No. 14 with some of my fellow prisoners who had stayed on at Dachau. There was a Lithuanian who felt he could never make the Americans understand that returning home would simply mean his being put into another Dachau.

"Why are they treating us this way?" he would ask. "With just a few formalities, I could get out of this damned place. Oh, the Americans are really a disappointment!"

I tried to explain to him that he was being unfair to the liberators, who had taken great risks for his sake. There were enormous logistic problems, I said; and besides, they had to try to avoid diplomatic incidents, to say nothing of transporting, feeding, and caring for millions of refugees. The Americans were doing the best they could. No one had a right to make demands upon them.

"But that's the very point of the whole thing," he retorted. "They talk about liberty as if it were a gift. The Americans crossed the ocean and came to dole liberty out to us as they hand out chewing gum. Liberty is not a gift; it is a right. We are born free. The American Constitution says so. I've read it. So they can't give us what already belongs to us."

A Polish comrade chimed in:

"The Americans didn't get into the war because they said, 'We won't tolerate some of our battleships being blown up at Pearl Harbor, and besides we don't like the looks of the Japs, and German industry is giving us too much competition.' No, the United States got into the war as the defenders of liberty and democracy. They asked us to rebel against our masters; to help them; to sabotage; to join the underground. Roosevelt appealed to us; he promised us a better world. It was because we listened to him, because we listened to the Voice of America, that we became prisoners. When a nation urges another people to revolt in the name of liberty, it has no right afterward to put a price tag on that liberty."

"You keep talking only about the United States," one of the Soviet comrades put in, "but we were liberators too. If it had not been for the Red Army at Berlin, there would not have been an American 45th Division at Dachau."

"Don't worry. We haven't forgotten that," I said to him. "But we haven't forgotten either that you were the first ones to make an alliance with Hitler and deported millions of your own people to slave camps, to say nothing of the Katyn Forest massacre, about which you still refuse to give any explanation. And besides, why do you close your borders to us? A Soviet soldier pointed his bayonet right at my nose one evening in Berlin when I tried to cross the demarcation line. When I protested and told him I had been a prisoner at Dachau, he just laughed in my face."

"Old wives' tales," the Russian countered. "Propaganda, propaganda! You guys are still all filled with the Goebbels poison. Your whole damned Europe is still thinking Nazi-fashion."

"All of which does not change the fact," said a Belgian, who was commuting between Dachau and Brussels as a courier for the camp command, "that your liberating troops acted like wild men. The Soviets pillaged everything; they raped any women they found on their path, whether they were old grandmothers, little girls, factory workers, movie stars, it didn't matter. It went on every evening, every night; everybody saw it. You can't deny that."

"Why should we try to deny it?" the Russian asked. "We are not ashamed of it. When anybody tells me about these rapes, I remember the answer I got from a comrade in a liaison group that came through Dachau. He was the driver for an inspector general, and he said: 'In my village, when I was a partisan, the Germans came through one morning. They couldn't find any men around, so they hung all the women from the trees and deported the kids, who were never heard from again. Among those women was my mother. So if we only rape their women, what have they got to kick about?' "

A Czech professor, who had been reluctant to go back home, preferring to head up the leathergoods depot at the

272 / **The Day of the Americans**

camp and make himself a little money that way, made a speech which seemed outlandish to me.

"Don't hold this rape business too severely against our Russian friends," he said. "It's true, their conduct was a bit brutal. If they had shown a little more patience, they would have achieved the same result, because the German women, living in houses which had permanent signs up reading, 'Woe betide any who even smile at a foreigner,' wanted nothing better than to give themselves to the conqueror. The Russians accomplished it through rape, the Americans with cigarettes and chocolate bars, the French with their charm, and others got there through stupidity, boredom, or a sense of adventure. But someday all this is going to have social significance. Let us make no mistake about it. We can already see it here in Dachau a few months after liberation: before long, Germany will be rehabilitated. She will deny her past, become strong and prosperous, and start to prepare her revenge. In twenty years, Dachau will be forgotten, just as the atrocities in Belgium were forgotten twenty years after 1914. In twenty years, Germany will be armed by her enemies of today, and the generals who conquered her will salute as her soldiers goosestep by.

"One thing she will never be able to erase, and which will decisively change her chemical make-up. In twenty years, Germany's new generation, the one that will be born six, nine, eighteen, twenty-four months from now, will no longer be of the Germanic race. Its fathers will have been French, Russian, Czech, Italian, Rumanian, or what have you. It will be an entirely bastard generation, and that might just make it our only true guarantee of peace."

A Rumanian comrade joined in: "We overdo it a little when we keep repeating 'Dachau, Dachau, Dachau,' as if it were Dante's Inferno. One of the SS men on trial asked me the other day: 'What have they got against us? That we locked you up in a camp instead of shooting you as we had every right to do under international law?'

"Let's be fair about it and compare the life here to the life of a soldier in the Rumanian army. A soldier is not a free man. We may have been beaten here in the camp, but in the Rumanian army the beatings never stop. The camp *Kapos?* They were no worse than our sergeants! They made us sleep like pigs in the barracks. Do you think a Rumanian soldier sleeps every night in a featherbed? We were hungry. Do you think the men who were fighting on the Russian front always had enough to eat? They say the camps meant death. Well, isn't the soldier sent to his death by his generals, without anyone asking his advice? Doesn't he have to face death continuously for six years? If one of us escaped and got across the border, he was welcomed as a hero. But if a soldier deserted. . . .

"The shoe was only on the other foot when it came to the farewells. When we left to come here, everybody cried. When the soldiers went off to war, they were feted, kissed, their brows wreathed with laurels. The bands played."

There was a German from Silesia. His homeland was lost forever. Nevertheless he dared to defend his fellow country-men:

"You accuse us, as a people, of all these atrocities. Yet you don't say a word when an American President wipes out a whole city with one atomic bomb. In Dresden, a whole art center was completely destroyed, 600,000 homeless people were burned alive. And what about our own prisoners, our own refugees, freezing and dying in Siberian concentration camps?"

Now it was my turn to answer:

"Yes, the atom bomb is something of a dilemma. But you Germans are in no position to criticize it, because if you had been able to make it in time you would have used it even more ruthlessly. And don't talk to us about bombardments and victims. Weren't you the ones who invented that kind of warfare? Warsaw, London, Rotterdam, Coventry—those were all cities filled with human beings. You raise your arms to the heavens and shriek, 'Dresden!' But if Dresden was bombarded it was because you asked for it, because you started the war, attacked the Russians. And the man you selected as your Fuehrer refused to give up even while going on with the struggle. Those responsible for the destruction of Dresden are Hitler and his people. Sure there were refugees in Dresden. But why had they become refugees? Because they believed the Nazi propaganda and also because they had guilty consciences and were afraid of the Russians. If they had stayed on their farms and in their homes, if they had accepted the unavoidable military occupation, those losses could have been avoided. The same goes for the prisoners in Siberia. Don't forget that they went in that direction, first of all, of their own accord.

"But let us admit for the moment that the atomic bombing of Hiroshima, the destruction of Dresden, the Russian POW camps, are all criminal acts, because everything connected with war is criminal. This would not wipe out a one hundred millionth part of the German people's responsibility. A crime remains a crime, even if elsewhere in the world the same crime is being committed a thousand times over. A criminal remains a criminal even if thousands like him get away scot-free. What we're talking about is the fault of the German people and nothing else."

The Czech professor resumed: "In ten years there will not be one German war criminal left in Allied hands. Right now, as you can see from what's happening at Potsdam, they're getting ready to prepare the next war, instead of wiping the slate clean of the one just ended. Human genius knows no frontiers. Soon we'll be traveling toward the moon, toward Mars, toward the stars. Yet this genius is unable to find a common-sense solution to end the struggle of man against man. The tragedy about our wars is that, when we come to the end of them, we no longer remember how they started."

"Well, I have a solution," said the Rumanian. "Please note something about generals: they command but they never, never fight. I read just the other day that during World War I only about three hundred German generals died, and most of those in their beds. This war cost more than ten times as many lives as the first one, yet the number of German generals who died was almost exactly the same: three hundred, except that a number of them were hanged by Hitler. The answer is that there ought to be only one rank in all the armies: general. An army of nothing but generals, all covered with medals, all holding their marshals' batons in hand. That way nobody would be left to fight because they would all be giving orders. War would become obsolete for want of fighters."

The Pole was thinking. "We survivors of Dachau," he ventured, "ought to form a secret society, a fraternity of *carbonari*. We would be everywhere; we would be able to observe everything. As soon as we were informed of a war criminal on the loose, we could seize him and try him. If a statesman were known to be preparing war, violating the rights of one of our comrades, we could sabotage his preparations, punish him, liquidate him. That way our secret society could rule the world."

"And who would rule us?" asked the Czech professor. "Anyway, gentlemen, let us have no illusions. There will be no Dachau solidarity, no spirit of Dachau to hold us together. We are alive, sure, but we are weary, exhausted, disillusioned, embittered. We are not ready to take up the struggle again. Those of us who may overcome this and assume the risks again will be drowned in a sea of mediocrity. We would merely be exploited. For us, truly, it is too late. There is no point in trying to turn back the hands of the clock. The time that has been lost can never be recaptured. Believe me, our words are wasted words."

I understood what he meant when I was asked to be a witness at several trials, including those at Nuremberg. The American investigator spoke only English and was surrounded by an army of interpreters. Words were translated from Rumanian into Hungarian, from Hungarian into German, from German into French, and when this was at last translated into the final version, a good half of the testimony had fallen by the wayside. When it came to my turn, I was asked whether I could remember the color of the eyes, the home address, the names of the parents of a prisoner I had seen die on the way to the crematorium. I was to be reminded of this type of investigator much later when I saw the *Perry Mason* show on TV. I was questioned about the SS man who had been so ruthless. Did I know where he lived? Where he was born? What make of watch he wore? Did he have a ring on his finger? Had I ever seen him kill a prisoner, of an evening, after sundown? Or several at once?

I felt sorely tempted to tell this investigator: "Mister, next time I'm in a concentration camp, I'll politely ask the SS man on duty to hold up the bestiality a moment so I can write down the color of his eyes, the make of his watch, and his telephone number, for use on the day when he is tried by his victorious enemies . . ."

Liberated Europe, in the meantime, was pockmarked by thousands of new camps in which those who had been liberated from the German camps were interned. These new Lagers were known as "Displaced Persons' Camps" and proved highly troublesome to those in charge as well as to the populations of the surrounding areas. No one, of course, worried about how the poor people inside of them felt.

The Turkish government, after thinking it over carefully, decided that it really had no reason to rejoice unduly because one of its nationals had been a victim of the camps. This fact, by its very nature, seemed to underline how very little the other 20,000,000 of its population had done to oppose Nazism. Therefore they asked me not to publish the story of my years in prison. The great Turkish newspaper *Akşam,* which had started to run the series, was ordered to drop it. The ambassador, against his will, begged me to refrain from discussing my wartime experiences, and especially never to mention the fact that it was another Turk who had turned me in to the Gestapo.

I have a curious conception of journalism: I believe that no government has the right to tell me what I may write and that my only loyalty is to my readers. A newspaperman who is a patriot first and a reporter afterward is in reality a swindler taking unfair advantage of his readers. I refused to be intimidated. The embassy, therefore, felt obliged to ask the American army to cancel my credentials. This maneuver only half-worked, since there were French publications ready to give me accreditation. After that, the Turks refused to renew my passport.

This was serious, but still not tragic. First of all, even before leaving Dachau, I had decided I would apply for American citizenship. Beyond that, I had several uncles in the Turkish diplomatic service and, luck being with me, all of them were consuls. So when my passport expired, I would go to see one of my uncles and ask him, nonchalantly, to issue a new one. Bureaucracy being alike in all countries, it took a long time for the uncle in question to be advised by Ankara of the ban against me and instructed not to favor me in the future. By the time I ran out of uncles, I was already in the United States. I was sadly mistaken, however, if I thought all that was necessary was to say the magic word "Dachau" to get an immigration visa. On the contrary, an American consul in London warned me, "Don't mention to anyone that you were locked up in a camp. The immigration people will consider it proof you're a Communist." I should have heeded his advice. The formalities turned out to be endless, complicated, pettifogging, and often insurmountable. If I were the Pope, I would canonize without hesitation anyone who has survived the interrogation of an American immigration official.

The U.S. Senate, in spite of all this, had passed a law giving priority to all persons who had been victims of Nazism. However, to take advantage of it, it was necessary to be still interned in a displaced persons' camp. It was actually suggested to me that I might leave America, my home, my work, and live as a refugee in one of these camps in Italy, in order to qualify! This was like telling a man to jump into a lake so as not to be drenched by the rain. Beyond that, I had to prove that my native country would persecute me if I went back. Since at the time Turkey had become an ally of the United States, which, as politics tends to paint everything black or white, could not foresee that its Turkish allies, whom it considered model democrats, would one day hang their own prime minister, the best friend of a U.S. President. Thus no one would believe that going back to Turkey involved the slightest danger for me. Of course, they were not the ones who would be running the risk. At the moment they knew of only one villain in the world, Soviet Russia.

I was therefore reduced to getting my naturalization papers by the normal methods—slow, to be sure, but more dependable. I am not really sorry about that. I would not want to be beholden to Dachau for anything.

I can still remember the day I first went to file my naturalization application (it took five years after that to get my final papers). I met two old Berlin friends at the immigration office. A newspaperman, after all, finds friends everywhere. These two were notorious Nazis, one of them had belonged to a very active section of the party, and neither of whom had changed his political opinions. Apart from that, they were very nice people who wished me the best of luck, because, of course, they were already American citizens and they had their precious passports safely in their pockets They had had no trouble at all in proving to the authorities that they could not go back home—the Soviet occupants would have persecuted them.

It suddenly dawned on me that I was one war, one enemy too late.

16

The Typewriter

My former comrades had piled in the jeep the widest variety of spoils. There were boots, bolts of khaki material probably once intended for the Afrika Korps, an SS helmet, a record with the song "Lili Marlene," cans of food and other military rations: in a word, everything that was to be found in the huge Dachau warehouses where, just as in the times of the SS, they were now working for the occupying forces. This loot, at a time when the black market was flourishing in every corner of Europe, had priceless barter value.

But they had not fulfilled my fondest wish: to get a typewriter. The Gestapo had confiscated those I had owned at the time of my arrest. Even in Paris, a typewriter was unobtainable. How can you be a newspaperman without a typewriter?

I lodged my complaint with the commander of the press camp at Bad Wiessee, an attractive locality some forty miles from Dachau. There was a lake, spicy little Fräuleins who bathed in it wearing less than a bikini, an excellent canteen, and a group of war correspondents who were busy writing or doing anything else they wished.

My palaver with the colonel, a very nice fellow but sticky

with regulations, turned out to be rather lengthy. I gave him a detailed account of the days of the Nazis, went deep into descriptions of life in the prisons and camps; outlined the methods of the Gestapo, established with Cartesian logic the indispensability of a typewriter to my being able to fulfill my orders—all signed Eisenhower. I begged him to give me a requisition for a typewriter from the German stocks held under seal by the military authorities.

"Impossible," the colonel assured me. "I can't do that without referring first to London and then to Washington. And that would take at least six weeks. We came here to establish law and order, but there are cases when exceptions have to be made. Nobody is going to stand in the way of your getting a typewriter on your own. Just one thing, though; don't break any of the rules."

One of those rules said that the municipality of Munich was supposed to establish a list of all persons having within their possession articles of military value such as tires, souvenir weapons, gasoline, and even typewriters. I went to see the Rathaus official in charge of these lists, and by good luck he turned out to be a former prisoner whom the Gestapo had continuously bothered. He therefore was very cooperative and willingly gave me the names and addresses of all the people in Munich who had dutifully declared that they owned type-writers.

Unfortunately, he could not give me a requisition order either for, as he explained to me, such *Bezugschein* had to be signed by the deputy mayor. "And," he went on, "the deputy mayor is a former Nazi sympathizer who only remains in his job because his daughter, a big blonde with heavy breasts and enormous feet, is the mistress of a colonel in the American administration. This colonel, incidentally, came directly to Munich from a school in Carolina where he was specially trained for occupation duty because his mother was born in Prussia.

"Go to some civilian and induce him to sell you his typewriter. Pay him in marks at the rate indicated on the list. Be sure to get a receipt and we will then certify the legality of the transaction."

One of my friends from the press camp agreed to go along with me on the first of these expeditions. He was a cartoonist for *Stars and Stripes* who wanted to sketch some faces of authentic German burghers, so it was a good opportunity for him. We had a jeep and a driver, a soldier from Santa Fe, New Mexico, who was delighted because I could speak Spanish with him. He had an irresistible way with the girls, which was a valuable asset, but he was also in the habit of arming himself to the hilt even when he was just standing around the PX; he was loaded with hand grenades, knives, submachine guns, bayonets, to say nothing of the case of ammo in the back of the jeep.

In Paris, the second secretary of the Turkish embassy had lent me a revolver ("This time we can't let you go back into Germany without protection," he had said), but up to now I had let it remain at the bottom of my military pack. I had intended to stop in one of the dense forests that bordered the Autobahn in order to learn how to use it, but the occasion had never arisen.

Our driver, Mexico, stopped the jeep with a screech of brakes at the house of the German who was top man on my list of typewriter owners. Shutters opened. All the heads in the neighborhood came to their windows at the noise and they followed our psychological maneuvers with fascination. My

283 / **The Typewriter**

friend the artist was holding a large sketch pad, but for all they knew, it could just as well have been some ominous military file. Don't forget that our audience had been conditioned by a dozen years of political terror. In theory, war correspondents were not issued arms and not allowed to carry them, so Mexico took the embassy secretary's revolver out of the pocket of his trenchcoat and handed it to me. I put the gun in my right-hand pocket. Then, after a brief hesitation, I took it out again, carefully examined the clip, checked the safety catch as if to make sure that it was ready to fire, and then slowly, ostentatiously, slipped it back into the left-hand pocket of my jacket, but awkwardly, so that it could still be seen.

We went into the house of the German who, quickly alerted, had the prettiest of his daughters come to stand by him, this being the argument that always carried the most weight with the occupiers. We went in slowly, looked around, said nothing for the moment. It never pays to hurry when you are carrying on a cold war.

The German had plenty of time to think over all the things that could be held against him. Such a summing-up inevitably took quite a bit of time.

Finally I addressed him in German, while my friend made some quick sketches. Our host undoubtedly thought he was making notes, but what worried him most was that I was talking to him in his own language. He had accumulated enough experience up until then to know that generally the Americans knew only two words of Goethe's language, *Fräulein* and *kaputt*. If I spoke German, it had to mean that I belonged to some mysterious secret service.

I introduced myself with elaborate politeness and ran down all my titles and functions, expressing them all in American terms so that the German understood almost nothing of my gobbledygook. During this time, Mexico had ostentatiously turned the jeep around, parked it in front of the door, and set about making room on the back seat, as if we were going to have another passenger—perhaps a prisoner.

Then I said with a disgusted and slightly pitying tone, "I have been told at the City Hall that you were terribly involved with the Nazis." I really knew nothing about it but nine hundred and ninety-nine times out of a thousand it was true and there was no risk of my making a mistake.

The inevitable reply came: "Me? Nazi? Never! Me, always against brown bandits. Me, always listen to American radio." And this was the signal for the pretty girl to go to the kitchen to prepare some ersatz coffee for us. My friend the cartoonist followed her.

The German gathered his courage at this point and started telling me he had a cousin living in Chicago, another in Minneapolis. He then told me how his family had suffered, what with the bombs, the boys away on the Russian front, the fear, his daughter so undernourished, and he himself not having had a cigarette since the Ardennes offensive began. Oh, that heartless Hitler!

I offered him a smoke as his daughter returned with the cartoonist, blushing furiously.

"I need your typewriter," I told him. "But we don't want to make any trouble for you"—my fingers absent-mindedly wandered to the pocket that had my revolver in it—"so we'll give you the standard price for it."

"But the typewriter is the only thing I have left—"

The daughter looked ready to start weeping, as if we had just said we were going to requisition her hope chest.

"Let me explain," I went on. "You know about Dachau?"

"Dachau?" he replied. "Never heard of it."

"Well, it's a prison, a KZ. I was locked up there and they took away my typewriter. That's war. Don't you want to make up a little for the harm that was done and let us have yours? It will all be returned to you by the government at the end of the occupation period."

I took out my municipality receipt pad, which had the stamp of American Military Government in one corner. As soon as he saw officially stamped forms, he was reassured, and his troubles seemed to take on an official character, not so serious after all.

I took out my wallet and went on:

"I note that, according to your own declaration which I have here, the value of the machine is set at 145 marks. To allow for the time you have lost on this, I'll make the price 175 marks. Please sign here."

At the time, 175 marks was the equivalent of a carton of Camels. However, the German was overwhelmed by my generosity and was eager to sign the receipt before I changed my mind. He must have thought he was getting the better of me in this bargain.

He even went to get me an extra part, a can of oil, and some paper, since he was getting such a good deal. Before leaving, after much handshaking, I tendered to him, in the name of that great anti-Nazi brotherhood in which we had been united for a dozen years, a package of American cigarettes. I was sure my artist friend had already given some chocolate to the girl in the kitchen and had made a date with her.

We left the place with the air of benefactors.

After getting a typewriter for myself, we had to find another for the cartoonist. Then Mexico decided there had to be one for the commander of his motor pool. The story got around the camp, and one after the other the war correspondents came around to ask me to do as much for them. Pretty soon, in this area of Munich, there was a traffic in typewriters that would have made the president of IBM green with envy. I think we even got hold of one that had belonged to Hitler personally. A visiting publisher preempted it and took it back to Oregon with him.

Almost all the typewriters were in bad shape. We could, of course, have had them repaired in army shops, but there was a risk. Anything that had been "liberated" by one soldier could be "re-liberated" with impunity by another. And then we would have had to start all over again. The official at City Hall came to my rescue by telling me about a shop that handled such work. The shop was on the outskirts of Munich, ironically on the road to Dachau, at Allach. There was no one there; only a phone number, whitewashed on the window, indicated how the proprietor could be reached.

The proprietor turned out to be a woman who was taking the place of her husband—he had been called up at the beginning of the war and was now somewhere in Norway.

"I can't work at home," she explained. "We have no electric power, but if you can take me with you to the American compound, I can make the repairs on the spot. It will be two marks an hour."

Mexico and I arrived punctually at six P.M. at the slum where she lived. She had told us she could work only evenings because during the day she worked for the farmer at whose home she was located.

Imagine our surprise to see a terrific babe appear, about twenty-five years old, dressed in bouffant black taffeta, a necklace around her neck, lips covered with lipstick, and wearing stockings as if she were going to a ball.

I could hardly hide my amazement.

"But Fräulein," I asked, "aren't you going to get your beautiful gown dirty, doing repair work?"

"That doesn't matter," she replied. "This is my first time out of an evening in a year. My first trip in a jeep. Please, don't drive too fast. I want the whole neighborhood to see me. Just think, me in a jeep with an American officer!"

There were some kind of regulations at the time against fraternization with German females, but in her case it was different: she was on a job. It was all legal, and she repaired the typewriter with skill and professional conscientiousness. I paid her what she asked, but I could not refrain from inviting her to the mess, where she had her first good meal in months. Then we went to dance at the club and I did not get her back home till well after curfew.

"Mexico," she begged the driver, "Please go slow, very slow. I want everyone to see me coming home. . . ."

After that, every time someone got a typewriter, I filled him in on how to get it serviced, and the girl in the black taffeta gown showed up often at the canteen and the club. I even suspect that some of the typewriter guys were not completely on the level when they said their machines needed service again.

One morning, just after breakfast, two huge MPs arrived, saying:

"The commander wants you. Come with us."

I was beginning to feel the shoe pinch. The commander, I figured, had heard about the typewriter caper and I was in for an arrest or a transfer out of the area. I was right; he was pretty unhappy.

"You've broken the rules, I'm afraid."

I went into a long digression, talking about the problems of

newspapers, about the war and Dachau, and how the Hitlerites had confiscated everything, but after a bit the commander
interrupted me:

"You know, a revolver was found in your room. You can't
keep it; it's against regulations. It's been sent to SHAEF in
Paris. You can pick it up there when you go back."

He poured me a shot of whiskey and in a strictly nonmili-
tary tone went on:

"You know, my son back in the States is going to graduate
any day now. In fact, he may already have graduated, but
letters are so slow in getting here. Anyway, I thought I'd like
to give him a present.

"A Hermes would be just what he'd like. Don't you think
you might find me one? Nothing illegal, of course. I'll pay for
it at the regular price in marks. You can use my jeep to get
it. . . ."

I headed back toward Paris at the end of the month. As a
reward for my efforts, I had been given a rebuilt Opel convertible from the motor pool. Everything went well until the
crossing of the Rhine at Mainz. The car got out of control, I
can't remember why—maybe a hole in the pavement. I have
only the faintest recollection, for I was found unconscious on
the road. After throwing me clear, the car had gone into a spin
and plunged into the Rhine. The "liberated" typewriter went
with it. And I arrived in Paris empty-handed.

17

The Syndrome

The Mayor of Berlin, Willy Brandt, having suggested that I go to see a doctor, because the authorities of the new West German government wanted to be reassured about the state of my health, I underwent a long examination at the hands of a specialist, a woman—and quite a pretty one—who used all kinds of shiny new instruments. Toward the end of the examination, the lady doctor turned to me and mumbled: "Dachau, huh? Well, you've nothing to kick about. At least you're alive."

It is difficult to talk about the wounds inflicted, the maimed limbs, the amputated breasts, the bodies broken by beatings, the castrations, when you are one of the lucky ones to survive. The German authorities in charge of damage payments seem to be of the same opinion, since after twenty years only 57 per cent of the 457,651 claims by survivors whose health has been permanently impaired have been processed, and, as late as 1965, there are still 75,882 living survivors who lost an eye, a limb, or are disabled and cannot make a living, whose compensation payments have not yet begun. But do not think this is because they are demanding fortunes in reparations. A woman who will never be able to be a mother because of concentration-camp treatment gets $37 a month from the Bonn government. A totally blind person is entitled to $137 a month. Yet in a great majority of cases the first payment of these compensation awards did not take place until twenty or twenty-five years after incarceration by the Gestapo.

So much for the physical scars. What about the psychological scars?

One of the leading New York psychiatrists, Dr. William G. Niederland, clinical associate professor of psychiatry of the State University of New York, who has twenty years of professional experience in this field, has given scientific evidence of the existence of a "post-concentration-camp syndrome" or what he also has coined the term "survivor syndrome." This syndrome affects at least 97 per cent of all liberated prisoners, even those who may consider themselves immune; those who have become rich, famous, powerful, even those who believe they are happy and are convinced they are now living a normal life.

In medical journals Dr. Niederland has published a number of papers on the subject that have attracted wide attention. He read a paper on the subject at the 1965 Annual Convention of the American Psychiatric Association, where his view was supported by Dr. Henry Krystal of Wayne State University. The scientific documentation which Dr. Niederland has collected on this score is most impressive and is based on the study of 2,000 cases. I will therefore limit myself to a few of the essential points, without going into scientific terminology which, I confess, is beyond me.

More than half the Jews who survived the extermination camps suffer from serious nervous disorders. According to Dr.

Niederland, many of their cases are hopeless. I should point out that his studies have been mainly, though not exclusively, devoted to Jewish survivors to whom he has had access. "It is not a racial problem," he states. "The fact is simply that Jewish prisoners more often than others were witnesses to the massacring of their close relatives, and so were much more affected. Their persecution also began earlier and often was more severe.

"They are the most difficult patients I have. A psychiatrist should have the confidence of his patients. But I can rarely get theirs. They refuse to recall the past; because any such recall is too painful and inwardly deeply upsetting. They remain aloof, withdrawn, depressed, and anxious."

These people live in fear and shame. When they see a policeman they are likely to cross the street. If there is an unexpected ring at their doorbell they may shake with terror. Disquieting news on the television upsets them greatly. Many fear that what happened in Germany will someday happen in the United States.

They live on two separate levels: though they may be here with us, they are at the same time back in Auschwitz, in Berlin, or in Lodz. Their lives are split between the present and that world which exists only in their visions, from which they have been unable to escape.

One of them claimed he has seen Himmler, of an evening, at the corner of 45th Street. Another says the mayor of New York is really the Auschwitz commandant in disguise. Others persist in believing that their wives did not die in the crematorium, even though they saw them with their own eyes, but that they are living here in New York, hiding, afraid to show themselves.

"These are the walking dead," says Dr. Niederland.

They have lost their memories except for memories of persecution, deprivation, and mistreatment. They constantly await new catastrophes. They do not want to discuss their lives in the camp because they are afraid those who hear them will not believe them or will mock them.

They do not shrink from having children. On the contrary, they seem to want families so as to replace those lost through murder, and to make sure that their names will not disappear forever. They want children to make up for the loss of those they saw die. But they are demanding, sometimes even hard on them, as if preparing them for another catastrophe, or perhaps unconsciously punishing them for being the ones who are left alive.

They are difficult mates. A good many marriages of camp survivors are unhappy.

They are permanent victims of a guilt complex.

Some of them shy away from the simplest of pleasures: a movie, an ice-cream cone, a dance, because they seem to be saying to themselves: "How can I go to the movies when my son is in ashes in the furnace? How can I dance when my wife went up in smoke in Ravensbruck?"

These symptoms did not appear immediately after the liberation. At that time there was still some hope that the wife, children, parents would return someday. Living conditions were still precarious. Then, facts had to be faced, and the survivor somehow went to a new home, a new trade, made money, started living in another country—for instance, America. Then the real remorse and despair set it. Then the nights became sleepless.

Now they suffer because they are alive while their mothers, fathers, sisters, wives, or children perished. "I should have been the one to die in their place. . . ." Hundreds among Dr.

Niederland's patients want to expiate the fact that they are still alive.

Others are haunted by remorse over perhaps having stolen a piece of bread from other prisoners, having hurt them in some way, turned them in, having let them be sent on a work detail in his place. In the camps it was easy to become responsible for the death of a comrade. Thus, for twenty years, a worm has eaten away at their souls.

Then there are those who were guilty of cannibalism. One girl remembers biting off her sister's finger. One patient confessed he had consumed a dead comrade's liver.

These confessions are never made directly. They are experiences the patient refuses to admit to himself, much less to the doctor. The psychiatrist has to piece them together by interpreting the dreams and symptoms of the patient.

Another psychiatrist, Dr. H. Bluhm, once said, "Death in a concentration camp requires no explanation. Survival does."

Even after twenty years, these victims who see ghosts everywhere cannot expect total cure. Many of them must be institutionalized. There are many suicides among them. Even after twenty years. Dr. Niederland feels that time, instead of improving their condition, may only aggravate it unless adequate treatment is provided.

The German Federal government is not deliberately ignoring the existence of these psychological phenomena and consequences of the persecution. Rather it is the opinion of certain doctors, accredited by the government, which often determines whether these illnesses resulted from captivity. Unfortunately, some of these doctors can hardly be called objective, many of them being German and a few of them former Nazi sympathizers.

A group of two hundred American psychiatrists sent a

petition to Chancellor Erhard, asking him to adopt a more humane attitude on the subject.

The American doctors' petition cites three examples:

CASE A: A baby was torn from its mother's arms by an SS man and dashed against a wall. Bits of brain tissue splashed onto the mother. Since then, she has partially lost her mind. *German's specialist's diagnosis:* No connection. Such an experience should be forgotten in two years or so.

CASE B: An SS man fired point-blank at a mother holding her child in her arms. The child died. The mother survived. She was liberated but has remained seriously disturbed throughout these years. *German specialist's diagnosis:* The woman's problems are serious but they are due to the fact that she is overweight and have nothing to do with her persecution.

CASE C: A child five years old lived for a long time hidden in a dark cellar, where he was fed only two or three times a week. His parents almost suffocated him to keep him from weeping or crying out, because the slightest noise would have revealed their precarious hideout. *German specialist's diagnosis:* The patient was too young to remember any of this.

The "survivor syndrome" affects every one of us, even those who have never consulted a psychiatrist and have not the least inclination to: even those who can now gaily laugh when they talk about the camps; who claim they no longer hate the Germans and spend their vacations in the Black Forest; who ostentatiously shake hands with the President of the German Federal Republic, and choose a Mercedes or a Volkswagen when they buy a new car

What are the symptoms?

Nightmares, lack of sleep, headaches, periods of depression which outwardly may appear to be connected with the stock market or the political situation, fear of solitude and yet craving to be alone, distrust, contempt for people, chronic anxiety, almost total lack of faith in humanity.

There is, especially, an exaggerated cult of the ego. They blow up every detail, every conception of their existence; this leads to an almost constant dual personality. They experience immense weariness and fatigue, which often turns into hopelessness and which makes them refuse to countenance talk of the past, makes them proclaim that they have no desire for revenge, and makes them feel that all previous events were crazy, stupid, useless. They seek to take personal responsibility for what happened to them. They feel they should have remained like the others, the ones who never did anything that led to imprisonment in the camp.

There is finally the malaise of having lost the faith, the religion which was theirs in childhood. According to the psychiatrists, 70 per cent of the survivors no longer have any religious beliefs. The rest have become superreligious, and now they interpret every event of their lives, their experiences in the camps, their liberation, their cure, as an uninterrupted series of divine interventions. At the same time they realize that their beliefs are only another acute form of superstition, from which they suffer also.

This syndrome is the invisible curse. It lies there, deep in our brain, as a mental cancer which tortures us and will continue to torture us until the day when once again we can link hands with those who never left Dachau. . . .

18

Return to Dachau

After the aimless wanderings, during the months that followed the catastrophe brought on by National-Socialism, I could not return to Germany before 1959, for no embassy was ready to replace the passport that had been stolen from me by the Gestapo.

In 1959, I became possessor of the precious green booklet. I call it precious not only because it elevated my human condition, but because the privilege of being an American citizen is certainly one of the greatest benefits on earth. I criticize, as we all do, the United States—its government, its people, its ways—because I love it, because we all passionately love this country, the freest in the world. We criticize it because we want it to be perfect. We cannot stand the idea that this magnificent diamond in the rough is not without a blemish.

At first, I had no intention of visiting Dachau. My wife and I had made this first voyage to a still-convalescent Europe to take part in a convention of the International Press Institute, an influential publishers' organization, which I feel honored to belong to. It energetically defends freedom of the press.

The congress was held in West Berlin, threatened by the Soviet "King-Kong," and the schedule included an excursion into "non-free" territory. At that time, the Wall had not yet been put up, but the contrast was nevertheless striking. The avenues of the West Zone were brilliant with neon lights, while the East was distinguished mostly by its ruins: the ruins of the palace where Hitler had lived and governed; the ruins of the War Ministry from which the orders had been sent that started the invasion of Europe; the ruins of the Wilhelmstrasse where Ribbentrop and Goebbels, each in his own domain, decided the best way, physically and morally, to subjugate much of the globe; the ruins of the Prinz-Albrechtstrasse where Himmler carried out the final solution of the Jewish problem. No, alas! all these ruins had not been replaced, as were their counterparts in West Berlin, by new buildings in which someday another German Chancellor, other Ministers of War, Foreign Affairs, Propaganda, another Chief of Police might in their turn put them to use.

A member of the Bonn government, Ernst Lemmer, then Minister of German Reunification, made a big speech about democracy, his great specialty. I knew Ernst Lemmer well, for when I was a correspondent in Berlin, Lemmer had worked as a tipster, filling the foreign newspapermen in on what was going on within the Hitlerian government circles. I had never used him then, for he was too expensive and was only a beginner, but I knew from my American colleagues that he was well informed and amazingly familiar with the ways of thinking of the Nazi officials. An admirable accomplishment, indeed, for a man who today alleges he was always a fanatical anti-Nazi. I spoke to him from time to time in those days, and it could only have been a coincidence—for there are such coincidences in life!—that I was later to be confronted, by the

Ministry of Propaganda, with things I had said to Lemmer. Poor fellow, they must either have tapped his telephone or hypnotized him, or used some kind of a truth serum on him!

But this also shows how naïve the Gestapo really was. Here was a German who had belonged to the Democratic party and yet openly associated with the foreign press, furnished it with tips; had all kinds of entrees at the Chancellery, the Wilhelm- strasse, the Ministry of Propaganda; was an active member of the underground Resistance movement; and yet the Gestapo did nothing about him, although it had no scruples about hanging generals galore, about sending poor devils to Dachau simply because their names, picked out of the telephone directory, sounded like that of the Premier of loyalist Spain.

Having been duly impressed by the speech of Minister Ernst Lemmer who, I repeat, had been a crusader of democracy, a champion of the Resistance, and a good and true German of his time, I was even more impressed by our trip around the "good" Reich. It was idyllic. Beautiful young girls, dressed in folk costumes (having disposed of their Hitler Youth uni- forms) poured Rhine wine for us at the various stops. We were taken through the huge Volkswagen factory where no one bothered to mention that the name of the Volkswagen was Adolf Hitler's idea.

They showed us operas, open-air swimming pools, castles, and demarcation lines, the brothels right out in the street in Hamburg and the vineyards of Bonn—but no concentration camps. I did not intend to let myself be upset by that omission, but my wife, a native American, after this trip through Alice's Wonderland, was beginning to think that my tales of those camps must be imaginary.

It must be said in my wife's defense that she comes from a

family which, because it emigrated to America some centuries ago on a broken-down old ship called the *Mayflower*, is deeply distrustful of those who reached these shores in later, more luxurious, and faster ships. I fear that they will always believe that my concentration camp experiences are really only an excuse to cover my inability to amass a fortune in dollars during the years 1943 to 1945.

That was why, one rainy afternoon, I went back with her to Dachau.

The place was deserted but for a lone American soldier standing guard before the crematorium. He was not there as an honor guard, but to prevent vandalism, for there had been young Germans who soiled its walls by emptying chamberpots over them.

Except for a statue hidden behind a bush and a few signs which time and the weather had made almost illegible, everything within the crematorium (the only part of the camp retained "in memory") had been left much as it was in the old days. All that was missing were the piles of corpses, but to me they were there—they always will be. An old woman, a Pole, was selling postcards, horror pictures, and a little explanatory pamphlet. This was how she eked out her meager living. She lived in the room adjoining the oven; the one in which corpses had been stacked for final inspection, which meant stripping them of their last elements of value. She prepared her meals on a little stove whose smoke went up the chimney of what had once been the crematory oven. This explained the thin white wisps that could be seen as one approached the camp, which had almost made me think the phantom souls of the victims were still being burned there. . . .

"Doesn't it bother you to live here?" my wife asked her.

The old woman replied: "A person has to sleep somewhere. The others, on the outside, wouldn't take me in."

The "others" she talked about were those who lived in the barracks of the Lager, for the new industrious and economical Germany had not, until then, felt shame enough to do away with these slaughterhouses. No, she had used them to house a few hundred of her own refugees who, after having enthusiastically taken part in the plan to conquer and subjugate other people's countries, had been forced to flee from them, with a sometimes light burden of personal possessions on their backs and an extremely heavy one on their consciences. Having come from Poland, Czechoslovakia, or the faraway Ukraine, they vegetated here in the Lager, which represented to them only an agglomeration of temporary slums. In fact, they had transformed our old barracks. They had installed kitchens in the rooms where so many prisoners had been executed under streams of freezing water and where so many others had died of dysentery. There were beds and wardrobes in the stable dormitories, and even flowers, geraniums and carnations in the windows. A well-stocked grocery store had been set up in the VIP prisoners' block and a café with outdoor tables adorned the principal square, the place where the fatal roll-calls had taken place. Where once the lists of names of the prisoners being sent to the commandos of death had been posted, you could now see an immense sign: "Drink Coca-Cola."

They used the former inmate kitchen for a handbag factory. (Have no fear, human skin was no longer used.) The building where the wicked Dr. Hintermeyer conducted his diabolical experiments became the children's rumpus room.

There were also election posters put up by the extreme right-wing party, which called itself the "Refugees' party," promising some vague kind of revenge. In the small streets, where each morning we had seen the whitewashed corpses of those who had died during the night, there were now Volkswagens quietly parked, lending a bit of color to the rainy gray countryside.

In the old Revier, where in the old days more patients died than were ever cured, there were dances on Saturdays to the sounds of a jukebox, or, when it was too late for that, a zither played by a refugee from Transylvania. The boys and girls danced, rubbed against each other, kissed, and then, excited by the music, the bodily contact, and the Schnapps, went outside to make love. The girls, with their skirts raised, would put their naked thighs down on this earth that had been drenched with blood, sweat, and tears; perhaps on the very same few square yards where a prisoner had been beaten or butchered. . . .

More years have gone by since then. Today the refugees have left too, and almost the entire camp has been razed. Under the auspices of the Bavarian provincial government, a few of the buildings will be rebuilt, made new, clean, and solid; flowerbeds will be planted; there will be ample parking for tourists, as well as a snack bar and a well-documented museum. The documentation will be highly imaginative, in order not to depress the tourists visiting Dachau, they have already begun to manipulate the facts of history and the claim now is that there never was any such thing as a gas chamber at Dachau. It is so easy, after all, to reinvent history when almost all the witnesses were killed in advance. . . .

I don't know whether this sort of Mme. Tussaud's Museum, with its figures in striped uniforms, its instruments of torture, its cardboard reproductions of dungeons and its meaningless statistics, is preferable to the abandoned and profaned Dachau of my first return visit. I am told that thousands upon thousands of foreigners working in Germany—Greeks, Spaniards, Turks, Algerians—come to spend their weekends at the place, and that they are thrilled by it. Is that what our sacrifices were intended to offer?

There are also several monuments to be seen, religious monuments put up "in memory." I am told there will be others—but one looks in vain for the only monument, the only commemorative plaque which would have any meaning for me: an inscription of regret from the German people, by the German people. Just the word "Regrets," and a list of the names of all the SS men who from 1933 on served in the garrison.

Most of the survivors have no desire to go back to visit Dachau (except for those with professional reasons, as I did).* Therefore they will have no occasion to be surprised that these new Hilton-type buildings—shining, whitewashed, and clean as Elizabeth Taylor's bathroom, are shown to the new generations as a faithful reproduction of the old blocks. Besides, no one ever claimed that our barracks were poorly constructed, that the plumbing worked badly, or that there was no order or organization at Dachau. What made us suffer was the horrible filth within those walls; the odor of death, of charred flesh exuding from every stone; the terror to be seen in the eyes of every one of us; the wind, the mud, the cold, the heat, the blood that soaked the pavements; the fleshless skeletons hanging from the ceilings of the shower rooms; and the fear, the fear of what might happen the next moment—a fear that was

* Yet, some of the former inmates have returned to Dachau only to look for buried treasures of confiscated gold they thought the SS had hidden in some spots known only to them.

continually renewed and to which no one ever grew accustomed.

Why then commemorate all that by building model pavilions, as if this were another World's Fair?

The day of my first return visit, my wife and I decided to have a drink in the village of Dachau itself, about a mile away from the camp. We had first tried to go to the PX of the American garrison that occupied the huge compound formerly housing the SS; but in spite of our passports, we were not allowed inside the military area. I found that most curious. During my career as a reporter, I had visited the most secret American bases. I was at Guantanamo at the height of the Cuban crisis; I was invited to the South Pole by the Navy commander; in Texas, I remember having gone through an experimental air base with my eyes closed because I did not want to compromise myself by seeing an entirely new and top-secret plane; I have even fingered an atomic bomb on the atomic aircraft carrier *Enterprise,* where I was allowed to go about freely just as I went about freely at Cape Kennedy. And yet, in five years, despite all my efforts and official requests to the Pentagon, I have never been able to get inside the American base at Dachau, formerly that of the SS. The public relations officer, notwithstanding the usual expansiveness of his kind, even refused me a photograph of the camp. I could only come to one of several conclusions: either something ultrasecret is being prepared at the Dachau base, or else the American army is ashamed of having liberated this camp twenty years before, or ashamed to have remained there after driving out its previous occupants.

I had never before visited the town of Dachau. Prisoners were almost always transported directly into the camp in windowless vehicles, the "Grüne Minnas." I had arrived there myself by train, but that was at night, and at the time had suited me just fine; for I knew that those who were taken through the locality by day were exposed to the catcalls of the local inhabitants, and that at times were even stoned by them. I thought, therefore, that Dachau was a more or less deserted little town, with a few dilapidated houses with closed shutters, some stables, an old garage, a few stores. Imagine my surprise at discovering a charming little city all flower-decked with wisterias, roses, peonies, petunias—with a castle, delightful inns, elegant streets—a veritable nook of heaven.

The municipality of Dachau distributes by the hundreds of thousands a small tourist pamphlet which starts with the words: "Dachau Is Worth Visiting," and goes on to say that Dachau is the very heart of that Bavarian good fellowship known as *Gemütlichkeit,* and that no one should come to Dachau without his camera. The castle of Dachau used to be the pride of the Wittelsbachs, and this is the place where the ex-president of the German Federal Republic, Dr. Heuss, is said to have completed his doctorate. Dachau, it is claimed, is also the favorite relaxing spot of German film stars. Each year, in the fall, a popular fete takes place in the town, and two thousand children parade in costumes through the streets. Dachau, it seems, still is partial to masquerade.

Many German intellectuals—the writer Ludwig Thomas, the painter Leopold von Kalkreuth, the sculptor Ludwig Dihl —lived in Dachau. It seems there was even a school of painting called the "Dachau School," and one cannot therefore allege that Himmler selected an unknown hamlet inhabited by illiterates and brutes as the location of his notorious concentration camp.

The township of Dachau was founded in 805. The word Dachau means "marsh" in Old German. The Bavarian Grand

Elector established a summer residence there in the sixteenth century, and the present castle was constructed in 1715 by the architect Josef Effner, who was responsible for such architectural marvels as the castle of Nymphenburg and the royal residence at Munich.

The tourist guide is not silent on the subject of the concentration camp. On the contrary, the booklet even carries a picture of the monument to the deportees and gives detailed instructions for visiting the site. "Don't forget to take your camera," the guidebook repeats, while insisting that the inhabitants of this town were totally ignorant of what went on in the camp.

The mayor of the city, one Herr Hick, who, although having been briefly interned in the camp himself, has never explained why he was arrested or even why he was released, makes the same claim, urging people to avoid further discussion of the past. Yes, the city of Dachau was unaware of everything.* The prisoners who came to work from dawn to dusk for the local peasants or craftsmen must have been invisible; the SS men who whipped these prisoners as they herded them through the streets must have been doing some strange sort of ballet; and the girls who came to the windows to see the prisoners go by, accompanied by their SS guards, laughing and flirting, must have been transient tourists. For the guidebook says that when the fog from the Dachau marshes evaporates, one may see, from the central square of

* In July, 1945, a team of official interrogators from the Seventh United States Army Intelligence took the following testimony from inhabitants of Dachau:
JOSEPH SHERRER: "Our people knew very well what was going on in Dachau camp. Most of them did a thriving business as a result of the presence of the camp and the clientele of the SS. The most outspoken anti-Nazis were those who in reality did not have any business with the Nazis yet resented the fact that they were not making money out of them."
JOSEPH ENGELHARD: "A scandal for all civilized people, the passivity of

the town, the Alps rising up about a hundred miles distant—
but no one was able to see as far of the edge of the town,
where 30,000 condemned were penned into a huge enclosure.

Among the many tourists who on Sundays drive over from
Munich, one may encounter a lovely young woman, her face a
little tired but with the figure of an adolescent. Her name is
Gudrun Himmler. She is Heinrich Himmler's only daughter.

Dachau is for her a familiar sight. She told me, as we were
talking one evening in Schwabing, Munich's Greenwich Village, where she lives in a small flat she has transformed into a
museum honoring the memory of her father.

"My father took me there when I was only twelve. Yes, I
saw inmates. My daddy told me that the ones with the red
triangle were political prisoners, the others with the black
triangle criminals. Was I impressed? My God, they looked like
all people in a prison—ugly, dirty, emaciated, and they scared
me. But I was not really interested in them. What fascinated
me was the herb garden. My father showed me every plant
and gave me detailed explanations for almost an hour. I was
allowed to take some flowers home with me. I was delighted."

The concentration camp was completed in 1933. In 1934,
Dachau became a city, the seat of its district. Its population
has quadrupled since then to more than 40,000 inhabitants.
The Dachau budget exceeds 16,000,000 marks. There are

---

our population. Ninety per cent of the people living in Dachau are filthy;
they have daubed themselves with the blood of innocent human beings."
EDOUARD GRASAL: "They [the people of Dachau] were cowards and acted
like cowards. They did not want to risk anything. And that's the way it
was in all Germany. The courageous can be counted on the fingers of your
hands."
Incidentally the main avenue going from Dachau town to Dachau Concentration Camp was designated by the mayor as the "Nibelungenstrasse."
(All testimony from "Records of the Seventh US Army, National Archives of the United States of America.)

several important industries: paper, cement, fertilizer, machinery. Dachau employs more than 3,000 foreign workers and is classified as one of the most important industrial and agricultural centers of Bavaria, after its capital. It is estimated that the income of the Dachau population had multiplied ten times since 1933, while that of the Federal Republic as a whole has not even tripled.

Is this prosperity due to chance, or to the convict labor that died while draining the marshes and making the Dachauer Moor a healthful region? Was it due to chance, or to the work of the prisoners at the nearby farms and factories? Was it due to chance, or to the machines, the merchandise, the gold, the clothing confiscated from the deportees, the Jews, and other victims of the Gestapo, which the SS stored in their great warehouses before offering them on the market place of Dachau?

Perhaps the people of Dachau do not know, or perhaps they have forgotten. There is no one to tell that pink-cheeked farm girl that the bracelet that weighs so heavy on her arm used to belong to a little Jewish woman in Warsaw. Dachau has forgotten everything; and yet, if ever you are in the neighborhood, look closely at the pretty girls between twenty and twenty-five years of age, walking about in their dirndls and their nylons, in the park of the château. Some of them are tall, fair-haired, with silken tresses; they remind you so much of the SS guards, those magnificent male specimens who, among other things, had taken on the task of re-Germanizing the race.

They will be walking arm in arm with other girls, sometimes their sisters or their cousins, who may be about twenty years old but who are dark, almost swarthy, with crinkly hair, short stature, some with irregular noses, strangely like certain Polish

or Russian prisoners who, in spite of all the puritanical watch-
fulness of the American commander of our camp, succeeded
each night in slipping out of the camp after the liberation for
adventure and—who knows?—perhaps a little vengeance in
the beds of the Dachau beauties.

We were seated, my wife and I, that afternoon of my first
return, near an immense veranda of the principal Gasthaus,
which afforded a magnificent view, that vaunted view of more
than a hundred miles to the mountains and the green-and-gold
foothills around Dachau.

Inside the room was a group of some thirty schoolgirls with
their teacher. Their ages varied from eight to twelve, so they
were all born well after the catastrophe. The girls looked at us,
whispering among themselves. Then, after much hesitation and
repeated urging by the teacher, one of them came over to my
wife, curtseyed, and timidly asked her in English for her
autograph and "Please tell us about Hollywood, because we
are studying English and we love American movies. . . ."

The girls had thought that my wife was a starlet, being
young, red-headed and American. My wife laughed. The ice
was broken; the girls swarmed around us. The teacher even
came over, and we talked about Los Angeles, New York, and
the ways of American teen-agers. The girls were from the
local school and were celebrating the birthday of a classmate.
They presented flowers to my wife in exchange for her auto-
graphs; there were roses, violets, lilies, and I, won over by
their charm, slipped away to the local candy store to bring
them a huge box of goodies.

It was only toward the end of our visit that the teacher
expressed surprise at the presence in Dachau of two American
tourists. "It doesn't happen often," she said. "You must have

come to see our marvelous château. Isn't it beautiful? It certainly deserves its reputation."

My wife hardly knew what to say. I looked at her, her arms full of the flowers. I looked at the teacher, who belonged to the other generation; at the schoolgirls of the new generation who were happily devouring the candies I had brought this late afternoon of the summer of 1959.

"Yes," I answered her with a smile. "We came to Dachau to visit your beautiful château. . . ."

Index

311

Acknowledgments

The author wishes to thank Mr. Harold E. Salemson for his invaluable assistance in the preparation of the English language edition of this book.

He also would like to express his gratitude to all who helped him with his research, and especially, His Excellency the Chancellor Dr. Kurt von Schuschnigg; the Marquise of Pallavicini; Countess Mottyo Andrassy; Consul Dr. Theodor Schmidt; Dr. William G. Niederland; Mr. Edmond Michelet; Dr. Lamberti Sorrentino; Mr. Albert Guerisse; Dr. Hans-Gerhard Knitter; Louis Lochner; Marguerite Higgins; Miss Gudrun Himmler; the Director of the Eden-Paradiso Hotel in Capri; the Munich section of the Dachau International Committee; the Book Section of the Department of Information of the United States Army, and the Pictorial Section of the United States Department of Defense.